797,885 Books

are available to read at

www.ForgottenBooks.com

Forgotten Books' App
Available for mobile, tablet & eReader

ISBN 978-1-331-68576-0
PIBN 10221307

This book is a reproduction of an important historical work. Forgotten Books uses
state-of-the-art technology to digitally reconstruct the work, preserving the original format
whilst repairing imperfections present in the aged copy. In rare cases, an imperfection in
the original, such as a blemish or missing page, may be replicated in our edition. We do,
however, repair the vast majority of imperfections successfully; any imperfections that
remain are intentionally left to preserve the state of such historical works.

Forgotten Books is a registered trademark of FB &c Ltd.
Copyright © 2015 FB &c Ltd.
FB &c Ltd, Dalton House, 60 Windsor Avenue, London, SW19 2RR.
Company number 08720141. Registered in England and Wales.

For support please visit www.forgottenbooks.com

1 MONTH OF
FREE
READING

at

www.ForgottenBooks.com

By purchasing this book you are
eligible for one month membership to
ForgottenBooks.com, giving you
unlimited access to our entire
collection of over 700,000 titles via
our web site and mobile apps.

To claim your free month visit:

www.forgottenbooks.com/free221307

* Offer is valid for 45 days from date of purchase. Terms and conditions apply.

Similar Books Are Available from
www.forgottenbooks.com

Every Man a King
Or Might in Mind-Mastery, by Orison Swett Marden

Self-Help
With Illustrations of Conduct and Perseverance, by Samuel Smiles

Improvement of the Mind
by Isaac Watts

A Dictionary of Thoughts
by Tryon Edwards

Methods of Obtaining Success
by Julia Seton

The Power of Truth
Individual Problems and Possibilities, by William George Jordan

How to Get What You Want, Vol. 1
by Orison Swett Marden

How to Be Happy Though Married
by Edward John Hardy

Self Development and the Way to Power
by L. W. Rogers

Beginning Right
How to Succeed, by Nathaniel C. Fowler

How to Make Money
Three Lectures on "The Laws of Financial Success", by B. F. Austin

The Pursuit of Happiness
A Book of Studies and Strowings, by Daniel Garrison Brinton

Your Forces, and How to Use Them, Vol. 1
by Prentice Mulford

Conquering Prayer
Or the Power of Personality, by L. Swetenham

He Can Who Thinks He Can, and Other Papers on Success in Life
by Orison Swett Marden

The Power of Thought
What It Is and What It Does, by John Douglas Sterrett

Plenty
by Orison Swett Marden

The Practice of Autosuggestion By the Method of Emile Coué
Revised Edition, by C. Harry Brooks

Thinking for Results
by Christian D. Larson

Calm Yourself
by George Lincoln Walton

AMERICAN NERVOUSNESS

ITS CAUSES AND CONSEQUENCES

A SUPPLEMENT TO NERVOUS EXHAUSTION

(NEURASTHENIA)

BY

GEORGE M. BEARD, A.M.M.D.

FELLOW OF THE NEW YORK ACADEMY OF MEDICINE, MEMBER OF THE NEW YORK
NEUROLOGICAL SOCIETY, EX-VICE-PRESIDENT OF THE AMERICAN
ACADEMY OF MEDICINE, MEMBER OF THE NEW YORK
ACADEMY OF SCIENCES, OF THE AMERICAN
NEUROLOGICAL ASSOCIATION.

———————————

NEW YORK

G. P. PUTNAM'S SONS

27 & 29 WEST 23D STREET

1881

COPYRIGHT, 1881, BY G. P. PUTNAM'S SONS.

PREFACE.

THIS work is designed as a supplement to my lately published work on Neurasthenia (Nervous Exhaustion).

That work, though it appeared but one year ago, speedily passed to a second edition in this country, and has already been translated into German. It is just to infer that at last, after long delay, an audience has been found for a scientific discussion of this class of subjects.

In the preface to Nervous Exhaustion it was stated that the chapter on the causes was designedly omitted, inasmuch as a thorough elucidation of that side of the subject, in all its relations and dependencies, would be of so complex a character as to require a special volume of itself. The present work is, therefore, to be regarded as a chapter on causes for the treatise on Nervous Exhaustion, with these qualifications — that it embraces the whole domain of nerve sensitiveness and nerve susceptibility, that lead to the more definite condition of nervous exhaustion, and that it is of a more distinctly philosophical and popular character than that treatise, which was specially addressed to the professional and scientific reader.

The various subjects discussed in this work have occupied my mind from the time when I first began to think; in the form in which they now appear they represent not far from a quarter of a century of research and toil; many of the sections having been so often re-written and re-cast, that they bear little resemblance to their original form. The criticism which will be given to the philosophy of this work has been to a considerable degree anticipated, since the researches, and generalizations based on the researches, have been published by me, in various ways, during the last fifteen years; and most of them have been extensively published and republished in England and Germany; and thus have repeatedly, and in various forms, received the attention of some of the strongest critics of our generation. Replies to these critics and improvements in the mode of statement inspired by their suggestions, will be found in the present volume. Among these criticisms, especially noteworthy are those of the London *Times*, London *Spectator*, and *Saturday Review*; in Germany there has been endorsement rather than criticism. Although the general philosophy of this work is, in substance, the same as that contained in my earlier writings on the same subject, yet, in details and illustrations, and in the arrangement and methods of argumentation, very many additions have been made which are here published for the first time. Many of the distinctive thoughts of this work are found in my lecture on American Nervousness given before the Medical and Surgical Society of Baltimore, and subsequently published in the *Virginia Medical Journal*, and in pamphlet form, and in papers on "English and American Physique," in the *North American Review*, on "The Future of the American People," in the *Atlantic Monthly* and on "The Consolations of the Nervous," in *Appleton's Journal*, and in a series of articles in the *Yale College Courant*. More recently I lectured on the general subject before the Philosophical Society of Chicago.

Some of the points have also been touched upon in a series of papers recently given through the New York *Medical Record*, in my paper on Writer's Cramp; also in my work on "Hay-Fever," and on "Neurasthenia" (Nervous Exhaustion), and in Beard and Rockwell's "Medical and Surgical Electricity." In a paper read before the British Medical Association, in Cork, 1879, and Cambridge in 1880, I also discussed the problems raised in this volume and the one that it supplements.

Throughout this book references and foot notes are resorted to but occasionally, since to make the list of authorities of sources of facts complete would require another volume at least half the size of the present one.

To those who are beginning the study of this interesting theme the following epitome of the philosophy of this work may be of assistance, as a preliminary to a detailed examination.

First. Nervousness is strictly deficiency or lack of nerve-force. This condition, together with all the symptoms of diseases that are evolved from it, has developed mainly within the nineteenth century, and is especially frequent and severe in the Northern and Eastern portions of the United States. Nervousness, in the sense here used, is to be distinguished rigidly and systematically from simple excess of emotion and from organic disease.

Secondly. The chief and primary cause of this development and very rapid increase of nervousness is *modern civilization*, which is distinguished from the ancient by these five characteristics: steam-power, the periodical press, the telegraph, the sciences, and the mental activity of women.

Civilization is the one constant factor without which there can be little or no nervousness, and under which in its modern form nervousness in its many varieties must arise inevitably. Among the secondary and tertiary causes of nervousness are, climate, institutions—civil, political, and religious, social and business—personal habits, indulgence of appetites and passions.

Third. These secondary and tertiary causes are of themselves without power to induce nervousness, save when they supplement and are interwoven with the modern forms of civilization.

Fourth. The sign and type of functional nervous diseases that are evolved out of this general nerve sensitiveness is, neurasthenia (nervous exhaustion), which is in close and constant relation with such functional nerve maladies as certain physical forms of hysteria, hay-fever, sick-headache, inebriety, and some phases of insanity; is, indeed, a branch whence at early or later stages of growth these diseases may take their origin.

Fifth. The greater prevalence of nervousness in America is a complex resultant of a number of influences, the chief of which are dryness of the air, extremes of heat and cold, civil and religious liberty, and the great mental activity made necessary and possible in a new and productive country under such climatic conditions.

A new crop of diseases has sprung up in America, of which Great Britain until lately knew nothing, or but little. A class of functional diseases of the nervous system, now beginning to be known everywhere in civilization, seem to have first taken root under an American sky, whence their seed is being distributed.

All this is modern, and originally American; and no age, no country, and no form of civilization,

not Greece, nor Rome, nor Spain, nor the Netherlands, in the days of their glory, possessed such
maladies. Of all the facts of modern sociology, this
rise and growth of functional nervous disease in the
northern part of America is one of the most stupendous, complex, and suggestive; to solve it in
all its interlacings, to unfold its marvellous phenomena and trace them back to their sources and
forward to their future developments, is to solve
the problem of sociology itself.

But although nervousness, and the functional
nervous diseases derived from it, are most frequent
in America, and were here first observed and first
systematically studied, they are now and for some
time have been, becoming more and more frequent
in E. .e.

Sixth. Among the signs of American nervousness specially worthy of attention are the following:
The nervous diathesis; susceptibility to stimulants
and narcotics and various drugs, and consequent
necessity of temperance; increase of the nervous
diseases inebriety and neurasthenia (nervous exhaustion), hay-fever, neuralgia, nervous dyspepsia, asthenopia and allied diseases and symptoms; early
and rapid decay of teeth; premature baldness; sensitiveness to cold and heat; increase of diseases not
exclusively nervous, as diabetes and certain forms
of Bright's disease of the kidneys and chronic ca-

tarrhs; unprecedented beauty of American women; frequency of trance and muscle-reading; the strain of dentition, puberty, and change of life; American oratory, humor, speech, and language; change in type of disease during the past half century, and the greater intensity of animal life on this continent.

Seventh. Side by side with this increase of nervousness, and partly as a result of it, longevity has increased, and in all ages brain-workers have, on the average, been long-lived, the very greatest geniuses being the 'longest-lived of all. In connection with this fact of the longevity of brain-workers is to be noted also, the law of the relation of age to work, by which it is shown that original brain-work is done mostly in youth and early and middle life, the latter decades being reserved for work requiring simply experience and routine.

Eighth. The evil of American nervousness, like all other evils, tends, within certain limits, to correct itself; and the physical future of the American people has a bright as well as a dark side; increasing wealth will bring increasing calm and repose; the friction of nervousness shall be diminished by various inventions; social customs with the needs of the times, shall be modified, and as a consequence strength and vigor shall be developed at the same time with, and by the side of debility and nervousness.

Some of the views herein contained have passed long since through the three stages through which all new truths must pass before they enter into the fellowship of science; the stage of indifference, the stage of denial, the stage of contests of priority ; others are passing out of the second and third of these stages, and others still have not yet passed, or are but beginning to pass out of the era of indifference. It is worthy of comment that some of the most iconoclastic of the truths here announced, those which, when first made known, years since, were believed to indicate insanity on the part of the author, and were felt to threaten the stability of the science to which they belong, have already become so interwoven with our medical literature, that their philosophy and their terminology are met with every day and every hour in reading and in conversation ; out of these researches a number of books have been published, in Europe and America, and numbers more, as I learn, are in preparation; in this new and immense field, there is room for an army of workers.

But despite all this rapid adoption and popularization of these facts, their reception is yet, and for a long future must remain, very far from being unanimous; indeed, only among the leading experts can they be said to have gained complete and unwavering acceptance; with the great body of science young and old, these truths are as though they had never been ; in all our cyclopedias of medicine, the terms hysteria, somnambulism, ecstasy, catalepsy, mimicry of disease, spinal congestion, incipient ataxy, epilepsy, spasms and congestions, anemias and hyperemias alcoholism, spinal irritation, spinal exhaustion, cerebral paresis, cerebral exhaustion and irritation, nervousness and imagination are thrown together recklessly, confusedly, hopelessly as in a witches caldron; and in all, and through all, one shall look vainly—save here and there, for an intelligent and differential description of neurasthenia, the most frequent, the most important, the most interesting nervous disease of our time, or of any time ; still hay-fever is classed as parasitic or infectious, although as justly insanity or epilepsy or neuralgia might be similarly classed ; still inebriety or dipsomania, is either not mentioned at all or grotesquely confounded with alcoholism or epilepsy ; still our medical graduates, after years spent in listening to lectures, must wait for their diploma before they are even ready to begin the study of this side of the nervous system. Meantime the literature of ataxia, which is but an atom compared with the world of functional nervous diseases, has risen and yet rising with infinite repetitions and revolutions to volumes and volumes.

The researches on the longevity of brain-work-

ers have a history which, at this stage, as an en-
couragement to young men who are giving themselves to original work, may properly be given
here. The investigations on this subject were made
by me while a student of medicine; were given as
a lecture before an association of army and navy
surgeons in New Orleans, were then put in a graduating thesis, which not only received no prize, but
not even an honorable mention. A popular essay
based on these researches, after being rejected by
one magazine was finally published in the " Hours
at Home," when all its statistics and reasonings were
called in question; after being put in a somewhat
different form the same was published in the first
volume of the " Transactions of the American Health
Association," and there for the first time, through
the transactions and through the reprint, was fairly
brought before the scientific world, and for the
first time began to have an audience. The essay
was reprinted in England in the London Journal
of Science, and a full abstract was published in
Germany, with the statement, that it was an evidence of the progress of science in the United
States that such researches could be made here.
Within the last few years the views of that essay
have been passing into general acceptance in the
scientific world; some of them having been used
of late as a base line whence to attack other

researches contained in this book. The philosophy and the facts which have met with so complete an endorsement, were in substance those contained in that graduating thesis which now rests in peace in the archives of my alma mater.

The philosophy of the work of neurasthenia of which the present work is a supplement, after a long period of indifference — has passed in the mind of many, if not the majority of experts on nervous diseases, through the three stages which new truths are destined to pass — so that, now we hear little but the dying away echoes of the contest of priority which always attends the latter part of the last stage in the evolution of ideas.

At the late meeting of the British Medical Association Dr. Crichton-Browne gave an address on this subject accurately stating and confirming my conclusions in regard to the increase of nervous diseases, and advocating throughout much of the philosophy embraced in that portion of this work which is devoted to the signs and causes of nervous exhaustion; and he also added some very suggestive and well-stated observations of his own; even going so far as to assert that the English are growing thinner, that they weigh less than their ancestors of a century ago.

The law of the relation of age to work which is announced and demonstrated in the chapter on longevity of brain-workers has not yet been accepted by any considerable number of human beings so far as known to me, and it is scarcely probable that it will be accepted, although it is easier of demonstration and absolute verification than any of the facts that are contained in these researches; men feel as though this discovery were an attack upon the human race, and by the instincts of self-preservation every one is enlisted to oppose it. It is probable, therefore, although any one with a cyclopedia can confirm all that I claim to have discovered on this subject, that a yet higher and wider development of the scientific sense will be required before even experts in pyschology shall be ready to receive a scientific truth so opposed to the almost universal convictions of mankind.

When, a number of years ago, I formulated some of the signs and proofs of this increasing nervousness, there was scarcely a responsive voice in any country; but the strongest, most numerous and comprehensive endorsements these views have obtained have thus far been in Germany and England more than in the United States, which is the nervous country by pre-eminence. So far as I know, there has been no hostile criticism of this philosophy in Germany, but in England, even now, these views are not unanimously sustained. At the time that Dr. Crichton-Browne gave his essay in which he not only asserted all that I had claimed on the increase of nervousness, but went even farther than I should have dared to go, on their increase in England, the distinguished microscopist, Dr. Lionel Beale, published a work on "Slight Ailments," in which he had occasion to refer to nervousness and to my researches in that subject, and he denies that there has been any increase; and implies that if our fathers had observed properly, they would have found as much as their descendants. Philosophy of this kind comes partly from defective observation; but more, it is to be feared, from defective reasoning; from conjoined inability and unwillingness to trace detailed facts back to the general laws whence they flow, or to take a wide survey of intricate and difficult problems. If this philosophy be driven to its logical conclusion, it must assert that, on the banks of the Nile and the Amazon, among the fading-away Indian tribes of our continent, in Greenland, in Iceland, in Lapland, in Russia, in China, in Turkey, in Australia, in India, in Japan, and in the Cannibal Islands there is just as much hay-fever, just as much epilepsy, just as much inebriety and insanity, just as much neurasthenia, as many phases of insomnia, of headache, just as much near-sightedness, as much hypochondria, hysteria, chorea, and as much mental and physical debility as there is in London and New

York. A conclusion so unscientific and non-accordant with general — to say nothing of special— observation, is a thousand times over refuted by facts contained in this volume; and that at this late hour, this delusion survives in scientific society is an argument more potent than all others I know, for such a re-construction of our system of education as shall make reasoning of that kind among educated men impossible.

The *London Times* in commenting on some of the views here brought forth has assumed and stated that I deplore the necessity of stating them. An inference so erroneous I trust may not be drawn from the present volume. Science fears not, nor does it hope — it does not even expect; but takes all that it finds in nature and makes it its own, trusting all, receiving all, and with equal welcome.

It has been said, it will be said here, that these subjects are unworthy of science, and that the time and force of scientific men expended upon them might have been more wisely used in other realms; and it will be urged, as it has been urged, upon those who would make the wisest use of their powers, to give little heed to the scientific study of this side of psychology and sociology.

As compared with politics, a topic like this must seem, and especially in a land like ours, very small indeed; so that only when we fix our eyes most closely upon it, is it possible to see it at all; but it is the office, the nature, the essence and the life of science to ennoble the ignoble, and out of smallness and meanness to evolve greatness and beauty; all science that is now known is but the organization of phenomena of nature that men have thought to be too trifling for the solemn attention of the human mind.

The philosophic study of the several branches of sociology, politics, charities, history, education, shall never be even in the direction of scientific precision or completeness until it shall have absorbed some, at least, of the suggestions of this problem of American Nervousness. We are, therefore, called to its study by the very presence in our minds of the seemingly weightier matters that would drive it out of sight; we are called to it by politics itself, which American youth are taught is the only theme worthy the attention of an ambitious nature; by the problems of merchandise, of invention, of property, and of social order. This subject also calls us to its study by the chance it gives through widely-opened doors for original, creative, pioneering, and productive work that shall make Europe follow us, instead of our following Europe. Long enough this babyland of science has fed on the crumbs that fall from Germany's table; corn and fruits we are carrying to the old country; let new ideas, and crops of fresh discoveries go with them. Better to criticise and confirm than to be idle; but wiser far to make others criticise and confirm. If we will cease to cross the sea in our search of materials for thought, and take those that fall in full showers at our doorsteps, we shall do our best service for other lands as well as for our own.

The hope may be expressed — that this theme may not be judged by the imperfectness and inexpertness of its representative; the insignificance of the author may weaken, but cannot destroy his cause; for, as little children sometimes return homeward from their play so laden and covered over with wreaths and flowers that they themselves are hidden, so this subject by its richness and importance quite conceals and overshadows its advocate.

G. M. B.

New York, May 1—
161 Madison Avenue.

CONTENTS

CHAPTER I.

NATURE AND DEFINITION OF NERVOUSNESS.

CHAPTER II.

SIGNS OF AMERICAN NERVOUSNESS.

CHAPTER III.

CAUSES OF AMERICAN NERVOUSNESS.

CHAPTER IV.

LONGEVITY OF BRAIN-WORKERS, AND THE RELATION OF AGE TO WORK.

CHAPTER V.

PHYSICAL FUTURE OF THE AMERICAN PEOPLE.

AMERICAN NERVOUSNESS

CHAPTER I.

NATURE AND DEFINITION OF NERVOUSNESS.

IF our fathers in medicine of the last century could be told of the subject of this work, their first question would be, "What is meant by the term nervousness?" They would say, and very truly, that the Greeks had no word for nervousness as we now understand that term; and that even down to the eighteenth century, nervousness was supposed to mean irritability of temper, disposition to anger, excitability—a mental quality, and not a physical disease.

The first step, therefore, in the study of nervousness is to define it. First of all, what does it not mean?

Nervousness does not mean unbalanced mental organization; a predominance of the emotional, with a relative inferiority of intellectual nature. Relative excess of the emotions may produce symptoms which appear to be precisely similar to those which come from nervousness, and have been, and usually are, classed as nervous symptoms; and from a want of

knowledge of this distinction, confusion without limit
has resulted in the minds of many in regard to this
whole subject. This dual meaning of the word "nervous" has been an important obstruction in the study
of nervousness in general and of many special nervous
diseases.

Whatever our philosophy of the relation of mind
to body may be, practically we are compelled to study
the mental as well as the physical side of the nervous
system both in health and disease. Psychology may
be but physiology out of sight, but psychology, as we
know it, and physiology as we know it, are not identical. Mental strength may coexist with physical weakness, and physical strength may coexist with mental
weakness.

A few illustrations familiar to all will make clear,
better than any quantity of abstract reasoning, this
distinction. The performers in the Middle-Age epi-
demies—those who were attacked with the various
symptoms of anæsthesia or paralysis, or with chorea
or hysteria in vast crowds, sometimes in large populations—these were not nervous, they were simply
unbalanced, that is, they had but little intellectual
strength and very much emotion, so that when these
psychical phenomena, as hysteria or chorea, once got
a start among them, it spread like fire on a prairie.
Trance, with its numerous, interesting and intricate
phenomena, a condition that has been known in all

ages, and among almost all people, is not nervousness, albeit nervous people are sometimes subject to it; it is more likely to be psychological than physical in its origin, and it is a condition that can only be studied satisfactorily by psychological methods.*

In the religious revivals of Kentucky, in the beginning of the present century, the phenomena of "The Jerkers," so called, were not manifestations of nervousness, but were in all respects similar to the Middle-Age epidemics. To the same order belong the performances of the "Holy Rollers," who, in certain parts of New Hampshire and Vermont, it is said, were wont to roll on the floor in the phrenzy of religious excitement. The "Jumpers," of Maine—the phenomena which I have recently studied, are not nervous, although they are called so by many of those who see them. As stated in my paper giving an account of my experiments with these remarkable people, none of them have the symptoms of nervous exhaustion, even in a mild form; they come from stalwart and hard-working ancestry, and they can themselves toil, and do toil systematically in the woods, and hold their own, side by side with their companions—they are not sleepless or neuralgic, nor do they suffer from morbid fears, or any of the various sensations of neurasthenics ·

* See my work on Trance, in which this distinction between physiology and psychology is discussed more fully and variously illustrated.

some of them are among the best examples of physical hardness and endurance ; but, despite all this muscular vigor, and all this broad margin of nerve-force which they certainly possess, they can no more help jumping, when suddenly struck, or on hearing a sharp sound, or throwing, or striking, or repeating automatically what is suddenly communicated, than they can avoid breathing. This interesting survival of the Middle Ages that we have right here with us to-day, is the most forcible single illustration that I know of, of the distinction between unbalanced mental organization and nervousness.

These Jumpers are precious curiosities, relics or antiques that the fourteenth century has, as it were, dropped right into the middle of the nineteenth. The phenomena of the Jumpers* are as interesting, scientifically, as any phenomena can be, but they are not contributions to American nervousness.

Brainlessness (excess of emotion over intellect) is, indeed, to nervousness, what idiocy is to insanity ; and, like insanity and idiocy, the two are very often confounded. Insanity is a disease of the brain in which mental co-ordination is seriously impaired ; but idiocy does not necessarily come from disease, but from defi-

---

* In the December number of *Popular Science Monthly* (1880), I described the phenomena of these Jumpers, and gave the results of my experiments with them, and showed their relations to mental and physical disorders more in detail than I can do here.

cient brain, or a brain unbalanced or badly organized ; as these psychical or mental disorders, like those of the Holy Rollers, the Jumpers, etc., do not come from disease, but from ill-balanced brains—a preponderance of emotion: and such mental disorders may appear, and usually do appear, in those who have an abundance of nerve-force, and can never become neurasthenic, or nervously exhausted.

Idiocy and insanity may sometimes run together ; so an emotional nature may sometimes become excessively nervous.

Nervousness is not passionateness. A person who easily gets excited or angry, is often called nervous. One of the signs, and in some cases, one of the first signs of real nervousness, is mental irritability, a disposition to become fretted over trifles ; but in a majority of instances, passionate persons are healthy—their exhibitions of anger are the expression of normal emotions, and not in any sense evidences of disease, although they may be made worse by disease, either functional or organic.

Nervousness is nervelessness — a lack of nerve-force.

If it be asked why I do not use the term nervelessness in preference to nervousness, the reply is, that nervousness already has the floor, and will hold it, and, with the above explanations, need not mislead. It is difficult, and sometimes beyond our power to drive out an old term, even although it be but partially correct. In medical science we are forced to retain terminology that is in the last degree unscientific, for the same reason that we retain our orthography, which in the English language is, as all know, very bad indeed. Such terms as Writer's Cramp, which gives but little idea of the condition to which it is applied, and Hay-Fever—one of the most unscientific and least expressive terms in medicine—we are compelled to adopt in scientific literature. Similarly, such common terms as hysteria and epilepsy are as strong in their positions as ever, although scientific men use them under reserved protest. It is, therefore, unwise to attempt to displace the term nervousness by nervelessness, or by any other word that might be framed. An attempt of this kind would doubly fail; it would not be understood, and would, therefore, bring confusion; and would not succeed in driving out the old and familiar term which has so long been growing in popular and professional literature.

Nervousness manifests itself by some one or many of a very large number of symptoms of functional debility and irritability, the majority of which symptoms are not found in those who have simply unbalanced mental organizations, and among these symptoms—which are described or illustrated in detail in my work on Nervous Exhaustion (Neurasthenia)—are the following:

Insomnia, flushing, drowsiness, bad dreams, cerebral irritation, dilated pupils, pain, pressure and heaviness in the head, changes in the expression of the eye, neurasthenic asthenopia, noises in the ears, atonic voice, mental irritability, tenderness of the teeth and gums, nervous dyspepsia, desire for stimulants and narcotics, abnormal dryness of the skin, joints and mucous membranes, sweating hands and feet with redness, fear of lightning, or fear of responsibility, of open places or of closed places, fear of society, fear of being alone, fear of fears, fear of contamination, fear of everything, deficient mental control, lack of decision in trifling matters, hopelessness, deficient thirst and capacity for assimilating fluids, abnormalities of the secretions, salivation, tenderness of the spine, and of the whole body, sensitiveness to cold or hot water, sensitiveness to changes in the weather, coccyodynia, pains in the back, heaviness of the loins and limbs, shooting pains simulating those of ataxia, cold hands and feet, pain in the feet, localized peripheral numbness and hyperæsthesia, tremulous and variable pulse and palpitation of the heart, special idiosyncrasies in regard to food, medicines, and external irritants, local spasms of muscles, difficulty of swallowing, convulsive movements, especially on going to sleep, cramps, a feeling of profound exhaustion unaccompanied by positive pain, coming and going, ticklishness, vague. pains and flying neuralgias,

general or local itching, general and local chills and
flashes of heat, cold feet and hands, attacks of temporary paralysis, pain in the perineum, involuntary
emissions, partial or complete ·impotence, irritability
of the prostatic urethra, certain functional diseases
of women, excessive gaping and yawning, rapid decay
and irregularities of the teeth, oxalates, urates, phos-
phates and spermatozoa in the urine, vertigo or dizzi-
ness, explosions in the brain at the back of the neck,
dribbling and incontinence of urine, frequent urination, choreic movements of different parts of the
body, trembling of the muscles or portions of the
muscles in different parts of the body, exhaustion
after defecation and urination, dryness of the hair,
falling away of the hair and beard, slow reaction of
the skin, etc.   Dr. Neisser, of Breslau, while translat-
ing my work on Nervous Exhaustion into German,
wrote me that the list of symptoms was not exhaustive.   This criticism is at once accepted, and was long
ago anticipated.   An absolutely exhaustive catalogue
of the manifestations of the nervously exhausted state
cannot be prepared, since every case differs somewhat
from every other case.   The above list is not supposed
to be complete,* but only representative and typical.

* Other symptoms of Neurasthenia have been described by me
in a series of papers in the New York *Medical Record,* on Nervous
Diseases connected with the male genital functions, published
during the last two years, ending February 19, 1881. It is quite
true, as Dr. Neisser states, that certain chronic catarrhs of the

Nervous Bankruptcy.

A nervous person suffering from any number of the above-named symptoms is one who has a narrow margin of nerve-force.

In finance, a man is rich who always lives within his income. A millionnaire may draw very heavily on his funds and yet keep a large surplus; but a man with very small resources—a hundred dollars in the bank—can easily overdraw his account; it may be months or years before he will be able to make himself square. There are millionnaires of nerve-force—those who never know what it is to be tired out, or feel that their energies are expended, who can write, preach, or work with their hands many hours, without ever becoming fatigued, who do not know by personal experience what the term exhaustion means; and there are those—and their numbers are increasing daily—who, without being absolutely sick, without being, perhaps for a lifetime, ever confined to the bed a day with acute disorder, are yet very poor in nerve-force; their inheritance is small, and they have been able to increase it but slightly, if at all; and if from overtoil, or sorrow, or injury, they overdraw their little surplus, they may find that it will require months or perhaps years to make up the deficiency,

nasal passages, pharynx and eyelids· are of a neurasthenic character, and are maintained by a depressed state of the nervous system.

if, indeed; they ever accomplish the task. The man with a small income is really rich, as long as there is no overdraft · on the account; so the nervous man may be really well and in fair working order as long as he does not draw on his limited store of nerve-force. But a slight mental disturbance, unwonted toil or exposure, anything out of and beyond his usual routine, even a sleepless night, may sweep away that narrow margin, and leave him in nervous bankruptcy, from which he finds it as hard to rise as from financial bankruptcy.

A man is not well and strong and properly organized and equipped for life, who has not a large amount of reserve force, much more than is needed in his ordinary duties. An electric battery that does not supply very much more electric force than is needful for the use to which the battery is put, is a failure, since, by the wasting away of the elements and the chemical changes that take place in the fluid, the force will tend to diminish, and unless there be originally a great reserve in excess of what is needed for the purpose—either medical or other use—there will be necessary frequent cleaning and overhauling. Scores of batteries of all sorts have been brought to me by hopeful and earnest inventors, which I have been obliged to condemn simply for this : that while, perhaps, they have every other desirable element in an instrument for medical use, they are deficient in reserve force. When in perfect order, with new fluid, the elements clean, all the connections perfectly bright, they will give, perchance, all the electricity that is needed, and thus deceive the inventor, the manufacturer, and the one who purchases; but in a few days the reserve is so drawn upon that they are useless, and in time become too feeble for the whole range of medical purposes, even after being thoroughly cleaned. I have been compelled to make myself very unpopular with inventors and manufacturers for giving this opinion in regard to their instruments. Men, like batteries, need a reserve force, and men, like batteries, need to be measured by the amount of this reserve, and not by what they are compelled to expend in ordinary daily life. Prof. Erb, of Leipsic, in his brief but very appreciative, scientific and suggestive chapter on "Neurasthenia," in Zimmsen's Cyclopedia of Medicine, emphasizes the fact that unusual exertion, out of the ordinary line of toil, is especially exhausting to neurasthenics. This is a fact which I observed for years in all my study of the subject, and it is an instructive and important fact in our study of the pathology of neurasthenia and of nervousness in general. The greater exhaustion that comes from unusual and unwonted exertion, has this twofold explanation, which is quite clear to those who are familiar with modern physics: First, unusual exertion, along the untravelled pathways of the nerves, meets with greater resistance, just as the electric force meets with greater resistance in a badly conducting circuit. Routine labor requires the evolution and transfer of force along well worn pathways, where the resistance is brought down to a minimum; hence a very slight evolution of force is sufficient to produce the result, just as a very slight amount of electricity will pass through a good conductor, like a large copper wire. To overcome this resistance of these unworn pathways, more nerve-force is required: the reserve is drawn upon; the man becomes tired. Hence we see that neurasthenics who can pursue without any special difficulty the callings of their lives, even those callings requiring great and prolonged activity, amid perhaps very considerable excitement, as that of statesmanship, politics, business, commercial life, or in overworked professions, are prostrated at once when they are called upon to do something outside of their line, where their force must travel by paths that have never been opened and in which the obstructions are numerous and can only be overcome by greater energy than they can supply. In the presence of unusual exertion, these persons are like men with moderate incomes, who, having long been accustomed to live within those incomes with ease, and who are therefore relatively rich, are called upon suddenly and unexpectedly to meet an unusual drain, and so become insolvent.

The purpose of treatment in cases of nervous exhaustion is of a twofold character — to widen the ✿margin of nerve-force, and to teach the patient how to keep from slipping over the edge.

Why American Nervousness ?

The very title of this work, "American Nervousness," may seem to some a giving away of this question; to others, perhaps, an insult. It is asked why not English, French, German, or Irish nervousness? Our answer is, that while modern nervousness is not peculiar to America, yet there are special expressions of this nervousness that are found here only; and the relative quantity of nervousness and of nervous diseases that spring out of nervousness, are far greater here than in any other nation of history, and it has a special quality. American nervousness, like American invention or agriculture, is at once peculiar and pre-eminent. Our title is justified by this, that if once we understand the causes and consequences of American nervousness, the problems connected with the nervousness of other lands speedily solve themselves.

He who has ascended the summit of Mont Blanc looks easily down on all the other mountains of the Alps, none of which he cares to ascend, for already he is higher than they; he who has solved the problem of nervousness as it appears in America, shall find its problems in other lands already solved for him; for as the greater includes the less, so the history of the rise and growth of the nerve maladies of the United States embraces all of a similar or allied nature that have arisen in other lands.

I have before me a most valuable book by Karl Hillebrand, on German Thought.

Neither by the title of this book nor by the treatment of the subject does the author imply that there is no thought outside of Germany. He does, however, imply, and directly state, that in modern times, up to a recent day, Germany has done the thinking in philosophy for all nations, and that there are peenliarities of German thought that entitle it to special study, and make it legitimate and proper to prepare a work on that subject and with that title. For the same reasons, American nervousness is a subject worthy of distinct and special study.

The philosophy of Germany has penetrated to all civilized nations; in all directions we are becoming Germanized. Similarly, the nervousness of America is extending over Europe, which, in certain countries, at least, is becoming rapidly Americanized. Just as it is impossible to treat of German thought without intelligent reference to the thought of other nationalities, ancient or modern, so is it impossible to solve the problem of American nervousness without taking into our estimate the nervousness of other lands and ages.

Nervousness distinguished from organic disease.

Nervousness is to be distinguished from nervous diseases of an organic or structural character. There is no evidence—certainly no evidence of a satisfactory character—that such serious diseases, for example, as locomotor ataxia, spinal paralysis, and various organic diseases of the brain, paralysis of a cerebral origin, with rupture of the arteries, have so very much increased in modern times, and there is certainly no evidence that diseases of this kind are any more common in America than in any other country. Indeed, so far as I have been able to estimate from information I have been able to obtain and from my own personal observation in the hospitals of Europe and of this country, I should say that locomotor ataxia and other diseases of the spinal cord are really more common in Europe than in America. Sufferers from ataxia and spinal meningitis and interior spinal sclerosis, are not usually very nervous people, certainly not exceedingly so. Indeed, nervousness, in its extreme manifestations, seems to save one from these organic incurable diseases of the brain and of the cord; with some exceptions here and there, the neurasthenic does not go into or die of nervous disease. A certain degree of nervousness may be necessary for the development of these structural diseases of the brain and cord, but not the extreme phases of nervousness. It is undeniable that these structural

diseases — some of them at least, are much more
common in civilized countries than in barbarian, but
they are not so common among the very nervous as
among those who are but moderately so ; they may
be regarded as stopping-places between the strength
of the barbarian and the sensitiveness of the highly
civilized. A point which I always make in dealing
with neurasthenic patients is, that their very frequent
fear of dying of some organic disease of the brain
and cord, is usually not well grounded, and that
their very nervousness is likely to save them from
what they so intensely fear. They may become insane—some of them do ; they may become bed-con-
fined invalids; they may be forced, as they often are,
to resign their occupations, but they do not, as a
rule, develop the structural maladies to which I
here refer.

Some of the nervous symptoms above mentioned
may be found in organic or structural disease, but
when so found they can be distinguished from the
same symptoms occurring in neurasthenia or the
neurasthenic state, by tests — as described in my
work on Neurasthenia — that need not often mislead us.

Although nervousness sometimes leads to insanity,
especially of the melancholic form, and to the types
known as inebriety and general paralysis of the insane,
just as it may lead to epilepsy or hysteria, yet there

is no necessary correlation between simple nervousness and the extreme or special manifestation of it in the form of insanity. Thousands and thousands are nervous who are not and never will be insane.

To compress all in one sentence; nervousness is a physical not a mental state, and its phenomena do not come from emotional excess or excitability or from organic disease but from nervous debility and irritability.

CHAPTER II.

FOR years, the philosophers of both continents have been asking, and in various and inconsistent ways have been answering, this question, Are nervous diseases increasing? and they have gone to the most distant regions and to the far away ages for arguments which, when found, did not aid them on either side. There is no need of this search, the proofs are all about us; we are overloaded, weighed down with excess of evidence; the proof shines so strong that our eyes are blinded by its light; it irritates and teases us until we are benumbed, and can feel no more.

Just as, in recent and famous trials in court, of persons accused of crime, there have been many escapes, from the very excess of evidence against the prisoner, whereby the overburdened jury have been compelled to give up the hope of finding the truth, so the magnitude, multiplicity and imminence of the phenomena of American nervousness overawe and weary us; the problem becomes harder to solve than if there were fewer facts to help us in the solution.

Just as, according to the old story, the passengers of a ship that had been long out of her calculations, being in danger of death from thirst, on saluting another passing vessel, and asking for water, were told to dip it up, for they were in the Amazon ;—so philosophers wandering in unknown regions, eager for information on this theme, may well pause where they are, and dip up facts enough all about them to solve the problem for all time.

Principles of evidence to be applied in the study of this subject.

Exact statistics in regard to the relative frequency of functional nervous diseases in ancient and modern times, or even comparing the last with the present century, cannot be secured, for the reason mainly, that persons do not die, or at least are not reported to have died of those diseases — even when death is a result directly or indirectly of neurasthenia, for example, it does not appear so in the death records; consequently, the tables of mortality are of no use in the study of this subject. The attempts that have been made to make comparison of the relative number of deaths that result from paralysis of cerebral origin in present and past times have failed in aiding the solution of this question, and partly for this—that rupture and other diseases of the blood-vessels are not, strictly speaking, nervous diseases; they are really vascular diseases ; but as rupture or lesion takes place in the vessels that go through the brain, the nervous system suffers. Diseases of this kind depending upon rupture in the brain or the breaking of the arteries are very old ; and, although they may have increased in modern times, they certainly have not increased as rapidly as functional diseases of the nervous system. Functional nervous disorders, which are an evolution of nervous diathesis, belong to a different order of disease ; they may increase, while structural diseases, such as some forms of paralysis, may decrease or remain stationary.

The development of nervousness and the increase of functional nervous diseases, under whatever names they may be known, have been so great in modern times, especially in the Northern portions of the United States, that there is no need of statistics — the facts can be demonstrated by the general observation of those who have opportunities to observe, and improve those opportunities so as to be able to draw correct conclusions. There is as much evidence that nervous diseases have increased in this country during the past fifty years as there is that the population has increased during the same time. Every ten years we have a census, but even if no census were taken, we should know that our population had increased largely; and that fact is no more certain after a census than before, although it has greater precision. A person visiting Chicago does not need to go through every house and count every inhabitant to know that it is a city of several hundred thousand, and that this population has multiplied from almost nothing in 1830 to half a million or more in 1880. Before the last census the citizens of Chicago estimated the population by general observation, and such estimates were not far from the truth. The citizens of St. Louis made estimates in the same way, and did not get so near to the truth. Both cities were influenced somewhat in their judgment by feelings of local pride, but both, in spite of this local bias, were correct in their conclusion that their respective cities had very materially augmented in population.

The evidence that nervous diseases have increased in the past century is quite as satisfactory; and even if statistics on this subject could be gathered as exact and particular as those of our census in regard to our population, such statistics, like those of the census, would merely give precision and confirmation to what we already know, and in regard to which our knowledge at present is practically sufficient.

Dr. Althaus, of London, has recently published a series of statistics which prove, or seem to prove, that *organic* or *structural* diseases of the nervous system have not increased in Great Britain during the past decade. These statistics are based on mortality reports, and are undoubtedly as correct as, in the nature of things, they can be; but for the reasons above given on the general subject of the increase of nervous diseases they shed absolutely no light. Nervous diseases or symptoms of the functional type, do not usually kill patients. No one dies of spinal irritation; no one dies of cerebral irritation; no one dies of hay-fever; rarely one dies of hysteria; no one dies of general neuralgia; no one dies of sick-headache; no one dies of nervous dyspepsia; quite rarely does one die of nervous exhaustion; and even when these conditions are the cause of death they are not noted as such in the tables of mortality; and yet a fleet of Great Easterns might be filled with our hay-fever sufferers alone; not Great Britain, nor all Europe, nor all the world, could assemble so large an army of sufferers from this distinguished malady; while our cases of nervous exhaustion would make a standing army as large as that of Russia. Even inebriety, as such, does not kill, or necessarily shorten life; it is the alcoholism and other effects of alcohol on the body that destroys inebriates, and not the disease inebriety. That these functional nervous diseases are multiplying on every hand, particularly in this country, is proved by the facts and reasonings here presented. But the tables of mortality give on this subject no information; these maladies might increase a hundred-fold and the death-rate would not be unfavorably affected by such increase. Take sick-headache, for example; in nearly every family of our brain-working, indoor-living classes there are cases; yet who dies of sick-headache? Seventy-five years ago hay-fever was almost unknown in this country or the world; now there are probably 50,000 cases in the United States alone, but who would suspect this increase from our tables of mortality? Persons may and do die with these diseases, but they do not die of them. Indeed, as I have elsewhere and often urged, these diseases favor longevity, and in a variety of ways; they make it necessary to be cautious, to avoid protracted over-exertion; they make it difficult or impossible to acquire destructive habits, and positively protect the system against febrile and inflammatory diseases. Hence the explanation of the apparent paradox that while there are more of these diseases in the United States than in all the rest of the world combined, there is no country where the longevity is greater than here.

Nervousness of constitution is, indeed, an aid to longevity, and in various ways; it compels caution, makes imperative the avoidance of evil habits, and early warns us of the approach of peril. Bulwer wisely says that it needs a strong constitution to be dissipated. Probably no great class of people in the world live longer than the professional and business men of America—the very class among whom these nervous disorders are so often found, the class that supplies the victims for our inebriate asylums.

I know not where to find a better demonstration
of the lack of logical and scientific training among
educated men, than in the published reports of the
discussion on this question of the increase of nervous
diseases, at the recent meeting of the International
Medical Congress in Philadelphia. While the weight
of opinion, so far as that goes, was in favor of the
views advocated by this paper, yet the speakers—men
of ability and distinction—nearly all illustrated the
very common habit—and with the laity quite excusa-
ble—of looking at one side of a subject. Thus, one
declared that there were no new diseases; another
that nervous diseases had only appeared to increase
through the mistaken observations of specialists. One
said that alcohol did not produce insanity; another
declared that it did, and that in connection with it,
tea, coffee, and tobacco caused more disease than brain
work. "Wickedness" was solemnly assigned as the
cause of the increase of nervous diseases, as though
wickedness were a modern discovery. One man wildly
declared that "the idea that a man could hurt himself
over books, was preposterous." But one of the strongest objections made was, that longevity had increased,
and that intellectual men are generally long-lived. To
me this objection was of special interest, from the
fact that when a number of years ago I first published
my investigations on the longevity of brain-workers,
showing that they lived longer than muscle-workers,

and that great men, on the average, lived longer than ordinary men, aud that longevity had clearly increased with the progress of civilization, I stated that nervous diseases of the functioual variety had increased *pari passu* with this increase of longevity, and that the facts, so far from being inconsistent, really explained each other, and for the reasous above noted.

Increase of the Nervous Diathesis.

It is observed that nearly all the sufferers from nervous exhaustion are those in whom the nervous diathesis temperament predominates. It is observed that the majority of these cases have what I have termed the *nervous diathesis*—an evolution of the nervous temperament.

I may quote here my remarks on the nervous diathesis as published originally in the first edition of Beard and Rockwell's "Medical and Surgical Electricity," p. 286:

By the term nervous diathesis we design to express a constitutional tendency to diseases of the nervous system. It includes those temperaments, commouly designated as nervous, in whom there exists a predisposition to neuralgia, dyspepsia, chorea, sick-headache, functional paralysis, hysteria, hypochondriasis, insanity, or other of the many symptoms of disease of the central or peripheral nervous system. What the gouty and scrofulous diathesis is to the blood, such is the nervous diathesis to the nerves.

The characteristic features of the nervous diathesis are ·

1. A fine organization. The fine organization is distinguished from the coarse by fine, soft hair, delicate skin, nicely chiselled features, small bones, tapering extremities, and frequently by a muscular system comparatively small and feeble. It is frequently associated with superior intellect, and with a strong and active emotional nature. By these general features the fine organization is so positively distinguished from one of an opposite character that it is most readily recognized even by those least accustomed to the study of temperaments. It is the organization of the civilized, refined, and educated, rather than of the barbarous and low-born and untrained — of women more than of men. It is developed, fostered, and perpetuated with the progress of civilization, with the advance of culture and refinement, and the corresponding preponderance of labor of the brain over that of the muscles. As would logically be expected, it is oftener met with in cities than in the country, is more marked and more frequent at the desk, the pulpit, and in the counting-room than in the shop or on the farm.

2. Liability to varied and recurring attacks of diseases of the nervous system. The nature of these attacks and the frequency of their repetition will be

variously modified by climate, the seasons, and other external conditions; by the personal habits and manner of life, and especially by sex and age. The typical manifestations of the nervous diathesis in infancy are convulsions, irritability, and sometimes grave cerebral disorder; of childhood, chorea, and analogous symptoms; of puberty, headache, chlorosis, spermatorrhœa, and occasionally epilepsy; of maturity, sick-headache, neuralgia, dyspepsia, with its accompaniments, constipation, insomnia, nervousness, and emaciation, functional and reflex and occasionally organic paralysis, hypochondriasis, neurasthenia, and, in women, hysteria, spinal irritation, and the long train of nervous conditions associated with diseases of the organs of reproduction; of old age, "softening of the brain," and slow paralysis. A child born with nervous diathesis may suffer in infancy from attacks of spasms of the glottis; in childhood, from chorea; at puberty, from spermatorrhœa; between the age of twenty and fifty or sixty, from the different grades and forms of dyspepsia, sick-headache, and neuralgia; and, in old age, may gradually fail beneath the slow advance of cerebral degeneration.

3. Comparative immunity from ordinary febrile and inflammatory diseases. The nervous diathesis appears, within certain limits to *protect* the system against attacks of fever and inflammation.

There seems, indeed, to be something in the nervous diathesis which is antagonistic to the febrile conditions, or at least to those forms which are developed by ordinary malaria for it is certain that on the average (with numerous exceptions, of course, on both sides) fevers and inflammations are less fatal among brain-workers than among muscle-workers, even when subjected to the same exposure. Now, it is among the brain-working class that the nervous diathesis is most distinctly marked and most frequently observed.

This great law also applies to races and nations. Although the question is so complicated by differences of external conditions that it is impossible to establish by statistics the relative quantity and quality of disease in civilized and barbarous lands, yet history and general observation seem to show that nearly all savage tribes are more liable to fatal attacks of certain forms of inflammatory and febrile disease than the civilized. The history of the North American Indians seems to point to this fact with considerable conclusiveness. Making all proper allowance for the better sanitary conditions, the higher prudence, and the stronger force of will of the civilized man, it would appear that he is less liable to contract certain forms of inflammatory disease than the barbarian, even when exposed to the same influences.

The nervous is the prevailing diathesis in the United States.

The nervous diathesis should be distinguished from

the tuberculous, with which it is frequently combined, and with which also it is liable to be confounded. The external appearances of the two are not very dissimilar, but their symptoms and their behavior under exposure, and especially their prognosis when existing separately, are radically different. The tuberculous diathesis frequently accompanies a fine organization; but fine organizations only in a certain proportion of cases have a tuberculous diathesis. The nervous diathesis is frequently not only not susceptible to tuberculosis, but apparently much less so than the average, and sometimes, indeed, seems to be antagonistic to it, for there are many nervous patients in whom no amount of exposure or hardship or imprudence seems to be able to develop phthisis, although they may appear to suffer intensely and constantly from the various phases of nervous disease. The tuberculous diathesis frequently appears in the coarsely organized, the plethoric, and the muscular. It develops most rapidly and perhaps commits its greatest ravages among the poor, the oppressed, and degraded. On the contrary, the nervous diathesis, though found more or less among all classes of civilized lands, is chiefly found among the higher orders. Both of these diatheses are the results and concomitants of depressed vitality; but the nervous is peculiar to brain-workers and civilization, while the tuberculous also afflicts the day-laborer and the savage. The one is perhaps an impoverishment of the blood, the other an impoverishment of the nervous force.

The distinction between the nervous and the tuberculous diathesis is seen again in the contrast in their prognosis. The nervous diathesis in many of its manifestations is speedily relieved, but rarely permauently eradicated; the tuberculous diathesis is less susceptible to actual relief, but in occasional instances may be absolutely cured. The nervous diathesis, by protecting the system against inflammations, seems to lengthen life; the tuberculous, by attacking and destroying a vital organ, most fearfully shortens it. In both the conflict between the remedies and the disease is always hard and sometimes long; in the nervous diathesis it is a guerrilla warfare, in which there are frequent skirmishes, with continual fightings and retreatings, where the enemy is disinclined to coneentrate his forces or allow himself to be drawn into a decisive encounter. In the tuberculous diathesis it is a pitched battle for the possession of a vital organ, where the enemy fights behind intrenchments, and usually obtains the mastery.

Increased susceptibility to stimulants and narcotics.

Among the signs of nervousness is increased sensitiveness to stimulants and narcotics. This is itself proof enough of the heightened nerve sensitiveness of the age. It is not only a fact demonstrated every day and every hour, but it is as unprecedented a fact as the telegraph, the railway, or the telephone. Until within twenty-five or thirty years, man, civilized or uncivilized, was an animal of tremendous alcohol power, organized for bearing, with only transient disturbance, enormous and repeated quantities not only of strong liquors, but also of other narcotics and stimulants of the various families.

Among Americans of the higher orders, those who live in-doors, drinking is becoming a lost art; among these classes drinking customs are now historic, must be searched for, read or talked about, like extinct or dying-away species.

A European coming to America sees a sight that no other civilized nation can show him—greater than Niagara—an immense body of intelligent people voluntarily and habitually abstaining from alcoholic liquors, females almost universally so, and males abstinent, if not totally abstinent. There is, perhaps, no single fact in sociology more instructive and far reaching than this, and this is but a fraction of the general and sweeping fact that the heightened sensitiveness of Americans forces them to abstain entirely, or to use in incredible and amusing moderation, not only the stronger alcoholic liquors, whether pure or impure, but also the milder wines ales, and beers, and even tea and coffee. Half of my nervous patients give up

coffee before I see them, and very many abandon tea
—next to chocolate the mildest of all table drinks.

Under the title of "The National Vice," Mr.
Richard Grant White has recently published in *The
Atlantic Monthly* what is a most accurate photograph
of the drinking customs of England as seen to-day.
Mr. White's observations are in harmony with my
own, among the very same classes, and in the same
districts.

Note the fact, also, that England is growing nervous, and that both her men and women drink far less
than formerly; and on all those subjects they are
passing through the stage in which we were thirty or
forty years ago. Every year the higher orders of
Great Britain are drinking less and less of strong
liquors; a simple substitute, a mild drink of a popular
sort, is having there a most extensive patronage. If
Mr. White had carried his studies into Germany he
would have found that the English, with all their
indulgence in alcoholic liquors, were but pupils and
beginners—amateurs, compared with the *habitués* of
the beer-gardens of Munich, Dresden, and Vienna.
Gallons upon gallons of their summer beer these Germans will drink day after day or in a single evening,
a quantity of fluid, considered merely as water, that
would suffice a brain-working, in-door living American for a week or month. An English physician of
much experience in nervous diseases asked me once

if it were true, as stated in one of my books, that my American patients could not bear smoking. I replied that there were very few nervous patients who were not injured by it, and very few who would not find it out without the aid of any physician. Our fathers could smoke, our mothers could smoke, but their children must ofttimes be cautious; and chewing is very rapidly going out of custom, and will soon, like snuff-taking, become a historic curiosity; while cigars give way to cigarettes. From the cradle to the grave the Chinese empire smokes, and when a sick man in China has grown so weak that he no longer asks for his pipe, they give up hope, and expect him to die. Savage tribes without number drink most of the time when not sleeping or fighting, and without suffering alcohol-ism, or without ever becoming inebriates; they have the vice of drinking, but not the nervous-disease inebriety.

It is much less than a century ago, that a man who could not carry many bottles of wine was thought of as effeminate—but a fraction of a man. But fifty years ago opium produced sleep; now the same dose keeps us awake, like coffee or tea;—susceptibility to this drug has been revolutionized.

The enormous quantity of alcoholic liquors, including beer, used in the United States, is used to a large extent by Germans and Irish, and those who live in the distant West and South.

Through all the Northern States the brain-work-ing classes find coffee more poisonous than whiskey or tobacco, and thousands are made wakeful by even a mild cup of tea. The incapacity for bearing the gentlest wines and beers is for thousands of our youth the only salvation against the demon inebriety. Thus the united forces of climate and civilization are press-ing us back from one stimulant to another, until, like babes, we find no safe retreat save in chocolate and milk and water. In the South, for climatic reasons, these substances are far better endured than in the North; but the very day on which this page is com-posed, I am called to see a Southerner paralyzed, to all appearance, through tobacco alone.

To see how an Englishman can drink is alone worthy the ocean voyage. On the steamer with me a prominent clergyman of the Established Church sat down beside me, poured out half a tumblerful of whiskey, added some water, and drank it almost at one swallow. He was an old gentleman, sturdy, vig-orous, energetic, whose health was an object of com-ment and envy. I said to him: "How can you stand that? In America, we of your class cannot drink that way." He replied, "I have done it all my life, and I am not aware that I was ever injured by it."

A number of years since I was present in Liverpool at an ecclesiastical gathering composed of leading members of the Established Church, from the bishops and archbishops through all the gradations; at luncheon, alcoholic liquors were served in a quantity that no assembly of any profession, except politicians, in this country could have tolerated.

Capacity to bear stimulants is a measure of nerve; the English are men of more bottle-power than the Americans.

This capacity for drinking measures the force of this stalwart people : long hours of brain-toil are better endured in Great Britain than in America; there is less exhaustion from the strain of overwork. This fact is observed by men in public life, as parliamentary leaders, etc., in England, that they can do more speaking, more sitting up late at night, as well as more eating and more drinking, than the politicians of America.

It has been said that the strength of a nation is the strength of the thighs rather than that of the brain; and, as an English physician of eminence has observed, the best population of the cities of Great Britain renews its strength from the large-limbed Highlanders of the north, but for whom there would be a constant degeneracy. It would appear, then, that the qualities which are necessary to make a good, strong nation are precisely the qualities which make a good horseman, and that he who can ride well makes a good founder of states. The English, as a people, have that balance and harmony of temperament. that always breed well. Large families are commanded by unrecorded law, and this little island has become the spawning-ground of empires.

The progress of total abstinence in both countries, is due, in part, no doubt, to the special efforts of reformers, but mainly to the general progress of culture, and perhaps, most of all, to that heightened nervous sensitiveness that makes it impossible for many to partake, even moderately, of wine without showing, instantaneously or speedily, the evil effects therefrom.

Temperance, indeed, is mostly a nineteenth century virtue, and the vice of intemperance is a survival of savagery in civilization. Going back yet farther, we find that with certain savage tribes, drunkenness is the rule, sobriety the exception. In these tribes every event of real or supposed importance, a birth, a funeral, the going to or return from battle, is celebrated by hard drinking. Reprove an Angola negro for being drunk and he will reply, " My mother is dead " as though that were excuse enough. Even as recently as the beginning of the present century, the custom of drinking at funerals yet survived with our fathers. At the present time both culture and conscience are opposed to such habits. It is among the depressed classes, who yet retain the habits, and the constitutions of the last century, that intemperance abounds; they drink as everybody drank, in the eighteenth century.

It is often claimed that we, of this generation, are more injured by drinking than our fathers, because of the adulterations of liquors. The reply to this is, that analyses show that most of the adulterations are, so far as their effect on the nervous system is concerned, comparatively harmless, and that few or none of them produce intoxication or inebriety. It is through the alcohol, and not the adulterations, that excessive drinking injures.

Inebriety.

This functional malady of the nervous system which we call inebriety, as distinguished from the vice or habit of drunkenness, may be said to have been born in America, has here developed sooner and far more rapidly than elsewhere, and here also has received earlier and more successful attention from men of science. The increase of the disorder has forced us to study it and to devise plans for it relief.

Like other nerve maladies, it is especially frequent here. It is for this reason mainly that asylums for inebriates were first organized in this country. England, however, is feeling the same need, and is beginning to follow our example.

In certain countries and climates where the nervous system is strong and the temperature more equable than with us, in what I sometimes call the *temperate belt* of the world, including Spain, Italy,

Southern France, Syria, and Persia, the habitual use
of wine rarely leads to drunkenness, and never, or
almost never, to inebriety; but in the intemperate
belt, where we live, and which includes Northern
Europe and the United States, with a cold and vio-
lently changeable climate, the habit of drinking either
wines or stronger liquors is liable to develop in some
cases a habit of intemperance. Notably in our country, where nervous sensitiveness is seen in its extreme
manifestations, the majority of brain-workers are not
entirely safe so long as they are in the habit of even
moderate drinking. I admit that this was not the
case one hundred years ago—and the reasons I give
in this work—it is not the case to-day in Continental
Europe; even in England it is not so markedly the
case as in the northern part of the United States.

For those individuals who inherit a tendency to
inebriety, the only safe course is absolute abstinence,
especially in early life; and in certain cases treatment
of the nervous system, on the exhaustion of which the
inebriety depends.

The use of tobacco in the form of smoking cigars
and cigarettes, is probably more common in America
to-day than it was a quarter of a century ago, but
smoking pipes and chewing and snuff-taking, are
habits which are passing away, among the better
classes. Thus is harmonized the paradox that while
there are more persons, perhaps, who make some

use of tobacco, there are fewer persons of the same classes who make an excessive use of it than formerly; and of those who do use it, even but lightly, there is an increasing number who are perceptibly injured by it.

Sensitiveness to drugs.

The increasing nerve susceptibility of our time and country is excellently illustrated by the effect of cathartic remedies. It took stronger doses to affect the bowels in the last generation than in the present —where formerly two or three powerful pills were required for a strong cathartic effect, now, one or two, or perhaps half a pill, suffices. This differential action of the same remedy on different temperaments can be well studied by those who have both hospital and private practice; the coarse and phlegmatic temperaments will require, in some cases, several-fold more powerful remedies to give a strong cathartic effect than the nervous and sensitive.

I am constantly obliged, in my practice, to prescribe half a pill for a cathartic, where for an old-fashioned constitution, such as we sometimes see, even now, two or three, or perhaps even more, are needed.

One very eminent physician finds that even chocolate, one of the mildest beverages, is a poison to him; and another experienced physician who consulted me one time in regard to himself, could not, he said, bear anything that I prescribed. I spoke of iron : he said iron, even in small doses, made his head ache; and when I tried it, even with other medicines, it produced that effect. I suggested quinine : he said quinine made him crazy. I tried a zinc combination : it disturbed his stomach. And yet this man, so variously sensitive, was actively engaged in one of our most laborious professions.

Thirstlessness.

Thirstlessness—a lack of desire for water, and the difficulty of assimilating it—is as common among the upper classes of Americans as lack of desire for solid food, and is a most serious symptom, expressive of a lower grade of nerve exhaustion. No people in the world drink so little fluid as we, either with or between meals. To see how other nations drink, and to learn how our fathers, half a century ago, used to drink, is, to a philosophic nature, worth a trip to Europe, though nothing else be seen; since one may live here for a lifetime and never take the pains to study the habits of recently-imported foreigners in our midst, or the habits of American-born citizens in the far distant West.

Relation of Indigestion to Nervousness.

Dr. Lauder Brunton, editor of *The Practitioner*, has lately published a very thoughtful and instructive

pression," the leading point of which is, that in the digestive track and particularly the intestines, various gases are formed, as sulphuret of hydrogen, marsh gas, etc., which, being absorbed into the circulation, have a paralyzing influence on the nerve centres. Dr. J. H. Salisbury, of Cleveland, has for years inculcated this same doctrine, and has treated his patients in accordance with it. Dr. Brunton argues, logically and truthfully, that much of nervous depression results from indigestion and from liver disorder, and that the old belief that hypocondria had its origin in the liver has thus a scientific explanation. While all this is quite true, it is also true, that, without special reference to digestion there may be impoverishment of nerve energy; the digestion even may be strong or tolerably so, while the individual is very weak, and, on the other hand, the person may be very strong, while the digestion is far from perfect; in a word, indigestion may excite and maintain neurasthenia and may result from it, but neurasthenia is none the less a condition of itself, though necessarily modified by the state of digestion. If, in an electric battery, however well constructed, the fluids are made impure by the products of chemical decomposition, the amount of force generated for use will be very much reduced, though the metals are new and the conduction is good; so in the body, though there may be much force in the nerve centres, yet if digestion be clogged and the waste matters are suffered to accumulate in the digestive apparatus and gases, and waste products circulate through the nerve system, the amount of force generated and usable will be very much diminished. When the fluid of a battery is filled with impurities by chemical decomposition, we may pour in acids as much as we will, but the battery will be weak, and the force you will get from it will be small; when the body is clogged with waste products, we may supply food, and the best of food, in any amount, and the person will be still feeble; hence it is that we so often find not only epileptics, but neurasthenics and nervous persons with other symptoms, are free and sometimes excessive eaters. They say their food does not give them strength, and it does not, for the same reason that the acid poured into the impure fluid of the battery does not give us electric force. There are those who all their lives are habitually small eaters and yet are great workers, and there are those who, though all their lives great eaters, are never strong; their food is either not digested or thoroughly assimilated, and so a much smaller fraction than should be is converted into nerve-force.

Sensitiveness of the Digestion.

Delicacy of digestion is one of the best known and first observed effects of civilization upon the nervous system. The history of the rise and fall of pork as an article of food is itself, without any re-enforcing fact, most instructive on this point. In America pork like the Indian, flees before civilization. In all the great cities of the East, among the brain-working classes of our large cities everywhere, pork, in all its varieties and preparations, has taken a subordinate place among the meats upon our tables, for the reason that the stomach of the brain-worker cannot digest it. Three times a day, and every day in the year almost, the flesh of swine in some form was, in the last generation, the dependence of our fathers, who could eat it freely without ever asking themselves whether it was easy or hard to be digested. This dethronement of pork has had, and is still having on one side, a disastrous effect upon the American people; for, as yet, no article of food with a sufficient amount of fat has been generally substituted; and fat in our dietaries is, if it can be assimilated, one of the imperative needs.

The demand for the pork of America is extensive in Europe, the exports reaching annually the value of one hundred millions, and the attempt made this very year to stop this exportation was an alarm to an immense body of capitalists. In our own country, pork is yet freely and in some districts almost exclusively employed, but chiefly in farming districts, and especially in the sparsely settled region of the South and West.

Americans moderate eaters.

Compared with Europeans, Americans of the middle and higher orders are, or have been, but moderate eaters. The bulk of our daily food is less than that of the English or Germans. With material for food in unlimited variety, we have made less use —certainly less frequent use of it at the table than any other nation of modern times. Four and five meals a day is, or has been, the English and, notably, the German custom. Foreigners have greatly surpassed us in the taking of solid as well as liquid food.

Twenty-five years ago nervous dyspepsia was diagnosed in Germany as the "American disease." This pre-eminence we deserve no longer—at least not as fully as then—for not only is it frequent in England, but Germany itself is a sufferer from this malady.

Increase of Near-sightedness and Weakness of the Eyes.

The *eyes* also are good barometers of our nervous civilization. The increase of asthenopia and short-sightedness, and, in general, of the functional disorders of the eye, are demonstrated facts and are most instructive. The great skill and great number of our oculists are constant proof and suggestions of the nervousness of our age.

The savage can usually see well; myopia is a measure of civilization. Well known German investigators have shown that near-sightedness increases in schools, from class to class, the proportion of near-sighted persons in the advanced classes being much greater than with those who have just entered. Near-sightedness, however, is but one of many maladies of the eye that civilization excites; the muscles are oftentimes weakened by excessive use, and in some cases where apparently there has not been over-use. And this muscular weakness is accompanied by great pain in the eye, and frequently by inability to read, sew, or do any work that requires close vision. The number of persons of both sexes who suffer in this way is very large indeed, and is certainly on the increase.

The special cause of this increase of near-sightedness in modern times is so apparent, that there has been but little dispute in regard to it—the over-use of the eyes for looking at minute objects, as in writing and reading.

In this form of local nervous and muscular debility, Germany has, it would appear, seemed to lead the world, and probably for these two reasons:

First. In the German schools and in the student life of certain classes of Germans, severe demand is made on the eyes by the illegible type and manuscript.

Secondly. The Germans, being less nervous than the Americans, excess in the use of any organ is more likely to induce in them local than constitutional disease, in accordance with the general law that in strong persons abuse of any function produces local disease and in the weak constitutional disease.   An American breaks down all over—becomes neurasthenic before his eyes give out; he cannot work long enough to injure his vision, but must give up while it is yet good.   Constitutional diseases prevent local diseases and *vice versa.*

Dr. Hasket Derby, of Boston, in a recent article asserts that, in the United States there is about one-third as much near-sightedness as in Europe, but that in New England, about one person in every ten who consults the oculist is near-sighted.   In regard to the development of near-sightedness with civilization and through the use of the eyes in schools, these propositions seem to be pretty clearly supported.

First, that among savages everywhere, near-sightedness is very rare, just as insanity, neurasthenia, hay-fever, the nervous disease inebriety, sick-headache epilepsy, hysteria, chorea, and nervous dyspepsia are very rare.

Macnamara declares that he took every opportunity of examining the eyes of Southall aborigines of Bengal, for the purpose of discovering whether near-sightedness and diseases of like character existed among them, and he asserts that he never saw a young Southall whose eyes were not perfect.

Secondly. Near-sightedness is rare in children who have not been to school.

Thirdly. Among the school-children of this country, between the ages of six and seven, three out of a hundred are found to be near-sighted.

Fourthly. This percentage increases with age, and at the age of twenty, twenty-six out of one hundred Americans are near-sighted. In Russia, forty-two out of a hundred, and in Germany, sixty-two out of a hundred are near-sighted.

Dr. Derby believes that spasm or cramp of the ciliary muscle, produced by over-use, is one of the first causes of near-sightedness.

Dr. Loring, of this city, in an excellent paper on this subject, avers that near-sightedness has a reactive effect on the mind, of an injurious character, and for that reason alone, should, if possible, be prevented.

At the recent Congress of German Naturalists, at Dantzic, Prof. Cohn delivered an address on "The Relation of School Hygiene to Myopia." He claims that it is rarely congenital, he having never met with it in children below five years of age. In rural schools but few myopes are found, the number increasing with the grade of the school. The figures in the Geneva high schools are alarming. In the "Malschulen" (corresponding to the scientific course of the high school) there were from twenty to forty per cent.; in the elementary schools from ten to twenty-

four per cent.; in the village schools five to eleven
per cent.; and in the " Gymnasien," or classical high
school, from thirtv to fifty-five per cent.—a regular
increase from the lowest school to the highest; showing clearly that over-use of the eyes in study is the
one exciting cause of this malady. He forms his
conclusion from the examination of over 10,000 school
children.

Early and rapid Decay of the Teeth

Teeth decay among other peoples, and the pain
called toothache is probably a thousand years old; nor
is man the only animal that suffers in this way. There
is no class of people of any race or color who lose
their teeth so early through decay, and so rapidly, and
need to keep themselves so constantly under the den-
tist's eye as the better class of Americans. American
dentists are the best in the world, because American
teeth are the worst in the world.

Necessity has been the parent of inventive skill.
Dr. J. N. Farrar, of New York, estimates that
$500,000 in pure gold is each year put into the
mouths of Americans, and four times as much cheaper
material, such as silver and platina; that each year
millions of artificial teeth are mounted, and that but
little more than one person in a hundred, take people as they are, has perfect teeth. All this is modern,
and, in this extreme manifestation, American.

This quick decay of teeth in America, and the various forms of nervous diseases that go with this decay, are the results not of climate alone, but of climate combined with civilization : the confluence of these two streams is necessary.   Irregularities of teeth, like their decay, are the product primarily of civilization, secondarily of climate.   These are rarely found among the Indians or the Chinese ; and, according to Dr. Kingsley, are rare even in idiots ; the cretins of Switzerland, the same authority states, have " broad jaws and well-developed teeth."

Special investigations have been made in order to determine whether negroes and Indians are troubled with decayed teeth.   Judging from all the sources of information, it is within the facts to assert that while the Indians, especially in advanced life, are liable to have the teeth decay, and while negroes, even in middle life, are similarly affected, yet, as compared with sensitive, nervous whites, they suffer but little in this way.   It is probable that negroes are troubled earlier than Indians.   The popular impression that negroes always have good teeth is erroneous—the contrast between the whiteness of the teeth and the blackness of the face tending not a little to flatter them.   Those who have sought to prove that the teeth decayed among savages, hundreds of years ago, just as rapidly, just as early, and just as badly as they decay now, among nervous, susceptible whites of this country, because they succeed in finding proofs of decay in skulls which they have examined, are guilty of reasoning quite the reverse of expert

Another fact of much instructiveness is, that decayed teeth in Indians and negroes are less likely to annoy and irritate than the same amount of decay in sensitive, nervous, and finely organized whites of any race.

Coarse races and peoples, and coarse individuals can go with teeth badly broken down without being aware of it from any pain; whereas, in a finely organized constitution, the very slightest decay in the teeth excites pain which renders filling or extracting imperative. The coarse races and coarse individuals are less disturbed by the bites of mosquitoes, by the presence of flies or of dirt on the body, than those in whom the nervous diathesis prevails. Nervous force travels more slowly, the reflex irritation is less perceptible by far, in the dark races and those who live out-doors, than in those who live in-doors, and are of a nervous diathesis. In the strong and coarsely built local irritation remains local, and does not reverberate through the body; while, on the other hand, in the feeble, the sensitive, and the highly and finely organized, any local irritation is speedily transmitted and puts the whole system into disturbance. The simple operation of sneezing illustrates this law in a most interesting and significant manner. It is said, for example, of the negroes of the South, that they rarely if ever sneeze. It is certain that the nervous, feeble, sensitive, and impressible of any race are far more likely to be provoked into sneezing from slight irritation of the nasal passages than those of an opposite temperament. In hay-fever, sneezing is one of the leading symptoms, and is provoked by irritations in themselves of the most trifling character, which those not victims of the disease can only be forced to believe by a personal battle with this enemy of the race.

Special explanations without number have been offered for this long-observed phenomenon—the early and rapid decay of American teeth—such as the use of sweets, the use of acids, neglect of cleanliness, and the use of food that requires little mastication. But they who urge these special facts to account for the decay of teeth of our civilization would, by proper inquiry, learn that the savages and negroes, and semi-barbarians everywhere, in many cases use sweets far more than we, and never clean their mouths, and never suffer, except in old age. The cause of the decay of teeth is subjective far more than objective—in the constitution of the modern civilized man. The young are early cautioned to clean their teeth, and properly so; but the only races that have poor teeth are those who clean them.

Baldness.

The increasing popularity of baldness is one of the minor but most instructive expressions of nerve sensitiveness. Among savages in all parts of the earth baldness is unusual, except in extreme age, and gray hairs come much later than with us. So common is baldness in our large cities that what was once a deformity and exception is now almost the rule, and an element of beauty. One may be bald without being very nervous; but the general prevalence of baldness comes from the general prevalence of nervousness. The beard and hair, accurately studied, are measures of nutrition of high delicacy and power.

A sudden emotional disturbance, as of grief, or the exhaustion of acute illness, or an exacerbation of chronic debility, may in a few days, or even in a few hours, cause the hair to fall or turn white and make it excessively dry.

Although woman is more nervous than man, yet she is less afflicted with baldness; the reason being that she has on her head more and longer hair, a greater proportion of her force being expended in that direction; hence, when she becomes nervous, she breaks down in other directions sooner than in this.

Sensitiveness to Heat and Cold.

Increased sensitiveness to both heat and cold is a noteworthy sign of nervousness. We must have the temperature of our rooms at least ten or twelve, if not fifteen degrees higher than our fathers desired, and at least ten degrees higher than the English, French or Germans of the present day desire. Dr. Bucknill, of England, when visiting the asylums of this country, noticed that the temperature was kept not less than ten or fifteen degrees higher than that of the asylums of Europe. In the winter we must dress warmer than our ancestors, we wear more under as well as over clothing; we cannot endure wet feet as they could, nor bear with impunity the same exposure. India-rubbers are far less used in Europe than here, although, on account of the abundant rains, they are more needed there. In America rubbers are for sale at every shoe-store; in Paris and in London I have hunted for hours looking for a pair. The heat of summer is not well tolerated; sunstrokes are, relatively, more frequent, or heat prostrations that suggest sunstroke, and which are followed in some cases by years of nervous disorders and symptoms. The months of July and August bear so heavily on our brain-working classes as to slow down or suspend business everywhere; a visitation of prolonged heat more fatal than yellow fever or cholera; we are to the mountains or the sea as by the march of an invading army.

Cold bathing is not borne as well as formerly. When the water system first became popular in the treatment of disease, great benefit was in many cases obtained by the use of very cold water, and the injurious effects arising from such treatment were not so common as now.

At present, in America at least, cold water is not used in hydropathic establishments as universally as when these institutions were first started; and one reason, among many others, why the hydropathic treatment declined in popularity among English-speaking people is, that nervous people (who were most likely to frequent these places) were also most in danger of being injured by the use of cold water. What their ancestors could not only bear, but be benefited by, they cannot bear at all. In ordinary bathing, not only in this country, but in England, it has been found of late years, that it is necessary to have water warmed somewhat, before applying it to the body—the old habit of cutting holes in the ice and plunging in is passing away; and the recently published protests in the *Lancet*, against the use of cold water in the morning bath, were wise and timely.

A large number of the nervous patients whom I treat professionally cannot bear the Turkish and Russian baths, as they are generally given; in many cases they are injured by them, and in some cases permanently injured, even for years.

In France, where the treatment of nervous diseases is very little understood, scarcely anything is advised by the best neurologists except the use of water, with a result, in the case of many of our American patients, of working serious injury. Two cases illustrating this have been brought to my attention this past month. Even while this paragraph is being written, I have received a letter from an American physician studying in Germany, in which he informs me that one of his patients—a Russian lady, I believe—was nearly killed by immersion in a deep tub of very cold water.

Water treatment is as good for some forms of nervous disease as it ever was; but it must be adapted to the constitution of the patient, and adapted also to the peculiar needs of each case.

Evolution of Nervousness.—Nervous Exhaustion (Neurasthenia).

More specifically, and to the eye of some, perhaps, more interesting than all, is the increase of neurasthenia, or nervous exhaustion, and effects allied to and correlated with it. Out of the soil of nerve-sensitiveness springs the nervous diathesis which runs into neurasthenia, or nervous exhaustion. Among the many branches of this neurological tree are, in the order in which they are very likely to develop in many cases—nervous dyspepsia, sick-headache, near-sightedness, chorea, insomnia, asthenopia, hay-fever, hypochondria, hysteria, nervous exhaustion in its

varieties, and ın the extreme cases—epilepsy, inebriety, insanity. (See Frontispiece). The disease, state,
or condition to which the term neurasthenia is applied is subdivisible, just as insanity is subdivided
into general paresis or general paralysis of the insane,
epileptic insanity, hysterical, climatic, and puerperal
insanity ; just as the disease or condition that we call
trance is subdivided into clinical varieties, such as
intellectual trance, induced trance, cataleptic trance,
somnambulistic trance, emotional trance, ecstatic
trance, etc. ; just so neurasthenia has sub-varieties, or
clinical varieties, the cerebral, the spinal, the sexual,
the digestive varieties, and so forth. These varieties
of nervous exhaustion are nowhere experienced, nowhere known, as they are here ; and even here they
have been known in great abundance only within the
past quarter of a century ; and they are even now
but just beginning to be scientifically and discriminately recognized and differentiated. The fathers and
mothers—the grandfathers and grandmothers—of our
neurasthenic parents of both sexes suffered from rheumatism, from gout, from lung fever, from all forms
of colds, from insanity now and then, and from epilepsy quite often ; but they were not neurasthenic

The influences and conditions that excite the
gout in the phlegmatic and strong develop to nervousness in the sensitive and weak ; neurasthenia is
more abundant in America, gout and rheumatism

in Europe. Lately I was consulted by a very nervous patient who comes from a line of gouty ancestors reaching back through several generations, the morbific force in his case having changed to the symptoms of insomnia, mental depression, and neuralgia.

The excessive nervousness of Americans seems to act as an antidote and preventive of gout and rheumatism, as well as of other inflammatory diseases. Many of the gouty and rheumatic patients in Europe are troubled with indigestion, and it happens very often indeed that attacks of rheumatism and gout— such as are familiar to the English and Germans—are preceded by so-called " bilious attacks," that is, symptoms of indigestion. The antagonism of disease to disease, and the force and value of disease in the treatment of disease, are illustrated very well by the frequency of functional nervous diseases in America, and the infrequency of gout and rheumatic troubles; and it would be most interesting to know whether as Europe becomes Americanized, and neurasthenia, with its train of symptoms invades Great Britain and the Continent, there shall take place a corresponding diminution in the frequency and severity of gout and rheumatism.

The purpose of the drawing (Frontispiece) should not be misunderstood; it is not to give a mathematical statement or history of the development of nervous symptoms as applicable to any one case, but a general view of the way in which these nervous symptoms develop, no two cases being precisely alike in this respect, or in any other respect. For clearness and convenience I use familiar terms rather than technical terms—those which are symptoms of disease rather than, strictly speaking, disease itself, such, for example, as hypochondria and insomnia.

The drawing gives a general view of the order in which these nervous symptoms are very likely to appear, although there is no uniformity.

Nervous dyspepsia is one of the first, then follows sick-headache—sometimes these come together, while the other symptoms of neurasthenia or nervous exhaustion are much later; and yet, hay-fever may come very early, even in babyhood; and near-sightedness and chorea in childhood, and neurasthenia or nervous exhaustion itself, in any of its varieties, may appear without many of the conditions which in this drawing seem to precede it; for many of these conditions are themselves symptoms of nervous exhaustion.

There is, it will be observed, no mathematical line between nervous diathesis and nervous exhaustion, the object being to represent what is truly the case, a growth and evolution; a passing from one state into another by successive increments.

Insanity and epilepsy are, occasionally, results of

protracted nervous exhaustion; but epileptics do not, as a rule, pass through this stage of neurasthenia before they become epileptics; indeed, neurasthenia saves us, in some cases, from insanity, although it may lead to insanity; on the other hand, inebriety (or dipsomania) may occur in those who are not neurasthenic, but simply of a nervous diathesis; or, it may be one of the sequels of neurasthenia, just like insanity in general.

One very important fact suggested by this drawing, that is, that many of the cases of nervous exhaustion and many of the cases of spinal trouble of various kinds, had in early life, nervous dyspepsia and sick-headache, from which, perhaps, they have either partially or wholly recovered, and which, indeed, they may have forgotten.

Increase of diseases not distinctively nervous.

Not only purely nervous diseases, such as are above described, but also diseases in which there is an important nerve element, have increased with the advance of civilization. Types of maladies of this class are diabetes and the so-called Bright's disease of the kidneys in its different varieties. The severe forms of Bright's disease do not, as a rule, occur in the very nervous, but oftentimes in those of fair if not firm constitution, and very frequently indeed in those of great apparent vigor—the class that suffer from locomotor ataxia and cerebral paralysis — but the milder and more chronic, and intermitting and relievable forms occur in those who are quite nervous and sensitive— even in the positively neurasthenic.

That diabetes is largely if not mainly a nervous disease is becoming more and more the conviction of all medical thinkers, and that, like Bright's disease, it has increased of late, can be proved by statistics that in this respect are in harmony with observation.

A single branch of our neurological tree, hay-fever, has in it the material for years of study; he who understands that understands the whole problem. In the history of nervous disease I know not where to look for anything more extraordinary or more instructive than the rise and growth of hay-fever in the United States of America. Straggling cases of this disease are found in Germany and France—possibly, also, in Italy and Spain; it is somewhat more frequent in Great Britain: but in the state of Illinois alone there are probably more cases every year, in its earlier, later, and middle forms, than in all the rest of the world, excepting the other States of the Union.

Hay-fever, as I have demonstrated in my work on that subject, is a nervous disease; it is subjective more than objective, though excited and maintained by invading objective irritations ; it is simply the sign of susceptibility, the peculiar idiosyncrasy of the nervous system to one or many irritants. Where can we find a more completely unprecedented fact than this, that for many years there has been here a large and powerful body called "The United States Hay-Fever Association," with a not unimportant branch in the West, and with a new branch projected in New York city? The fall or autumnal form of hay-fever is peculiarly American, and was but little known, if known at all, in this country seventy-five years ago. A just estimate on these matters is always impossible; but that there are in this country, crowded together mostly in the northern and western sections, diminishing in number as we go south, like all other nervous diseases, an army of fifty thousand (a respectable city in population) sufferers from this disease, is very probable. As I have myself studied or known of not less than one thousand cases, this estimate cannot be very excessive.

Chronic Catarrhs.

Catarrh of the nose and nasal pharyngeal states — so-called nasal and pharyngeal catarrh — is not a nervous disease, in the strict sense of the term, but there is often a nervous element in it; and in the marked and obstinate forms it is, like decay of the teeth and irregularities of the teeth, one of the signs or one of the nerve symptoms of impairment of nutrition and decrease of vital force which make us unable to resist change of climate and extremes of temperature.

That there has been an increase in nasal and pharyngeal catarrh in America during the last half century, seems to be pretty clearly established by the recorded experiences of large numbers of physicians in general and special practice; and it would seem that these catarrhs are more obstinate and difficult to yield to the most judicious treatment known to our modern art. Quite true it is that catarrh is but a symptom, and a symptom of various and differing diseased states of the nasal passages and the nasal and pharyngeal spaces; and quite true it is that bulging of the septum and hypertrophy of the turbinated bones are common pathological conditions in the disease known as nasal catarrh. But these hypertrophies and bulgings of the septum are themselves oftentimes a result of imperfect nutrition; and true also it is that, of themselves, they might not cause annoyance of an important character; but when acted upon by cold and damp they become sources of great and life-long distress.

There is every reason for the belief that, fifty years ago, catarrh was relatively more infrequent than now; that is, the number of cases, according to the population was not so large. Indeed, this malady is now so common that each city or locality in the northern and eastern portions of the country is asking itself whether there is anything in its location or climate to account for the frequency and severity of the catarrhs with which it is infested.*

It is certain, also, that the greatest sufferers from chronic catarrh are not those who are most constantly exposed to the dangers of out-door life — cold and damp—but those who live mostly in-doors ; who have only intermittent or occasional exposure ; many ladies, whose lives all the year are passed under cover are the most severe sufferers. All these statements are in no way inconsistent with these two facts ; first, that cold and damp are exciting causes of catarrh, when acting on the predisposed constitution ; and, secondly, that the greater attention which physicians of late years—general practitioners as well as laryngologists —have given to the treatment of catarrh has forced the subject more constantly and impressively upon our notice ; but to reason, therefore, that catarrh has not increased, is to imitate the illogical and unscientific example of those who have, until lately, contended that insanity and neurasthenia have not increased in modern times. To my own mind, there is no doubt that catarrh is much more frequent in the northern and eastern portions of the United States than in any portion of Europe.

* Very recently a committee of the Kings County Medical Society in Brooklyn have been investigating the question, whether residents of Brooklyn are more liable to suffer from catarrh than residents of New York city.

Habit of taking Drugs.

America is a nation of drug-takers. Nowhere else shall we find such extensive, gorgeous, and richly supplied chemical establishments as here; nowhere else is there such general patronage of such establishments. Not only in proprietary medicines, but in physicians' prescriptions, as well as in self-doctoring, this continent leads the world; a physician can live here on half the number of families that would be needed to support him in Europe, on the same terms.

But with all our drug-taking we are, as a people, sensitive to medicine. The difference between American and European constitutions, on the side of the nervous system, is illustrated in the different treatment that our nervous patients receive when they consult European physicians of distinction and skill. American physicians whose patients go abroad are astonished at the powerful medicines and the largeness of the doses ordered by the best authorities in Great Britain and on the Continent; and on the other hand, English and Continental physicians are astonished at the sensitiveness of Americans to strong remedies given in ordinary doses.

An American physician, long afflicted with severe neurasthenia, who for some time had been under my professional care, on reaching London, consulted a medical gentleman whom I knew to be familiar with those conditions as they exist in Europe, and who is judicious in their treatment. In this case he ordered a combination, such as he was accustomed constantly to give in his own practice in London, which produced not only a powerful but poisonous, and almost fatal effect; so that, indeed, for some hours it was a question whether the patient would survive.

I remarked to the London physician, when I saw him, not long after, that I should not have dared to have given such a dose to that patient in America; he said, however, that it was a very common draught with him. When my patient returned, I put him on drop doses of Fowler's Solution and Tincture of Cantharides, with most excellent results.

Relation of Nervousness to Beauty.

The phenomenal beauty of the American girl of the highest type, is a subject of the greatest interest both to the psychologist and the sociologist, since it has no precedent, in recorded history, at least; and it is very instructive in its relation to the character and the diseases of America.

This entrancing beauty, remarkable at once for its intensity and its extent among the comfortable classes of America, appears to be a resultant of two factors · the peculiarities of climate, to be hereafter referred to, and the unusual social position of women in America.

The same climatic peculiarities that make us nervous also make us handsome; for fineness of organization is the first element in all human beauty, in either sex.

In no other country are the daughters pushed forward so rapidly, so early sent to school, so quickly admitted into society; the yoke of social observance (if it may be called such), must be borne by them much sooner than by their transatlantic sisters— long before marriage they have had much experience in conversation and in entertainment, and have served as queens in social life, and assumed many of the responsibilities and activities connected therewith. Their mental faculties in the middle range being thus drawn upon, constantly from childhood, they develop rapidly a cerebral activity both of an emotional and an intellectual nature, that speaks in the eyes and forms the countenance; thus, fineness of organization, the first element of beauty, is supplemented by expressiveness of features—which is its second element; by the union of these two, human beauty reaches its highest.

Among the higher classes of America, the diminution of the friction of daily life, by avoiding the responsibility of housekeeping, united with generous living and all comforts, have assisted in adding the third element of beauty — that is, a moderate degree of embonpoint, a feature which, in the ex-

treme, and not re-enforced by these preceding elements—fineness of type and sprightliness of countenance, becomes the worst element of ugliness.

Handsome women are found here and there in
Great Britain, and rarely in Germany; more frequently in France and in Austria, in Italy and
Spain; and in all these countries one may find
individuals that approximate the highest type of
American beauty; but in America, it is the extent—
the commonness of this beauty, which is so remarkably, unprecedentedly, and scientifically interesting.
It is not possible to go to an opera in any of our
large cities without seeing more of the representatives of the highest type of female beauty than can
be found in months of travel in any part of Europe.

Among the middle and lower orders of the old
world, beauty is kept down by labor. A woman
who works all day in the field is not likely to be
very handsome, nor to be the mother of handsome
daughters; for, while mental and intellectual activity in the middle range heightens beauty, museu-
lar toil, out-doors or in-doors, destroys it.

One cause, perhaps, of the almost universal home-
liness of female faces among European works of art
is, the fact that the best of the masters never saw a
handsome woman. One can scarcely believe that
Rubens, had he lived in America, or even in England,
at the present time, would have given us such im-

posing and terrible types of female countenances.
If Raphael had been wont to see every day in Rome
or Naples what he would now see every day in
New York, Baltimore, or Chicago, it would seem
probable that, in his Sistine Madonna he would have
preferred a face of, at least, moderate beauty, to the
neurasthenic and anemic type that is there represented.

To the first and inevitable objection that will be
made to all here said — namely, that beauty is a
relative thing, the standard of which varies with age,
race, and individual—the answer is found in the
fact that the American type is to-day more adored
in Europe than in America; that American girls
are more in demand for foreign marriages than any
other nationality; and that the professional beauties
of London that stand highest are those who, in appearance and in character have come nearest the
American type.

American vs. *English Female Beauty.*

While the beauty of the English girl may perhaps
in some cases endure longer than that of her American sister, yet American beauty has this sovereign
advantage—that it best bears close observation.   The
English beauty is most beautiful at a distance, and
grows homely as we approach her: the typical American beauty appears most attractive near at hand; in

her case, nearness brings enchantment. The American face bears the microscope mainly by reason of its delicacy, fineness, and mobility of expression—qualities that are only appreciated on inspection. The ruddiness or freshness, the health-suggesting and health-sustaining face of the English girl seem incomparable when partially veiled, or when a few rods away; but, as they come nearer, these excelling characteristics retreat behind the irregularities of the skin, the thickness of the lip, the size of the nose; and the observer is mildly stunned by the disappointment at not finding the nimble and automatic play of emotion in the eyes and features, without which female beauty must always fall below the line of supreme authority. The English beauties of national and international fame, at whose feet the empire of Great Britain is now kneeling, in this country would be held simply as of average rather than exceptional excellence.

It is no hard task for one travelling in Great Britain or on the Continent to distinguish American ladies from those of any other nationality, by the finely cut features and mobility of expression; the practised observer would make a mistake but rarely. At the great watering-places, as Homburg and Baden-Baden, on the lines where travel is thickest, as on the Rhine and through Switzerland, we may often see a face which, far away, seems to be purely American, but which, as we gain a closer view, is found to be all English; should there be a doubt, the voice — the speaking of a single word — often solves the problem.

Riding once from Paris to Calais, there stepped into the coach a lady whom, for various reasons I assumed to be English, although her whole appearance—her voice, her manner, her conversation—were completely American. I concluded that at last I had found a case where it was impossible to make a differential diagnosis between an American and an English woman; and I very soon found that my reasons for believing her English were not well founded—that she was an American, and a typical American, in her face, expression, gait, and bearing, and even in the functional nervous disease which she had long endured.

It were well if these two extremes could be united; an American beauty slowly approaching, an English beauty slowly vanishing, present together a picture of human beauty the fairest that could fall on mortal vision. An American lady who unites the American qualities of intellect, of manners, and of *physique,* and who at one period lived for years in English territory, compresses it all in one sentence: "The English face is molded, the American is chiselled."

The superior fineness and delicacy of organization of the American woman, as compared with the women of Great Britain, Germany, and Switzerland, is shown in every organ and function—revealing itself in the .play of the eyes, in the voice, in the response of the facial muscles, in gait, and dress, and gesture. The European woman steps with a firmer tread than the American, and with not so much lightness, pliancy, and grace. In a multitude, where both nations are represented, this difference is impressive. In the hourly operation of shaking hands one can tell, in some cases, the American woman of the higher order from a European, Swiss, or German, in the same rank. The grasp of the European woman is firmer and harder, as though on account of greater strength and firmness of muscle. In the touch of the hand of the American woman there is a nicety and tenderness that the English woman destroys by the force of the impact. It is probable that the interesting and remarkable feat of muscle-reading, popularly called " mind-reading," would not be so skillfully and successfully performed by English as by American ladies, for the reason that they are physically more delicate and nimble, and their susceptibility to external impressions far greater.

There is, perhaps, no one test of both muscular and nervous susceptibility so delicate as this test of muscle-reading; for in these experiments the operator —the so-called " mind-reader "—is blindfolded, takes the subject to be operated upon by the hand, and leads him to some minute spot or locality on which the subject's mind is concentrated; and this is done oftentimes with a rapidity, a facility and a precision of movement that are almost beyond credence. In these experiments the operator's nervous system must be so susceptible as to detect the exceedingly minute and unconscious tension of the arm of the subject on whom he operates in the direction of the object on which his mind is concentrated; and he must also detect the unconscious muscular relaxation when the locality is reached. All persons cannot attain this precision; but of the female sex there are many who by practice, perform at the *séances* with a success almost unfailing. This delusion of "mind-reading" was born in this country, and within the past few years. It may be rationally claimed that it could not have originated, or at least have attained so wide popularity in England, Germany, or Switzerland, since not enough could be found there who were capable of performing it to the amusement and astonishment of large audiences.*

The physiological problem, whether the surface of the eye alone, independent of the muscles that cover and surround it, can express emotion, a near study of the American girl seems to answer quite in the

* See my paper, "Physiology of Mind-Reading," *Popular Science Monthly*, February, 1877.

affirmative. The time that nerve-force takes in traversing the fibres from centre to extremity is now mathematically measured, and it is known to vary with the individual, the temperament, and the season; with race, and climate, and sex it must also vary; in the brain of the American girl thoughts travel by the express, in that of her European sister by accommodation.

America, if archæology is to be trusted, is a modern Etruria, the delicate features and fine forms of prehistoric Italy emerging from the entombment of ages and reappearing in a higher evolution in the Western hemisphere.

Relation of Dress to Nervousness.

The dress is the woman: all of female character is in the clothes for him who can read their language. The American girl of the higher order is exquisitely susceptible, is impressed by mild irritation acting upon any of the senses; she dresses in taste, and, where the means are at hand, with elegance, in colors that are quite subdued, and noticeable only at a short distance.

A psychologist once asked me, " Why are bright colors beautiful in sunset, but out of taste in dress? Why should it be a sign of coarse taste to dress one's self in the most brilliant colors, when all go to see an imposing sunset? "

The answer is, that higher culture and sensitive nerves react to slight irritation; while low culture and insensitive nerves require strong irritation. Loudness of dress is, therefore, justly regarded as proof of coarseness of nerve-fibre.

If we could clothe ourselves in sunsets; if all this resplendency of crimson and scarlet and gold, and all these variations in hue and form could descend upon the delicate maiden, and fall about her in palpitating folds like a rich garment, the eye of that maiden and of those who gaze upon her would soon weary; the irritation of such splendor would become a pang, and only be worn as a badge and sign of a nature in the lower stages of evolution. Bright-colored scarlet and red, so common in Switzerland and in certain parts of Germany, are never seen in America in any class. And, among men, the custom of wearing gorgeous and jewelled apparel in public assemblies, as at courts or on occasions of state, is a survival of the barbarian period through which all Europe with the rest of the modern world has passed, or is now passing.

There is a fable that one day the most powerful of the fairies concluded to assist at the birth of women and assign to them the gifts which it was in the power of each fairy to bestow upon each one of the new born. The English woman received her brilliant color, the Italian woman her eyes, the Spanish her figure, the German woman her beautiful hair, the French woman her little foot and her *chic*. The fairies were going to leave, when a little thin voice was heard, and a little woman whom nobody had seen came and demanded her share. "Who are you?" asked the queen of the fairies.

"I am the Parisienne."

"You will not have any special gift like your sisters, but something from all the gifts of all the others." This was before the discovery of America. For the Parisienne can now be substituted the American.

Dentition, Puberty and Change of Life.

Another evidence of the nervousness of our time is the difficulty which we experience in teething, at puberty, and change of life. These normal physiological processes in recent times, make so important a draft upon the nervous system that various sorts of illness result therefrom. During dentition, stomach and bowel difficulties arise; at puberty chorea, chlorosis, sick-headache and hysteria oftentimes appear; and at change of life, a vast array of cerebral symptoms, and many of the above described symptoms of neurasthenia appear, and cause great disturbance, continuing sometimes for years. The system has an insufficient quantity of nervous force, and the draft which is made upon it by these processes exhausts it.

Cholera infantum has a nervous factor in its causation, and it is pre-eminently an American disease and is most prevalent during the excessive heats of our summer.

Parturition, Nursing, and Diseases of Women.

The process of parturition is everywhere the measure of nerve-strength. Had we no other barometer than this, we should know that civilization was paid for by nervousness, and that our cities are builded out of the life-force of their populations.

I was consulted, not long ago, by a Spanish lady of middle life, who had children to the number of fourteen, and always was up and about on the following day.

A case of this kind, in private practice, I have never before seen; certainly not among our in-door living classes.

For our savage ancestors, parturition was but a trifle more exhausting, either in time or expenditure of nerve-force than an attack of vomiting. On the march, an Indian woman, when taken with the pains of labor, would delay the company but half an hour.

All modern civilization demands prolonged rest for the parturient female; and how many there are in our own land, for whom the conventional nine days is extended to double that time; how many, also, to whom the simple act of giving birth to a child opens the door to unnumbered woes; beginning with lacerations and relaxations, extending to displacements and ovarian imprisonments, and ending by setting the whole system on fire with neuralgias, tremors, etc., and compelling a life-long slavery to sleeplessness, hysteria, or insanity.

One of the most amazing of all sights on the Continent of Europe and Ireland is that of the women toiling in the fields—mowing, raking, digging, driving carts, chopping wood, carrying water, which the same class on landing in this country rarely if ever do. Custom, which is the resultant of many and hard-to-be-traced influences, in part explains this difference; but in the second and third generations, the force of climate is potent and imperious. Our women cannot endure such exposure to heat or to cold, and soon become unable to bear the muscular strain that such labor makes necessary. The direst straits of poverty American women, even of direct German and English descent, will endure rather than labor at the hard, muscular employments of men. Subject a part of the year to the tyranny of heat, and a part to the tyranny of cold, they grow unused to leaving the house; to live in-doors is the rule; it is a rarity to go out, as with those of Continental Europe it is to go in.

How many thousands of mothers there are who cannot, if they would, nurse their own infants, who have not sufficient milk for them, and who cannot

bear the fatigue and drain upon the nervous system
that nursing causes. It is not so much the dislike as
the impossibility of nursing that makes wet nurses in
such demand. So also the processes of gestation and
child-bearing are borne in a most unsatisfactory way
by large numbers in American society. In a state of
perfect or almost perfect health, these processes are
physiological; but for the last half century, among
the upper classes of this country, they have become
pathological; they have become signs of disease.

Lacerations of the Womb and Perineum.

The large numbers of cases of laceration in childbirth, and the prolonged, and sometimes even life-
enduring illnesses resulting from them, are good reason for the terror which the process of parturition
inspires in the minds of many American women to-
day.

*The womb and perineum tear at childbirth be-
cause they have previously been reduced to the tearing
point by general nervous exhaustion.*

When Dr. Pallen and Dr. Sims discussed this subject of the laceration of the cervix at the last meeting of the British Medical Association, in Cambridge,
and spoke of the operations of Emmet for the cure
of that condition, the European surgeons expressed
astonishment and doubt in regard to the frequency
if not the existence or importance of the disease.

Allowing for imperfect observation—the confounding of ulceration with laceration, it is probable that the disease is more frequent in American women, and also more likely to cause reflex constitutional disturbance among them.

The difference between an average of a half-dozen children in a family, which obtained fifty years ago, and an average of less than four which obtains now, is very great, and, abating certain obvious qualifying facts, pretty accurately measures the child-bearing and child-rearing power of the woman of the past and the woman of to-day. But on this subject statistics are scarcely needed. Consider the large number of childless households, the many families that have but two or three children, or but one, and with them contrast the families that prevailed at the beginning of this century. The contrast, also, between the higher and lower orders in this respect, cannot, it would seem, be entirely explained by excess of prudence on the one hand, or want of it on the other.

American children cry more than other children—they are more nervous, more fretful, more easily annoyed by heat, or by irritating clothing, by indigestible food, as well as by nervous and emotional influences. The generalization that children in civilization cry and worry more than children in savagery seems to be sustained by the experiences of all travellers who are trustworthy reporters on these matters. Thus

Miss Bird—whose observations are always worthy of attention, and in the main, in harmony with facts—states in her work on "Unbeaten Tracks in Japan," that the children are more calm and quiet, and less troublesome than the children of higher civilizations.

Travellers in Brazil make the same report in regard to the children of the dark or mixed races in that country. In our own land the contrast between the black and the white children in this respect is very noticeable indeed; and that Indian children are cold, phlegmatic, and enduring is well known to all who have studied Indian life.

Relation of American Oratory to American Nervousness.

American oratory is partly the product of American nervousness. For success in the loftier phases of oratory, fineness of organization, a touch of the nervous diathesis are essential; the masters in the oratorical art are always nervous; the same susceptibility that makes them eloquent, subtile, and persuasive causes them to be timid, distrustful, and sometimes cowardly. We blame Cicero for the pusillanimity of his old age, and for his terror in the presence of death, and praise him for his spirit and force and grace in the presence of audiences, not thinking that the two opposite modes of conduct flowed from a single source. A nature wholly coarse

and hard, with no thread or vein of nerve sensitiveness must always fail in the higher realms of the
oratoric art, just as it must fail in all arts; everywhere it is the fine organization that conquers.

Jefferson, after acting his Rip Van Winkle for
years, even now enters upon the stage at each performance with a feeling of responsibility; and of
more than one orator has it been affirmed that he
always dreaded to speak. I know a clergyman of
exceptional power, who has preached thousands of
times, and yet who confesses to me that he can never
eat at a dinner where he is announced to make one
of his speeches.

"Give me an army of cowards," said Wellington;
it is the man who turns pale in the face of the
enemy that will fight to the death. This delicacy
of organization, united with Saxon force, makes
America a nation of orators. The preacher whom all
will allow to be the greatest and boldest we have ever
had in these States, admits that when he sees one
whom he knows to be his enemy in his audience, the
fire of his eloquence is at once extinguished; and
Gough, who has delivered eight thousand lectures,
whose life has been spent in the presence of crowded
assemblages, declares that he never goes on the platform without a certain anxiety lest he fail: he has
not yet outgrown the school-boy's timidity.

At a banquet in England I once sat next to a well-known man, of science, who had been appointed to respond to one of the most important and difficult toasts of the occasion. We conversed on many themes, but I noticed a deepening anxiety in his manner, and before his turn came he confessed to me that he would give one hundred pounds if he could be excused from speaking ; and knowing my interest in psychological studies he admitted that all the day long he had been apprehensive of the evening, and had even taken, without avail, a solitary row on a stream near-by, to divert and calm his mind. When he rose to respond, his manner was absolutely easy, and he spoke most elegantly and eloquently. Near us, also, there sat one of the speakers who is justly honored for his eloquence, and who is wont to prepare himself for important efforts by months of thought. This man likewise, it was easy to see, was nervous and anxious up to the moment that he was called upon, and only appeared collected and at home when he was doing that which he somewhat dreaded to do. The two best speeches of the evening were made by those who were most afraid of speaking.

Philosophy of American Humor.

The power to create or to appreciate humor requires a fine organization. American humor, both iu its peculiarities and in its abundance, takes its origin, in part, in American nervousness. It is an inevitable reaction from the excessive strain of mental and physical life; people who toil and worry less have less need than we for abandonment — of nonsense, exaggeration, and fun. Both the supply of and demand for humor of a grotesque and exaggerated form are maintained by this increasing requirement for recreation; not the vulgar, the untrained alone, but the disciplined, the intellectual, the finely organized man and woman of position, dignity, responsibility and genius, of strong and solid acquisitions, enjoy and follow up and sustain those amusements which are in our land so very common, and which are looked upon, and rightly so, as American—such as the negro minstrels or experiments in induced or mesmeric trance.

"The Gilded Age," the most popular play ever written on this continent, owes its success to those elements of exaggeration and nonsense, of absurdity and grotesquesness, that made it fail in Great Britain. Pinafore, popular as it was in Great Britain, was incomparably more so in America, where great numbers of troupes were playing it simultaneously, and in New York five theatres kept it running for weeks and months: its success at home was partly a reflex of its success here. In this country at present, no lecturer can attract very large crowds unless he be a humorist and makes his hearers laugh as well as cry; and the lectures of the humorists—now a class by themselves—are more required than those of philosophers or men of science, or of fame in literature. Americans, who are themselves capable of originating thought in science or letters, scholarly, sober, and mature, prefer nonsense to science for an evening's employment; and so, with the increase of our nervousness and intelligence there has been a fading away in the popularity of the instructive and dignified lecturers for whom our lyceums were first organized.

The American Language.

A new language is being evolved in this new world. It was once held — perhaps is held even now, in England, by some — as a certain reproach against Americans, that they spoke a different language from that of their mother country.

Criticism of this kind must come only from those who have studied but fractionally the psychology of language, and the philosophy of its development. The American language is as necessary as the American flag. As the English of England to-day differs from the English of England in the past, so must the American language differ from the language of England, and continue to diverge along certain lines, at least—more and more, with time and development.

Language is a resultant of very numerous factors working simultaneously or successively; and among these factors, climate, races, institutions, general and special, accidents of situation and of travel, of class, of war and peace, of industry and inventions, of wealth and the lack of it, are pre-eminent. Only by violating natural laws could Americans speak the English language as it is spoken in England. Every decade marks differences, subtractions, alterations — qualitive and quantitive — to the language which our fathers brought to these shores; and with heightening sensitiveness there are at the same time changes in pronunciation, in articulation, in phraseology, as well as in the choice and handling of terms. Treatises and criticisms on Americanisms we have perhaps enough — and not without a considerable value; but none of them would seem to give sufficient force to the study of the relation of language to nervousness, that is, to the effect of the nervous organization on our idioms, articulation, or lack or want of articulation.

Nervousness causes us to clip words, to leave off or slide endings of words like *ing*, the full and clear enunciation of which makes severe draughts on time and force. Voltaire said of the English that in conversation of a day they would gain two hours over the French, because they used fewer vowels and more consonants, vowels requiring more time than consonants for their distinct articulation; and an American can surely gain as much over the English as the English over the French by the use of compressed idioms, elisions, and the simple rapidity of utterance. The Americans effect much saving of force, also, by allowing the voice to fall at the end of sentences, although those who listen must expend more force if they would hear correctly.

I once attended, in company with Mr. A. C. Wheeler (Nim Crinkle), a matinée performance of our leading American actress, Clara Morris, in the powerful and emotional play of *Camille.* It is well known on this side of the Atlantic, and not entirely unknown abroad, that this actress is a representative of American female nervousness, and that she has suffered, and I believe still suffers at times, severe depressions and pains, so that only by stimulation and care and long rests is it possible for her to fulfil her parts

In studying her acting, at the performance referred to, we both observed—as indeed we had both observed before, that while in the expression of strong emotion through the vowel sounds she was remarkable, even surpassing Bernhardt, she was very much inferior to the French actress in her average elocution, disregarding in a most wonderful way the consonant sounds, and so making it a difficult task to hear the lines. For an actress so famous and successful her elocution is phenomenally bad, and it is a result, in part, of her extreme deficiency in nerve-force; unconsciously, no doubt, she expends the nervous energy that other actresses give to articulation in the spasmodic expression of feeling through the vowel sounds, and were she a better rhetorician she would be a less powerful actress, since her success is entirely in emotional characters, and it consists more of spontaneous and piercing outbursts of emotion than in a uniform manifestation of art. In this respect this actress is a type of her sex in America, on and off the stage—a type, to a degree, of both sexes.

The condition described by Mr. Richard Grant White, as heterophemy (saying the opposite of what we mean), is probably more common in America than in Europe, although instances of it have been pointed out in the writings of some of the leaders of English literature; as a symptom of disease and a result of brain exhaustion I have observed it in a number of cases; coming on or growing worse as the patient's brain-force diminishes.

Rapidity of Speech and Pitch of Voice.

The American speaks more rapidly than the European; he makes more muscular movements of the larynx in a minute: in his nervousness he clips words, articulating indistinctly, and allowing his voice to fall at the end of a sentence, sometimes so as to be inaudible. The Englishman speaks more slowly, enunciates more clearly, says fewer words to a minute, and, as is well known, keeps the voice up, where an American would let it fall. The American woman says more than the Englishwoman, is easier and more alert for converse, quicker to seize a delicate irony, more facile to respond to a suggestion, than the English lady in the same walk of life. I believe, also, that the English, Germans, and Swiss cannot hear as many words in a minute as Americans; the auditory nerve and the brain behind it being incapable of receiving and co-ordinating as many sounds in a given time. Hence it is necessary to speak to them with more calmness and clearness, whatever language may be employed.

The American voice is pitched higher than that of the European; and it would appear that the pitch has been gradually rising during the past century. Our musical instruments, according to some authorities, are keyed higher than those of European manufacture.

Greater susceptibility to Trance in America.

Americans are, without question, more susceptible to certain forms of trance than any other civilized people. As I have indicated in my writings on trance, the special variety known as induced trance is very much affected by the state of the atmosphere as well as by the general condition of the nervous system. Those who are very strong physically, are easily entranced, oftentimes; but the influence of the weather is very apparent to any one who studies the subject thoroughly, and makes experiments on large numbers of human beings at different times and seasons. I have observed, myself, that in dull, heavy, rainy, unpleasant weather, the phenomena of induced trance appear far more slowly, require more effort to develop them, are capricious, tricky, and uncertain; and the subjects are more disposed to slide out of the conditions in which they are placed in the trance state, than when the weather is sparkling and clear. A dry atmosphere is favorable to the induction of trance states; and a sensitive, nervous temperament — provided the psychology be favorable — is more likely to develop the higher manifestations of trance than the heavy and the dull. Hence it is that in the North-western sections of our country — in Minnesota and Iowa—where the air is not only excessively dry, but frequently very cold, the proportion of persons who go into trance through the ordinary manipulations and manœuvrings employed is greater than on the sea-board, and greater, probably, than in the South.

America is the only country, ancient or modern,

in which large numbers of people make it a life-business to amuse people by trance exhibitions; and those who have studied these exhibitions, as they are given by the best experts, well know that there is no form of evening amusement that can in any way be compared with them. All these phenomena are, it is true, known in Europe, and they have been known all over the world, some of them for centuries! but what is here claimed is, that they are more easily obtained here, and the manifestations are more certain and more interesting, partly because this trance has been studied in America more thoroughly than in Europe.

Change in Type of Disease.

The question often agitated is, Whether diseases have changed their type in modern times? This is a question which so far as *chronic* disease is concerned should not be discussed; to raise it, is to answer it. There is no doubt that chronic diseases have changed their type in the last half century. The only question is, What are the degrees of the change, and what are the causes which produce these results? *Acute* diseases, like pneumonia, may perhaps have been but little changed in type, but it is easily demonstrable that chronic nervous diseases have increased in recent periods, and that, with this increase of nervous symptoms, there has been also an increase in the asthenic forms of disease, and a decrease in the sthenic forms; and, correspondingly, that there has been a change in the methods of treatment of diseases; neurasthenia — nervous susceptibility — has affected all, or nearly all, diseases, so that nearly all illnesses occurring among the better class of people—the brain-workers —require a different kind of treatment from that which our fathers employed for the same diseases.

The four ways by which we determine these facts are—*first*, by studying the literature of medicine of the past centuries; *secondly*, by conversation with very old and experienced practitioners—men between the ages of seventy and ninety—who link the past with the present generation, and remember their own personal experience and the practice of medicine as it was fifty years ago; *thirdly*, from our own individual experience and observation; *fourthly*, by studying the habits and diseases of savages and barbarians of all climes and ages, and of the lower orders about us. Statistics on this subject are of very little value, for reasons that will be clear to those who are used to statistics, and who know how they can be handled.

We do not bear blood-letting now as our fathers did, for the same reasons that we do not bear alcohol, tobacco, coffee, opium, as they could. The change in the treatment of disease is a necessary

result of the change in the modern constitution.
The old-fashioned constitution yet survives in numbers of people; and in such cases, the old treatment
is oftentimes better than the modern treatment.

The diseases of savages can be learned from
books of travel and from conversations with travellers. Many of these books, it is true, are of a non-
expert character, but some of them are written by
physicians and scientific men of various degrees of
eminence, whose observations, on a large scale, compared together, enable us to arrive at the approximate truth. In the study of this subject, I have
compared a very large number of books of travel, and
I have arrived at this fact, in regard to which there
can be no doubt whatever, namely, that nervous disease of a *physical* character, scarcely exists among
savages or barbarians, or semi-barbarians or partially
civilized people. Likewise, in the lower orders m
our great cities, and among the peasantry in the
rural districts, muscle-workers, as distinguished from
brain-workers — those who represent the habits and
mode of life and diseases of our ancestors of the last
century — functional nervous diseases, except those
of a malarial or syphilitic character, are about as
rare as they were among all classes during the last
century. These people frequently need more violent and severe purging, more blood-letting, more
frequent blistering than the higher orders would

endure. If we would compare the nervous diseases of our time with those of the past, we have only to look about us among those classes of people whose temperaments take us back a half or three-quarters of a century; in these classes such diseases as neurasthenia, heavy fever, sick-headache are very rare indeed; so that it is very difficult for a hospital for nervous diseases to succeed in getting a sufficient number of patients of this character. On the other hand, hospitals for inflammatory and febrile diseases are enormously patronized among them. It is partly for this reason that the literature for nervous functional diseases is so poor and unsatisfactory; our medical books and lectures are made up far too often of hospital, charity, and dispensary practice.

In regard to the incapacity for observing, which has been so often charged upon all the physicians who were so unfortunate as to be born prior to the last half century, I may say, that even conceding the general truth of the charge, as applied to the mass of the profession, it certainly does not apply to all the great leaders in medical thought. The greatest medical minds of the last century were, to use the most measured language, the equals of those who lead the profession of our day, and were capable of observing, and did observe, and they recorded their observations; some of the grandest discoveries of all time were made by them.

Syphilis growing milder.

One reason, though not perhaps the only reason, why syphilis is growing milder with civilization, is, without much question, as it seems to me, the increasing nervousness of our time. This disease, dreadful as it is and must always be, is not so hideous and revolting in its symptoms as it once was; independent of the treatment, before any treatment is used, its manifestations are less repulsive than formerly, and they are less violent and obstinate among the higher than among the lower classes; syphilis, plus a nervous constitution, is a different disease from syphilis plus a strong phlegmatic constitution; it has less to feed on, and like febrile and inflammatory diseases, is not so furious and dangerous in a sensitive organism as in a strong one.

Nervous syphilis is apparently more common than it was; indeed, it simulates in very many of its manifestations the symptoms of neurasthenia, so that without the history of the case, it would be almost impossible to make a sure differential diagnosis.*

Nervousness increased by Inheritance.

Nervousness develops very rapidly in our climate, and, by the remorseless law of inheritance

---

* The very able and original prize essay of Dr. C. L. Dana, of this city, on " The Benignity of Syphilis," is worthy of careful study in relation to this question. (See New York *Medical Record*, February 5, 1881.)

soon becomes an element in the family history of recent importations.

A very considerable portion of those whom I see professionally for nervous diseases of a functional character are descendants of parents who were born in Germany, or some portion of Europe — descendants of ancestors who, in the old country, never knew what nervousness meant. I have never seen more severe cases of neurasthenia than some of this class. Some patients who were born in Europe, after a long residence here, themselves develop the full symptoms of nervous exhaustion.

Intensity of Animal Life in America.

In a paper of much interest on the Cosmopolitan Butterfly, a naturalist of Cambridge, Samuel V. Scudder, has shown that among all the butterflies properly comparable on the two continents, there is no single instance where the European butterfly has more broods than the American.

This author, speaking of the species of butterfly called the *V. Cardui,* asserts that "all observers in Switzerland and Germany agree that it is single-brooded; whereas, in New England it is double-brooded;" and, on comparing the histories of several other and different species also, he derives the general law that animal life on this continent is more intense than in Europe.

CHAPTER III.

THE causes of American nervousness are complicated, but are not beyond analysis: First of all modern civilization. The phrase modern civilization is used with emphasis, for civilization alone does not cause nervousness. The Greeks were certainly civilized, but they were not nervous, and in the Greek language there is no word for that term. The ancient Romans were civilized, as judged by any standard. Civilization is therefore a relative term, and as such is employed throughout this treatise. The modern differ from the ancient civilizations mainly in these five elements — steam power, the periodical press, the telegraph, the sciences, and the mental activity of women. When civilization, plus these five factors, invades any nation, it must carry nervousness and nervous diseases along with it.

Civilization very limited in extent.
All that is said here of American nervousness refers only to a fraction of American society; for

in America, as in all lands, the majority of the people are muscle-workers rather than brain-workers; have little education, and are not striving for honor, or expecting eminence or wealth. All our civilization hangs by a thread; the activity and force of the very few make us what we are as a nation; and if, through degeneracy, the descendants of these few revert to the condition of their not very remote ancestors, all our haughty civilization would be wiped away. With all our numerous colleges, such as they are, it is a rarity and surprise to meet in business relations with a college-educated man.

A late writer, Dr. Arthur Mitchell, has shown that if, of the population of Scotland, a few thousands were destroyed or degenerated and their places unsupplied, the nation would fall downward to barbarism. To a somewhat less degree this is true of all lands, including our own land. Of our fifty millions of population, but a few millions have reached that elevation where they are likely to be nervous. In the lower orders, the classes that support our dispensaries and hospitals, in the tenements of our crowded cities, and even on farms in the country, by the mountain side—among the healthiest regions, we find, now and then, here and there cases of special varieties of nervous disease, such as hay-fever, neurasthenia, etc.; but the proportion of diseases of this kind among these people is much smaller than among the in-door-living and brain-working classes, although insanity of the incurable kind is more common among the lower or the middle than in the very highest classes.

Edison's electric light is now sufficiently advanced in an experimental direction to give us the best possible illustration of the effects of modern civilization on the nervous system. An electric machine of definite horse-power, situated at some central point, is to supply the electricity needed to run a certain number of lamps—say one thousand, more or less. If an extra number of lamps should be interposed in the circuit, then the power of the engine must be increased; else the light of the lamps would be decreased, or give out. This has been mathematically calculated, so that it is known, or believed to be known, by those in charge, just how much increase of horse-power is needed for each increase in the number of lamps. In all the calculations, however widely they may differ, it is assumed that the force supplied by any central machine is limited, and cannot be pushed beyond a certain point; and if the number of lamps interposed in the circuit be increased, there must be a corresponding increase in the force of the machine. The nervous system of man is the centre of the nerve-force supplying all the organs of the body.

Like the steam engine, its force is limited, although it cannot be mathematically measured—and, unlike the steam engine, varies in amount of force with the food, the state of health and external conditions, varies with age, nutrition, occupation, and numberless factors. The force in this nervous system can, therefore, be increased or diminished by good or evil influences, medical or hygienic, or by the natural evolutions—growth, disease and decline; but none the less it is limited; and when new functions are interposed in the circuit, as modern civilization is constantly requiring us to do, there comes a period, sooner or later, varying in different individuals, and at different times of life, when the amount of force is insufficient to keep all the lamps actively burning; those that are weakest go out entirely, or, as more frequently happens, burn faint and feebly—they do not expire, but give an insufficient and unstable light—this is the philosophy of modern nervousness.

The invention of printing, the extension of steam power into manufacturing interests and into means of conveyance, the telegraph, the periodical press, the political machinery of free countries, the religious excitements that are the sequels of Protestantism—the activities of philanthropy, made necessary by the increase of civilization, and of poverty, and certain forms of disease — and, more than all, perhaps, the heightening and extending complexity of modern education in and out of schools and universities, the inevitable effect of the rise of modern science and the expansion of history in all its branches—all these are so many additional lamps interposed in the circuit, and are supplied at the expense of the nervous system, the dynamic power of which has not correspondingly increased *

* The London *Times*, in an editorial article of much ability and interest, giving a *résumé* of my researches in American nervousness, illustrates the philosophy here advocated very appropriately, by the analogy of the steam engine.

" The nervous system, as a whole, is the immediate motor power of the human machine ; and in this machine it may be very roughly said that the steam generated in a single boiler works through the agency of scattered engines, technically called special nerve-centres, or ganglia, which are charged with the maintenance of particular functions. If one such engine is hard at work, and is therefore using a great deal of steam, so much the less will be available to support the activity of the rest. For all functions of primary importance to the existence of the human race there are engines coeval with the race itself in antiquity, which have been perfected by long exercise, and handed down from generation to generation in a state of gradually acquired stability and aptitude. Such, for example, are the nerve-centres which combine in harmonious action the very large number of muscles that are collectively subservient to the maintenance of the erect posture, or the smaller but very distinct group that governs the conjoined movements of the eyes.

" When the progress of civilization calls for the performance of a new function, whether it be of body or mind, a new engine must be gradually provided for the purpose ; and this which becomes developed in individuals long before it can be considered the common property of the race, will for a long period be inferior to move established centres in its power of endurance. Dr.

Necessary Evils of Specialization.

One evil, and hardly looked for effect of the introduction of steam, together with the improved methods of manufacturing of recent times, has been the training in special departments or duties — so that artisans, instead of doing or preparing to do, all the varieties of the manipulations needed in the making of any article, are restricted to a few simple exiguous movements, to which they give their whole lives — in the making of a rifle, or a watch,

Buzzard has felicitously used these principles in explaining one of the causes of the disease called writer's palsy. The art of writing, measured by the antiquity of man, is only a thing of yesterday, and the special nervous engine which controls it is liable to derangements from which those of older formation are comparatively exempt. In our own day, even when compared with quite recent times, there has been an enormous increase of brain-work, of education, of competition between educated people ; and there can be no doubt that we are living in the midst of a consequently greatly increased development of nervous tissue and of nervous force, a large share of which, in very many people, is applied to intellectual or other purposes which are more or less novel in their nature. In a certain number of such people, to continue the illustration, the engines most in use are those which are deficient in stability, while, at the same time, the individuals have no excess of power for the maintenance of the activity of others. A man whose thinking centres are exerted to the full measure of their capabilities has no reserve of force to enable him to dispose of more food than he requires ; and he has either to find out how little he should live upon, and to live upon that little, or to pay a penalty in the shape of indigestion. He has no reserve of force with which to burn off fat for the maintenance of his animal heat, and it is sound economy for him to live in a warm room, and to devote his energies to higher uses than those of a perambulat-

each part is constructed by experts on that part. The effect of this exclusive concentration of mind and muscle to one mode of action, through months and years, is both negatively and positively pernicious, and notably so, when re-enforced, as it almost universally is, by the bad air of overheated and ill-ventilated establishments. Herein is one unanticipated cause of the increase of insanity and other diseases of the nervous system among the laboring and poorer classes. The steam engine, which would relieve work, as it was hoped, and allow us to be idle, has increased the amount of work done a thousand fold; and with that increase in quantity

ing furnace. If he fails to surround himself by a sufficient external temperature, he will suffer from cold. In this way certain forms of nervous disorder have been brought into what may be described as unnecessary prominence, and at the same time their relative prominence has been increased by the diminished frequency of many of the diseases which are caused by the neglect of obvious precautions or by the prevalence of unwholesome habits of living. There are fewer epidemics because, in spite of many shortcomings in our sanitary arrangements, the spreading of infectious diseases is hindered to a very real extent. There is less inflammation because people have learned, partially at least, the wisdom of taking proper care of their bodies.

Lastly, it must not be forgotten that the increase of nerve-force to which we have referred is an increase of the " boiler " power itself, and is therefore originally capable of being applied to any or all of the demands of the organism. When compared with our ancestors, we are athletes, and we may be physical or intellectual athletes, as we please.

" It is not given to ordinary humanity to reach a summit of ambition in more than one direction at once."

there has been a differentiation of quality and specialization of function which, so far forth, is depressing both to mind and body. In the professions — the constringing power of specialization is neutralized very successfully by general culture and observation, out of which specialties spring, and by which they are supported; but for the artisan there is no time, or chance, or hope, for such redeeming and antidotal influences.

Clocks and Watches.—Necessity of Punctuality.

The perfection of clocks and the invention of watches have something to do with modern nervousness, since they compel us to be on time, and excite the habit of looking to see the exact moment, so as not to be late for trains or appointments. Before the general use of these instruments of precision in time, there was a wider margin for all appointments; a longer period was required and prepared for, especially in travelling—coaches of the olden period were not expected to start like steamers or trains, on the instant—men judged of the time by probabilities, by looking at the sun, and needed not, as a rule, to be nervous about the loss of a moment, and had incomparably fewer experiences wherein a delay of a few moments might destroy the hopes of a lifetime. A nervous man cannot take out his watch and look at it when the time for an appointment or train is near, without affecting his pulse, and the effect on that pulse, if we could but measure and weigh it, would be found to be correlated to a loss to the nervous system. Punctuality is a greater thief of nervous force than is procrastination of time. We are under constant strain, mostly unconscious, oftentimes in sleeping as well as in waking hours, to get somewhere or do something at some definite moment. Those who would relieve their nervousness may well study the manners of the Turks, who require two weeks to execute a promise that the Anglo-Saxon would fulfil in a moment. In Constantinople indolence is the ideal, as work is the ideal in London and New York; the follower of the Prophet is ashamed to be in haste, and would apologize for keeping a promise. There are those who prefer, or fancy they prefer, the sensations of movement and activity to the sensations of repose; but from the standpoint only of economy of nerve-force all our civilization is a mistake; every mile of advance into the domain of ideas, brings a conflict that knows no rest, and all conquests are to be paid for, before delivery often, in blood and nerve and life. We cannot have civilization and have anything else, the price at which nature disposes of this luxury being all the rest of her domain.

The Telegraph.

The telegraph is a cause of nervousness the potency of which is little understood. Before the days of Morse and his rivals, merchants were far less worried than now, aud less business was transacted in a given time ; prices fluctuated far less rapidly, and the fluctuations which now are transmitted instantaneously over the world were only known then by the slow communication of sailing vessels or steamships; hence we might wait for weeks or months for a cargo of tea from China, trusting for profit to prices that should follow their arrival; whereas, now, prices at each port are known at once all over the globe. This continual fluctuation of values, and the constant knowledge of those fluctuations in every part of the world, are the scourges of business men, the tyrants of trade — every cut in prices in wholesale lines in the smallest of any of the Western cities, becomes known in less than an hour all over the Union ; thus competition is both diffused and intensified. Within but thirty years the telegraphs of the world have grown to half a million miles of line, and over a million miles of wire—or more than forty times the circuit of the globe. In the United States there were, in 1880, 170,103 miles of line, and in that year 33,155,991 messages were sent over them.

Effect of Noise on the Nerves.

The relation of noise to nervousness and nervous diseases is a subject of not a little interest: but one which seems to have been but incidentally studied.

The noises that nature is constantly producing— the moans and roar of the wind, the rustling and trembling of the leaves and swaying of the branches, the roar of the sea and of waterfalls, the singing of birds, and even the cries of some wild animals—are mostly rhythmical to a greater or less degree, and always varying if not intermittent; to a savage or to a refined ear, on cultured or uncultured brains, they are rarely distressing, often pleasing, sometimes delightful and inspiring. Even the loudest sounds in nature, the roll of thunder, the howling of storms, and the roar of a cataract like Niagara—save in the exceptional cases of idiosyncrasy — are the occasions not of pain but of pleasure, and to observe them at their best men will compass the globe.

Many of the appliances and accompaniments of civilization, on the other hand, are the causes of noises that are unrhythmical, unmelodious and therefore annoying, if not injurious; manufactures, locomotion, travel, housekeeping even, are noise-producing factors, and when all these elements are concentred, as in great cities, they maintain through all the waking and some of the sleeping hours, an unintermittent vibration in the air that is more or less · disagreeable to all, and in the case of an idiosyncrasy or severe illness may be unbearable and harmful. Rhythmical, melodious, musical sounds are not only agreeable, but when not too long maintained are beneficial, and may be ranked among our therapeutical agencies.

Unrhythmical, harsh, jarring sounds, to which we apply the term noise, are, on the contrary, to a greater or less degree, harmful or liable to be harmful; they cause severe molecular disturbance.

In regard to this general subject of the relation of noises to the nerves these three general principles are to be recognized :

1. That what is disagreeable may not of necessity be especially injurious to the health.

2. That it is possible to adapt the system to noises that are at first disagreeable, so that they cease to have any appreciable or at least demonstrable effect.

3. That there may be idiosyncrasies against noises as against all other forms of irritation—as there may be idiosyncrasies against certain articles of food or drink, or against the various stimulants and narcotics or different articles on the materia medica.

Although it is usually assumed that the disagreeable and the unhealthful are identical, although offensive odors in large cities have been regarded as nuisances in 'the eye of modern law, yet there is no scientific proof that there is any such necessary correlation. The odor of a tanyard is not only unpleasant, but enormously so; one, at first, wonders that any human being could live, even for a day, in such an atmosphere; and yet investigations that I made a number of years ago convinced me that those who regularly worked in these yards were not in any perceptible way injured in health, and that their longevity compared favorably with that of other muscle-workers in the various trades.

Likewise there are many vile odors in all' our cities that are legislated against as nuisances, and for permitting which the members of the Board of Health of the city of New York were lately indicted, but which certainly cannot be proved to be injurious to health; there is no evidence that they directly excite either acute or chronic disease, or that they tend to shorten life, although they are so disagreeable as to subtract largely from the comfort of those who are exposed to them. On the other hand, it is well established that the sewer gas and other poisons that give rise to most serious disease have little or no odor, and only make their presence felt by their effects.

With disagreeable sounds the same principle, up to a certain point at least, applies; the rumble of omnibuses, the jangling of car-bells, and the clatter of many carriages, with the tramping and shuffling of vast multitudes in our crowded streets, all jar on a sensitive frame; but whether they excite, in any considerable number of people, symptoms of either acute or chronic disorder, must be regarded as doubtful. That in connection with the bad air of cities and the confinement, they do tend to increase the nervousness of civilization is quite probable, but any claim more definite than that cannot well be maintained.

In case of illness or idiosyncrasy, however, it is quite different, for the evil effects of noise on those confined with grave or debilitating disease are oftentimes so speedy, direct, and severe that no doubt can be raised, and the cessation of the nuisance or the removal of the sufferer is an urgent need.

This must without dispute be allowed, that one may have an idiosyncrasy against a certain form of sound just as against a certain odor, taste, or action of food or medicine. How painful the noise of filing a saw may be is well known; but it is not so well known that this is but one of many noises that are specially offensive to individuals. The scraping of the foot on a corn cob or rubber mat is to some as painful as though a pin were stuck into the skin; and at one time, when somewhat exhansted by overwork, the noise of the tearing of a newspaper was to myself unpleasant in the extreme.

These peculiarities, however, are not necessarily the result of disease or symptomatic of any recognizable state; they are found in the strongest and hardiest. One who for a number of years has been my guide in the White Mountains, a man of rare endurance and vigor, who in a long and laborious life has never known a day of real illness, tells me that the noise of the filing of a saw has always been exceedingly distressing. A professional gentleman whom I know, says that the noise of the elevated railway trains in New York city are so harassing to him that he never goes on the avenue where these trains run unless compelled to do so; the effect he declares is rasping, exasperating, amounting to positive pain; and yet this man is not only well, but is remarkably tough and wiry, capable of bearing confinement and long and severe application.

This elevated railroad, it may be observed, has been a convenient means of illustrating all the principles here brought forward in regard to the relation of noise to nerves. When first organized, during the heat of summer, while people lived with doors and windows open for the admission of air, the noise of the trains was a source of distress to all or nearly all, who lived on or very near the avenue and streets through which it passed; a new structure usually makes more noise than an old one, and this fact not being understood caused the complaints to be almost as loud as the noise. Those who were so unfortunate as to be confined to the house by any form of sickness in some cases suffered so severely that it was feared their lives would be sacrificed; and some were obliged to dispose of their property and move away.

The majority of the residents, however, in the course of a few months became so used to the din that, except when their attention was specially directed to it, it ceased to be painfully annoying; they had adapted themselves to their environment; the nervous system had become in a degree benumbed, so that the vibrations striking on the ear gave rise to no conscious or rememberable sensation. This process of the moulding of the internal to the external was made much easier and shorter by the coming of cold weather, which closed the doors and windows; and by the fact that the structure of the road had been so affected by use that its vibrations were less rasping to the nerves. It would appear that the vibrations were both changed in quality and diminished in loudness, although so far as I know no scientific proof of this has ever been offered.

In some cases of idiosyncrasy it is probable that instead of adaptation to environment directly the reverse will take place, and the more the noise is heard the more distressing it will become. The analogy of hay-fever gives us a suggestion of truth on this subject. In this malady there is usually an idiosyncrasy against some one or a number of vegetable or other irritants, as dust or roses, or certain fruits, as strawberries, or peaches, or grapes, or water-melons; and this idiosyncrasy cannot be overcome by any effort of the will, and the sufferer, instead of getting used to any of these irritants by long dwelling among them, becomes thereby worse and worse; and the only relief is to run away and escape the irritation; the effect of a long absence being in some cases to make the sensitiveness less; avoidance of the irritant doing for them just what long subjection to it does for others. To sum up briefly, any irritation constantly or repeatedly acting, may have two precisely opposite effects — it may benumb or it may increase the sensitiveness — this latter effect occurring chiefly in cases of idiosyncrasy.

Railway Travelling and Nervousness.

Whether railway travelling is directly the cause of nervous disease is a question of not a little interest. Reasoning deductively, without any special facts, it would seem that the molecular disturbance caused by travelling long distances, or living on trains as an employé, would have an unfavorable influence on the nervous system.

In practice this seems to be found ; that in some cases — probably a minority of those who live on the road — functional nervous symptoms are excited, and there are some who are compelled to give up this mode of life.

A German physician has given the name " Fear of Railway Travelling," to a symptom that is observed in some who have become nervously exhausted by long residence on trains; they become fearful of taking a journey on the cars, mainly from the unpleasant sensations caused by the vibrating motions of the train.

That railway travel, though beneficial to some, is sometimes injurious to the nerve system of the nervous, is demonstrable all the time in my patients ; many while travelling by rail suffer from the symptoms of sea-sickness and with increase of nervousness.*

Rapid Development and Acceptance of New Ideas.

The rapidity with which new truths are discovered, accepted and popularized in modern times is a proof and result of the extravagance of our civilization.

Philosophies and discoveries as well as inventions which in the Middle Ages would have been passed by or dismissed with the murder of the author, are in our time—and notably in our country—taken up

* See my work on Sea-sickness, last edition.

and adopted, in innumerable ways made practical—modified, developed, actively opposed, possibly overthrown and displaced within a few years, and all of necessity at a great expenditure of force.

The experiments, inventions, and discoveries of Edison alone have made and are now making constant and exhausting draughts on the nervous forces of America and Europe, and have multiplied in very many ways, and made more complex and extensive, the tasks and agonies not only of practical men, but of professors and teachers and students everywhere; the simple attempt to master the multitudinous directions and details of the labors of this one young man with all his thousands and thousands of experiments and hundreds of patents and with all the soluble and insoluble physical problems suggested by his discoveries would itself be a sufficient task for even a genius in science; and any high school or college in which his labors were not recognized and the results of his labors were not taught would be patronized only for those who prefer the eighteenth century to the twentieth.

On the mercantile or practical side the promised discoveries and inventions of this one man have kept millions of capital and thousand of capitalists in suspense and distress on both sides of the sea. In contrast with the gradualness of thought movement in the Middle Ages, consider the dazzling swiftness with which the theory of evolution and the agnostic philosophy have extended and solidified their conquests until the whole world of thought seems hopelessly subjected to their autocracy. I once met in society a young man just entering the silver decade, but whose hair was white enough for one of sixty, and he said that the color changed in a single day, as a sign and result of a mental conflict in giving up his religion for science. Many are they who have passed, or are yet to pass through such conflict, and at far greater damage to the nerve centres.

Increase in Amount of Business in Modern Times.

The increase in the amount of business of nearly all kinds in modern times, especially in the last half century, is a fact that comes right before us when we ask the question, Why nervousness is so much on the increase?

Of business, as we moderns understand the term, the ancient world knew almost nothing; the commerce of the Greeks, of which classical histories talk so much, was more like play — like our summer yachting trips — than like the work or commerce of to-day.

Manufacturers, under the impulses of steam-power and invention, have multiplied the burdens of mankind; and railways, telegraphs, canals, steamships, and the utilization of steam-power in agriculture, and in handling and preparing materials for transportation, have made it possible to transact a hundred-fold more business in a limited time than even in the eighteenth century; but with an increase rather than a decrease in business transactions. Increased facilities for agriculture, manufactures, and trades have developed sources of anxiety and of loss as well as profit, and have enhanced the risks of business; machinery has been increased in quantity and complexity, some parts, it is true, being lubricated by late inventions, others having the friction still more increased.

Dr. Mosso, of Turin, Italy, has invented an apparatus, of simple construction, by which it is possible to prove that even a slight excitement of the brain causes increased circulation in it. The instrument consists in glass vessels large enough to hold a man's outstretched hand, in which there is an orifice in which the arm of the person to be experimented on is placed, so that the warm water with which the vessel is filled cannot escape, the water being connected with a thin glass tube like a thermometer, which shows the least rising or falling in the circulation of the arm. Experiments show that when a person has his attention attracted even slightly — as by the reading of a book or paper—the bulk of the blood in his arm diminishes; and the inference is that correspondingly the bulk of the blood in the brain increases.

With this experiment before us, let us consider the heightened activity of the cerebral circulation which is made necessary for a business man since the introduction of steam-power, the telegraph, the telephone, and the morning newspaper.

Buying on a Margin vs. *Gambling.*

The custom of buying on a margin that has lately grown so much in popularity is more exciting to the nervous system than ordinary gambling, which it in a measure displaces, in these two re spects—

First, the gambler risks usually all that he has; while the stock buyer risks very much more than he has.

Secondly. The stock buyer usually has a certain commercial, social and religious position, which is thrown into the risk, in all his ventures; whereas, the ordinary gambler has nothing to lose but his money.

For these reasons it is quite clear that gambling— formerly far more prevalent than now — is less pernicious in its action on the nervous system, than buying stocks on a margin.

Increased capacity for Sorrow—Love and Philanthropy.

Capacity for disappointment and sorrow has increased with the advance of civilization. Fineness of organization, which is essential to the development of the civilization of modern times, is accompanied by intensified mental susceptibility.

In savagery, life is mostly sensual, with much mental force held in reserve, as with North American Indians, while the intellect has but slight strength; in a highly civilized people, some of the senses and all the emotions are quickly excited, and are attended with higher, sweeter, and more complex and rapturous pleasure than in savagery, and but for the controlling and inhibiting force of a better trained reason, would make progress, and even existence, in civilization, impossible. Relatively to the intellect, the savage has more emotion than the civilized man, but in absolute quantity and quality of emotion, the civilized man very far surpasses the savage; although, as the civilized man is constantly kept in check by the inhibitory power of the intellect, he appears to be far less emotional than the savage, who, as a rule, with some exceptions, acts out his feelings with comparatively little restraint. The civilized man enjoys his food better than the barbarian; has vastly more complex modes of cookery, and appreciates, when ın health, nice distinctions in what he eats, far more than is possible to the savage.

Of the poetry of love, as distinct from the physical type, the lower savages know nothing — their friendships, their married life, their home life with their offspring, show but fugitive traces of that enormous and tyrannous emotion out of which all our novels, romances, and dramas are builded. This potency of loving, including not only sexual, but filial, brotherly and sisterly affection, in all its ranges and ramifications, is a later evolution of human nature; like all other emotions, it is matched by a capacity for sorrow corresponding to its capacity for joy. Love, even when gratified, is a costly emotion; when disappointed, as it is so often likely to be, it costs still more, drawing largely, in the growing years of both sexes, on the margin of nerve-force, and thus becomes the channel through which not a few are carried on to neurasthenia, hysteria, epilepsy, or insanity.

Jealousy is the shadow of love and like other shadows greater than the original; it deepens and widens and lengthens with increasing refinement.

Organized philanthropy is wholly modern, and is the offspring of a higher evolved sympathy wedded to a form of poverty that could only arise out of the inequalities of civilization. Philanthropy that is sincere suffers more than those it hopes to save;

for while "charity creates much of the misery that it relieves, it does not relieve all the misery that it creates."

Repression of Emotion.

One cause of the increase of nervous diseases is that the conventionalities of society require the emotions to be repressed, while the activity of our civilization gives an unprecedented freedom and opportunity for the expression of the intellect; the more we feel the more we must restrain our feelings. This expression of emotion and expression of reason, when carried to a high degree, as in the most active nations, tend to exhaustion, the one by excessive toil and friction, the other by restraining and shutting up within the mind those feelings which are best relieved by expression. Laughter and tears are safety-valves; the savage and the child laugh or cry when they feel like it — and it takes but little to make them feel like it; in a high civilization like the present, it is not polite either to laugh or to cry in public; the emotions which would lead us to do either the one or the other, thus turn in on the brain and expend themselves on its substance; the relief which should come from the movements of muscles in laughter and from the escape of tears in crying is denied us; nature will not, however, be robbed; her loss must be paid and the force which might be expended in muscular actions of the face in laughter and on the whole body in various movements reverberates on the brain and dies away in the cerebral cells.

Constant inhibition, restraining normal feelings, keeping back, covering, holding in check atomic forces of the mind and body, is an exhausting process, and to this process all civilization is constantly subjected.

A modern philosopher of the most liberal school, states that he hates to hear one laugh aloud, regarding the habit, as he declares, a survival of barbarism.

Domestic and Financial Trouble.

Family and financial sorrows, and secret griefs of various kinds, are very commonly indeed the exciting cause of neurasthenia. In very many cases where overwork is the assigned cause—and where it is brought prominently into notice, the true cause, philosophically, is to be found in family broils or disappointments, business failures or mishaps, or some grief that comes very near to one, and, rightly or wrongly, is felt to be very serious.

The savage has no property and cannot fail; he has so little to win of wealth or possessions, that he has no need to be anxious. If his wife does not suit he divorces or murders her; and if all things seem to go wrong he kills himself.

Politics and Religion.

There are two institutions that are almost distinctively American — political elections and religious revivals; for although in other countries both these institutions exist, yet they are far less numerous and far less exacting, and have far less influence than in America. Politics and religion appeal mostly to the emotional nature of men, and have little to do with the intellect, save among the leaders; and in consequence, the whole land is at times agitated by both these influences, to a degree which, however needful it may be, is most exciting to the nervous temperament.

Liberty as a Cause of Nervousness.

A factor in producing American nervousness is, beyond dispute, the liberty allowed, and the stimulus given, to Americans to rise out of the position in which they were born, whatever that may be, and to aspire to the highest possibilities of fortune and glory. In the older countries, the existence of classes and of nobility, and the general contexture and mechanism of society, make necessary so much strenuous effort to rise from poverty and paltriness and obscurity, that the majority do not attempt or even think of doing anything that their fathers did not do : thus trades, employments and professions become the inheritance of families, save where great ambition is combined with great powers. There is a spirit of routine and spontaneous contentment and repose, which in America is only found among the extremely unambitious. In travelling in Europe one is often amazed to find individuals serving in menial, or at least most undignified positions, whose appearance and conversation show that they are capable of nobler things than they will ever accomplish. In this land, men of that order, their ambition once aroused, are far more likely to ascend in the social scale. Thus it is that in all classes there is a constant friction and unrest—a painful striving to see who shall be highest; and, as those who are at the bottom may soon be at the very top, there is almost as much stress and agony and excitement among some of the lowest orders as among the very highest.

Consider how much nerve-force the American people have expended in carrying through our late nominations and elections.

Last June, just after the nominations were made, I was in Cleveland, assisting in organizing a national association for the protection of the insane, and in my address I referred to the campaign for the nominations as one of the reasons why we needed such an organization. To-day, just after the inauguration, those whose minds are philosophically bent, may well occupy themselves with making an estimate of the cost in brain and nerve of these months of excitement and disappointment; for it is the very essence of politics to disappoint those who have to do with it, and disappointment, like love, is one of the most expensive of human emotions.

Before the late election one of my patients informed me, to my alarm, that he was getting interested in politics. He had been treated most successfully for nerve troubles, two years ago, and had been put into working order, and had been able to work hard; but I knew that, like most of his class, he was living on a small reserve of nerve-force. He said that great issues were before us, and the neglect of politics on the part of intelligent men was the ruin of their nation. I said to him: "My friend, presidents and politicians are chips and foam on the surface of the sea; they are not the sea; tossed up by the tide and left on the shore, but they are not the tide; fold your arms and go to bed, and most of the evils of this world will correct themselves, and, of those that remain, few will be modified by anything that you or I can do." To this advice he, of course, paid no heed, and a day or two before the election came to my office, entirely prostrated, and confessed a most interesting fact—that five minutes' conversation on politics had taken all his nerve from him, doing more to exhaust him than months of steady work. He was a Hancock man, and the unpleasantness of defeat supplemented the discussions and electioneerings of a long campaign, doing more of evil for him than he had done of good to his country.

Take that case, which is not an exception, but a type of others in varying degrees; multiply it by thousands and thousands of thousands; add to it a million of our citizens whose existence depends, near or remotely, on the victory or failure of parties, and who must work all through their lives on the treacherous edge of precipices; pile on the infinite wranglings and . controversies, public and family, of these months that the nation believed to be a crisis in its life: throw in the concentrated agony of half our population on the morning following election and the long-drawn-out disappointments of the coming years; then need we ask if there is any mystery in American nervousness, even to those who reject every other accredited cause? The experiment attempted on this continent of making every man, every child, and every woman an expert in politics and theology is one of the costliest of experiments with living human beings, and has been drawing on our surplus energies with cruel extravagance for one hundred years.

Protestantism, with the subdivision into sects

which has sprung from it, is an element in the causation of the nervous diseases of our time.

No Catholic country is very nervous, and partly for this — that in a Catholic nation the burden of religion is carried by the church. In Protestant countries this burden is borne by each individual for himself; hence the doubts, bickerings, and antagonisms between individuals of the same sect and between churches, most noticeable in this land, where millions of excellent people are in constant disagreement about the way to heaven.

The difference between Canadians and Americans is observed as soon as we cross the border, the Catholic church and a limited monarchy acting as antidotes to neurasthenia and allied affections. Protestant England has imitated Catholicism, in a measure, by concentrating the machinery of religion and taking away the burden from the people. It is stated —although it is supposed that this kind of statistics are) unreliable—that in Italy insanity has been on the increase during these few years in which there has been civil and religious liberty in that country.

If this statement could be mathematically proved — as probably it cannot, in the face of so many sources of error to complicate the calculations — it would be a vigorous illustration of the philosophy here inculcated. Certain enough it is that, if such statement were proved to be true, it would be in unison with all that we know of the increase of insanity in those countries which have the most civil and religious liberty.

There would seem to be evidence that, among the negroes of the South insanity has increased, to a certain degree, since their liberation.

The anxieties about the future, family, property, etc., are certainly so wearing on the negro, that some of them, without doubt, have expressed a wish to return to slavery.

This very year (1881) a bill has been introduced into the House of Representatives in Washington, for a government commission to investigate the causes of the increase of insanity, or, more specifically, to empower the National Board of Health to undertake that task. Although advances in science are not usually made by committees—indeed, are almost never made by them, least of all by government committees — yet the offering of such a resolution is a suggestion of an advance in the popular interest in one of the great questions of this age or of any age.

In this department of science, as in all departments of organized knowledge, the discoveries and advances must be made by young men, working obscurely and alone, and all that committees of congress or health boards can do is, to diffuse what these young men have already discovered.

The people of this country have been pressed constantly with these three questions: How shall we keep from starving? Who is to be the next president? And where shall we go when we die? In a limited, narrow way, other nations have met these questions; at least two of them, that of starvation and that of the future life; but nowhere in ancient or modern civilization have these three questions been agitated so severely or brought up with such energy as here. In European civilizations accumulated family wealth has put the first problem, that of getting a living, fairly aside; whereas, in our country, until the past quarter of a century, the poor-house has been a life-long apprehension.

Consider the difference of expenditure of nerve-energy between a person who, always from the mother's arms to the tomb, has not had a thought for money, and one, otherwise similarly situated, who must always hasten and toil, lest he starve.

Habit of Forethought.

Much of the exhaustion connected with civilization is the direct product of the forethought and fore-worry that makes civilization possible. In coming out of barbarism and advancing in the direction of enlightenment the first need is care for the future.

There is a story of an American who, on going to an Italian bootmaker to have some slight job performed, was met with a refusal to do the work required. On being asked why he refused, he replied that he had enough money to last him that day, and that he did not care to work. "Yes" said the American, "but how about to-morrow?" "Who ever saw to-morrow?" was the Italian's response.

Those who live on the philosophy suggested by that question, can never be very nervous. This forecasting, this forethinking, discounting the future, bearing constantly with us not only the real but imagined or possible sorrows and distresses, and not only of our own lives but those of our families and of our descendants, which is the very essence of civilization as distinguished from barbarism, involves a constant and exhausting expenditure of force. Without this forecasting, this sacrifice of the present to the future, this living for our posterity, there can be no high civilization and no great achievement; but it is, perhaps, the chief element of expense in all the ambitious classes, in all except the more degraded orders of modern society. We are exhorted, and on hygienic grounds very wisely, not to borrow trouble — but were there no discounting of disappointment, there would be no progress. The barbarian borrows no trouble; stationary people, like the Chinese, do so but to a slight degree; they keep both their nerve-force and their possibilities of progress in reserve. Those who have acquired or have inherited wealth, are saved an important percentage of this forecasting and fore-worry; like Christian, they throw off the burden at the golden gate, but, unlike Christian part of it they must retain; for they have still the fear that is ever with them of losing their wealth, and they have still all the ambitions and possible disappointments for themselves and for their children.

On the highly civilized man there rests at all times a three-fold burden — the past, the present, and the future!. the barbarian carries through life but one burden — that of the present; and, in a psychological view, a very light one indeed; the civilized man is ever thinking of the past — representing, repeating, recasting, and projecting the experiences of bygone days to days that are to come. The savage has no future, and but little of the past, and that little is usually pleasant, and not burdensome.

The difference between civilization and savagery, and an impressive and instructive illustration of the cause of nervousness, is given us whenever any representatives of our Indian tribes visit the east. The utter want of curiosity in matters that do not come immediately home to them is a feature in their character most noticeable and most interesting, contrasting, as it does with the excess of Yankee curiosity. The barbarian cares nothing for the great problems of life; seeks no solution — thinks of no solution of the mysteries of nature, and, after the manner of many reasoners in modern delusions, dismisses what he cannot at once comprehend, as supernatural, and leaves it unsatisfactorily solved for himself, for others, and for all time; the curiosity of the Yankee, which, when harnessed, trained, and held in check, becomes the parent of invention, science, and ideas, inquiring into everything with eagerness, unrest, impatience, palpitating anxiety and breathlessness, draws heavily on the units of nerve-force.

The North American barbarian is not peculiar in his indifference to nature's mysteries; this feature is but a type of the barbarian and immature mind everywhere, the Indians of South America and Central America — the negroes of Africa and of our own country, young children everywhere, and adults who have never matured in the higher ranges of intellect are, in this respect — in varying degrees — like the Indians of the Western plains, living not for science or ideas, but for the senses and emotions.

Formal attempts are now being made to educate and civilize the Indians, and, at the present moment, with not success enough to warrant any fear less they should become specially nervous; but were the scheme to be carried forward in triumph, and the Indian develop into a thinker, questioner, and holder of property, with all the care, economy, and forecasting that property requires, then we shall see correspondingly, a development of nervousness in the Indians, if not in this generation, in those that are to come.

The very few cases of insanity among Indians that I have been able to trace or get account of, are among those who have been brought into close relations with the whites, and some of them were of purely religious origin.

Single instances illustrate the predominance of civilization as a factor in the causation of nervousness over all other secondary and tertiary factors in a most convincing way. Thus, one who while living in-doors and carrying on some brain-harrying occupation, and who cannot smoke, or drink, or eat any but the plainest and most easily managed food, and who, despite all his cares, is always suffering through, perhaps, the whole range of his nervous system, if he but plunge into the forest, or even from the city into the country toward any point of the compass, shall find himself another person, within perhaps, less than twenty-four hours, and in a few days or weeks can eat the most indigestible food with a disregard of time or method, use tobacco and alcohol freely as the impulse pleases, bear strong exertions of mountain climbing or sport; in short leading the life of a barbarian, he has the barbarian's health, and he finds not the alcohol nor tobacco, nor food, singly or unitedly, have made him nervous.

The human system in its animal state, before modern civilization appeared, was capable of bearing greater strain in all its functions without appreciable harm. He who has a constitution that requires watching and tenderness and anxious caution, that resents every over-indulgence of irregularity or disobedience to the law, has a very poor constitution.

Comparative Size of the Ancient and Modern World.

Little account has been made of the fact that the old world is small geographically. The ancient Greeks knew only of Greece and the few outside barbarians who tried to destroy them. The discovery of America, like the invention of printing, prepared the way for modern nervousness; and, in connection with the telegraph, the railway, and the periodical press increased a hundred-fold the distresses of humanity.

The sorrows of any part of the world, many times greater geographically than the old world as known to the ancients, through the medium of the press and the telegraph are made the sorrows of individuals everywhere.

The burning of Chicago — a city less than half a century old, on a continent whose existence was unknown a few centuries ago — becomes in a few hours the property of both hemispheres, and makes heavy drafts on the vitality not only of Boston and New York, but of London, Paris, and Vienna. With the extension and complexity of populations of the globe, with the rise and growth of nations and peoples, these local sorrows and local horrors become daily occasions of nervous disorders.

Our morning newspaper, that we read with our breakfast, has the history of the sorrows of the whole world for a day; and a nature but moderately sympathetic is robbed thereby, consciously or unconsciously, of more or less nervous strength.

The railroads of the world measure, 200,000 miles, all but $\frac{1}{14}$ portion being divided between Europe and America; and over these roads pass 66,000 locomotives, 120,000 passenger and 1,500,000 freight cars. On the seas there are 100,000 vessels and 12,000 steamers with a tonnage of 20,000,000. In proportion to population, Americans write far the most letters; next comes the English; then Switzerland, Germany, the Netherlands, Denmark, Austria France, Sweden, Norway, Spain, Hungary, Italy, Portugal, Greece, Russia, Servia, Roumania, Turkey.

Letter writing is an index of nervousness; those nations who writes the most letters being the most nervous, and those who write scarcely at all, as the Turks and Russians, knowing nothing or but very little of it.

Life in Ancient Athens and New York contrasted.

When we consider the life of an American child, from its early school-days until the hour it leaves the university or seminary, the many and tiresome hours of study, the endless committing and repeating and reciting, the confinement in constrained positions, the overheated and overdried atmosphere, the newspapers and novels that he is and must be prepared to criticise, the sermons and lectures which he is compelled to listen to and analyse, the strife and struggle for bread and competence against inflammatory competition, the worry and concentration of work made both possible and necessary by the railway, mail service, and the telegraph; in view of these facts, we wonder not that the Americans are so nervous, but rather wonder at the power of adaptation of the human frame for unfavorable environment. The education of the Athenian boy consisted in play and games and songs, and repetitions of poems, and physical feats in the open air. His life was a long vacation, in which, as a rule, he rarely toiled as hard as the American lad in the intervals of his toil.

All that the world has done for two thousand years — all the history it has made, all its art, science, religion, politics, morals, and social life, the Greek boy could know nothing of, could not even anticipate; the world to him was young, and Greece was all the world. No scholar can graduate with even a moderate stand from one of our public schools, without mastering in a certain way, and after years of labor, many of the good or evil thoughts and deeds that have occupied the human race since the time of Socrates and Aristotle. From all these events of history, which every year are rolling up as an increasing burden for the future, the Athenian scholar was joyously free; education was to him but a delicious union of poetry, philosophy, and art. What they called work, gymnastics, competition games, and conversations on art and letters, is to us recreation. Equally striking is the contrast in the life of Athenian and American adults. We have our occasional holidays, and a picnic or other pleasure party is cautiously allowed, or some anniversary is celebrated; but the Greek's life was a long holiday, a perpetual picnic, a ceaseless anniversary.

The Greek wife was half a doll, half a slave. Save a few of the more brilliant among the *etairae*

— the *demi monde* of the time — they had no more voice in the interests of state, or art, or learning, or even of social life, than the children of to-day; the mental activity of woman is indeed almost all modern. The American mother is not only the acknowledged queen of society, but also aims to lead, and oftentimes does lead, with the highest success, in literature, on the platform, in the pulpit, in philanthropy and reform, and in the practice of the medical art.

The offspring of those whose brains are thus kept in constant motion must be affected for better or for worse, sometimes in both ways. If the brain of the average American is tenfold more active than the brain of the average Athenian, the contrast in the cerebral activity of the women must be even greater. But waiving all attempts to bring the subject under mathematical law, these contrasts make clear, and bring into strong relief, the fact that in every direction the modern brain is more heavily taxed than the ancient. In accordance with all analogies, therefore, nervous sensitiveness and nervous diseases ought to increase with the progress of modern civilization; and neurasthenia would naturally be more abundant in the present than in the last century.

It might theoretically be objected to this reasoning that the capacity of the brain for work, and of the nerves for endurance, would grow with the growth of culture. This consideration is surely one of import. Up to a certain point work develops capacity for work; through endurance is evolved the power of greater endurance; force becomes the parent of force. But here, as in all animate nature, there are limitations of development which cannot be passed. The capacity of the nervous system for sustained work and worry has not increased in proportion to the demands for work and worry that are made upon it. Particularly during the past quarter of a century, under the press and stimulus of the telegraph and railway, the methods and incitements of brain-work have multiplied far in excess of average cerebral development. It is during this period that various functional nervous disorders have multiplied with a rapidity for which history gives us no analogy. Modern nervousness is the cry of the system struggling with its environment.

Extremes of Heat and Cold.

When we wish to obtain a powerful stimulating effect on any part of the body, we apply, in rapid alternation, ice and hot water: used for a short time, this application strengthens; used for a long time, it weakens. What the temporary effect of an alternation of heat and cold to the whole body may

be, every one who has taken a Turkish or Russian
bath well knows, and what the general effect of
such baths kept up constantly, or for a large part
of the time, may be, one can without difficulty
imagine; there are, indeed, constitutions that cannot
take even a short bath without fainting or weariness. The inhabitants of the Northern and Eastern
portion of the United States are subjected to.
severer and more sudden and frequent alternations
of extreme heat and cold than the inhabitants of
any other civilized country. Our climate is a union
of the tropics and the poles: "half the year we
freeze, half the year roast," and at all seasons a day
of painful cold is liable to be followed by a day of
painful warmth. Continuous and uniform cold as
in Greenland, like continuous and uniform heat as
on the Amazon, produces enervation and languor;
but repeated alternations of the cold of Greenland
and the heat of the Amazon produce energy, rest-
lessness, and nervousness. The climate of England
and the Continent differs from that of America,
in respect to uniformity, far more than is usually recognized even by those who have passed
years abroad: of the cold of our winters, of the
heat of our summers, England has but little expericuce. Invalid travellers who, as is the case with
many Americans, are sensitive to cold complain that
from the time they leave America to the time

of their return they never know what it is to be really warm. A clerical friend of mine, who resided several years in England, tells me that lack of warmth was a constant and severe affliction. All the houses that he visited were kept at a temperature at least ten degrees below what was comfortable for himself and wife; and yet neither of them were invalids, though both were ideal representatives of . the American type of susceptibility.

Our extremes give rise, among many other symptoms of nervous impressibility, to sensitiveness to heat and cold; midsummer and midwinter are borne with difficulty, and many whom I have known find it necessary to keep constantly on the run before climatic changes. For such, no section of the country is habitable more than three or four months of the year: in the winter they must take refuge in Florida; in the spring, to escape the heat and malaria, they hasten home, whence, in a few weeks, they are driven to the sea-side or farm-house. To live twelve months in one place is what very few of the brain-working classes of our large cities can endure. In this susceptibility to cold and heat, and the consequent necessity of hot-air furnaces and summer retreats, there has been a vast change within a quarter of a century. Our fathers were comfortable in a temperature of sixty degrees, while we require from seventy to seventy-five degrees, and even then suffer half the year from creeping chills and cold extremities. The metropolitan heats they bore right through midsummer, without the need or thought of vacation; and, without taking cold or experiencing severe discomfort, sat for hours in damp and fireless churches. Foreigners often complain of our over-warm rooms, which to them are as annoying as their under-warm rooms are to us; a temperature of sixty degrees contents them, as it did our ancestors half a century or less ago.

During the summer of 1868 the thermometer in England ranged between eighty-two and eighty-eight degrees, and at one time rose to ninety-two degrees, and all complained of the excessive heat. In the winter ice is not abundant; snow falls only to the depth of two or three inches, and remains on the ground for but a few days; skating and coasting and sleighing are almost forbidden joys. Through the entire year, in midwinter even, the meadows are fresh and green, and there is not a month when the public parks cease to be visited. In the coldest seasons a temperature of zero, or even ten degrees above, is very rare; at Greenwich the average of the thermometer during the month of January for half a century was thirty-seven degrees, a temperature that will not only allow but invite various and active out-door recreations. The English winter, indeed, is not unlike our March shorn of some of its bitterness and on its good behavior.

We Americans, on the contrary, for a part of the year are prisoners to our climate, in the summer not daring to walk abroad for fear of sunstroke, in midwinter hemmed in by biting cold and impassable drifts of snow; at no season able to predict or calculate the temperature for a day, or even half an hour, in advance. These sudden leaps of the American climate from distressing heat to severe cold, or the reverse, are quite unfamiliar to England, where spring slowly unfolds into summer, and summer in turn descends into a moderate winter.

Dryness of the Air.

The element of dryness of the air, peculiar to our climate as distinguished from that of Europe, both in Great Britain and on the Continent, is of the highest scientific and practical interest.

Among the usually observed evidences of the dryness of our atmosphere, these facts are noteworthy: the hair easily becomes harsh and dry, requiring oil and pomade; barbers are more popular and more patronized here; clothing hung out on lines gets dry more quickly, to the astonishment of foreign washerwomen; bread dries more rapidly and sooner becomes stale—hence the habit of using it fresh — eating it while warm; cellars can be used for the storage of provisions without fear of being injured by dampness; and articles of all sorts are less likely to be ruined by mould — less liable to corrode or decay; paint on houses dries more speedily, and the second coat can be sooner put on; inlaid floors are more easily cracked; makers of musical instruments must be more careful in selecting the material; the plaster in newly built houses dries so quickly that occupants move in far sooner than they would dare to do abroad; skins in tanyards do not need to hang out so long for drying; matches are more easily lighted;—if there be exceptions to all these facts they are found at the seacoast, on the shores of the great lakes, in damp, woody sections, or on the borders of the Gulf.

Extremes of dryness of the air teach us much on this subject. As the United States has a drier atmosphere than Europe, so the West is drier than the East. The climate of Colorado has been well studied by Dr. Dennison and others. This territory is, on the average, 6,500 feet above the level of the sea, while the peaks of the Rocky Mountains beyond reach as high as 13,000 or 14,000; and the temperature is not unlike that of New York, Indiana, or Illinois.

P. J. Huncke, United States signal officer at Denver, reports, that "between October, 1873, and September, 1874, the average humidity was 49.3 per

cent. There were no regular dews, fogs, or dampness at night; on the average there were in two
months, 19⅔ days that were clear and sunshiny."
On the nervous system this unusual dryness and
thinness of the air have a many-sided influence; such
as increase of headaches, neuralgias, and diminished
capacity for sustaining cerebral toil.

At Pike's Peak station, 14,000 feet above the
level of the sea, the signal officer of the United
States reports that the pulse beats from 90 to 100
per minute the first month, and from 82 to 90 the
second month; and when, as is often the case, there
is much electrical disturbance, the pulse goes to
110 and 120. All this is complicated with the element of error that comes from simple elevation;
but in Peru, as I am told, in latitude fifteen degrees South, at an altitude of from 4,000 to 6,000
feet, the climate is favorable to the nervous; and
certain districts of Switzerland are famed as refuge-
places for neurotic patients. At Leadville, Colorado,
the cigars exposed for sale are covered with a wet
sponge to keep them from drying up; men lose flesh
on coming to this region; catarrhs are very common;
there is a lessened capacity for cerebral toil. This
whole American continent, in its northern regions,
is Colorado on a smaller scale.

The organs, pianos, and violins of America are
superior to those made in Europe at the present

time. This superiority is the result, not so much of greater skill, ingenuity, or experience, but—so far as I can learn, from conversing with experts in this line —from the greater dryness of the air, which causes the wood to season better than in the moist atmosphere of Europe.

I am told, furthermore, that American pianos taken to Europe bear well the greater moisture of Europe; while, on the other hand, musical instruments brought from the other side of the Atlantic to this country, do not bear well the greater dryness of our atmosphere.

The causes of his great lack of moisture are found in the relative infrequency of lakes, the vast extent of unbroken territory, and the scarcity of rain. Eastern Europe is surrounded by immense bodies of water: hence the air is always freighted with moisture; hence, in part, the ruddiness, the solidity, and the bulk of the representative Englishman. The influence of the Gulf Stream is likewise of great importance on the climate of Great Britain, making it both damp and equable.

Not only are there many more days of rain in Great Britain than in America, but there are more clouds in the sky, even when it does not rain. Clouds, by well-known physical laws, interfere with evaporation; and thus the dampness remains longer in the earth than in a land where sunshine

is more free. Thus, the number of days of rain
and the amount of rain being the same in Great
Britain and America, Great Britain would be more
moist. This persistent moisture, as is well known,
is the cause of the greenness and long-continued
beauty of the foliage of Great Britain, of Ireland,
and of the Scotch lakes.

My friend Professor Ball, of Paris, told me there
is in this respect a great difference between Great
Britain and France. In Paris, at least, where the sky
is far clearer, more like that of America, the streets
dry up much more quickly after a rain. The
French, as also is well known, are more nervous in
some respects than the English, with a finer type
of organization, more nearly resembling Americans.

In regard to the electrical state of a dry atmosphere, this general fact is quite clear: that the
electricity which is found in all states of the atmosphere is less evenly and uniformly diffused, and
more liable to various disturbances through inequalities of tension, when the air is dry than when it is
moist. Moisture conducts electricity, and an atmosphere well charged with moisture, other conditions being the same, will tend to keep the electricity in a state of equilibrium, smce it allows free
and ready conduction at all times and in all dirce-
tions. The human body, therefore, when surrounded
by a moist atmosphere never has its own electrical

condition seriously disturbed, nor is it liable to sudden and frequent disturbances from the want of equilibrium in the air in which it moves.

In regions where the atmosphere is excessively dry, as in the Rocky Mountains, human beings— indeed all animals, become constantly acting lightning-rods, liable at any moment to be made a convenient pathway through which electricity going to or from the earth seeks an equilibrium. Hence it is that in that section, especially in the more elevated portions, the hair of the head and the tails of horses not unfrequently stand erect, and travellers over the mountains are astonished and alarmed bv flames of lightning on the rocks, and even on their walking-sticks. In the valley of Sacramento, and, to a less extent, in other sections of the Pacific coast, there occur at certain times what are called "north winds," which, coming from the desert of the North, are excessively dry, and consequently, for the causes above given, are attended by important electrical disturbances, similar in kind, but severer in degree, to those that at all times are liable to take place in that section. During the prevalence of these winds, which may last several hours or days, fruits and foliage, especially on the side toward the wind, tend to shrivel and wither; the grass, likewise, shows the effect of the same influence, and human beings and all animals are unwontedly irritable and nervous.   Even in the East our neuralgic and rheumatic patients, during and just before thunder-storms, are often suddenly attacked by exquisite pains that at once disappear with the appearance of fair weather.   There are those so sensitive that for a hundred miles and more, and for a full day in advance, as Dr. Mitchell has shown, they can predict the approach of a storm. The atmospheric conditions and disturbances in relation to moisture, dryness, and electricity which these sensitives thus visibly and painfully appreciate, affect us all, though invisibly and painlessly; but through a lifetime and through the generations these perpetually acting influences result in nervousness and nervous exhaustion, with all the maladies to which they lead.

The exceeding cold of our winters compels us to pass a large part of our time not only in-doors, but in rooms overheated with *dry* air; thus one of the bad features of our climate plays into the hands of the other, re-enforcing, extending, multiplying, its capacity for evil.   The high temperature and unnatural dryness of our closed rooms are both harmful, and are both made necessary by excessive external cold, and by the alternations of heat and cold that produce a sensitiveness of organization which can only find comfort in a somewhat high temperature.

How Dry Air causes Nervousness.

Dryness of the air, whether external or internal, likewise excites nervousness by heightening the rapidity of the processes of waste and repair in the organism, so that we live faster than in a moist atmosphere. The rationale of this action of dryness on living beings—for it is observed in animals as in men — is as follows: Evaporation from the surface of the body is accompanied by dissipation of heat, and by the numerous and complex vital changes of which the evolution and dissipation of heat through evaporation are the results. In a moist atmosphere such evaporation takes place slowly, because the air, being already saturated with water, cannot rapidly take up the vapor that comes from the surface of the body; hence this vapor accumulates in the form of sensible perspiration. A dry atmosphere, on the contrary, is eager and hungry for the bodily moisture and rapidly absorbs it, so that it does not accumulate on the surface, but passes off as insensible perspiration. We perspire the least when we are apparently perspiring the most; on sultry August days our clothing is soaked, because the moisture of the body has no chance for ready escape, and consequently the vital changes that produce the moisture are obstructed and move with corresponding slowness. A day that is both moist and warm is hotter to the nerves of sensation and far more oppressive than a far warmer day that is also dry, for the conversion of the fluids of the body into insensible vapor, which process takes place so rapidly in dry air, is attended with escape of bodily heat, which gives relief. Hence it is that in California and on the Pacific coast and in the Rocky Mountain region, where the thermometer sometimes runs as high as one hundred and ten or even one hundred and twenty degrees in the shade, sunstrokes were formerly unknown, and even now are exceedingly rare. Hence it is that the hot room in the moist Russian bath is so much harder to bear than the hotter rooms of the dry Turkish bath. Hence it is also that our August dog-days are so much more wearying and painful than the hotter days of mid-June and of early July.

One great climatic advantage of Europe is the non-existence of dog-day weather, as we, in this country, understand that term; the moisture of the Northern European atmosphere is never, for any considerable time, combined with high temperature. The English, who, except by travel in Africa or India or America, know nothing of hot weather, warn Americans against visiting Italy in summer; but those who do not heed this advice will find in Venice and Milan and Rome, and even Naples, no warmer days than in America at the same season.

Dryness of the air is one cause of the long-observed leanness of the Americans as compared with the Europeans. We are taller, thinner, lankier, than the original stock in England and Germany, partly because in our dry atmosphere we so rapidly evaporate; the animal fluids disappear into the aerial fluid; we have little chance to accumulate fat. Remembering that the body is composed mostly of water, it is clear that rapid evaporation must be attended by a rapid loss of bodily weight. A thousand Americans, taken at random, weigh less on the average than a thousand Englishmen or Germans of the same ages and social status; even the dark aborigines, in spite of their indolence, were almost always lean.

The moisture of the atmosphere of England is one cause of the success of her manufactures, and one reason why America finds it hard to compete with England in this respect is the dryness of American atmosphere. Certain threads, I am told, cannot be made in this country, under any condition yet suggested, and, for the manufacture of cotton, moisture is of high service. Even in England, there are certain districts more moist than others, and, therefore, better fitted for manufacturing purposes. The greater prevalence of moisture in the North of England has been assigned as the cause of the greater success of manufacturing in that section;

and one of the Manchester mill owners asserted that, during a season of dry weather, there was, in weaving alone, a loss of five per cent. in quantity, and another loss of five per cent. in quality; in spinning, also, an equal loss is claimed. To maintain moisture in mills, sundry devices have been tried, which have met, I believe, with partial success in practice.

Climate alone cannot produce a high order of nervousness, else the North American Indian should have been nervous, but climate plus an intense civilization. Dr. Benjamin Howard, whose opportunities for studying the comparative climatology of Europe and America have been abundant, has brought to my notice, in conversations on this theme, the fact that, in England the difference between the out-door temperature and the in-door temperature is much less than in the United States. An American does not need to be very long in England before noticing this fact, after his attention has been attracted to it. Even in the quite chilly weather of summer and autumn the English keep their doors and windows open and do without fire; and in seasons when fire is imperative, they keep the temperature so low (a little above or below 60 degrees) that one going out doors is sensible of only a slight change — it may be ten, twenty, or thirty degrees; whereas, in America, in our long winters, the houses especially in our cities (though not exclusively in cities), the temperature is seldom less than seventy or seventy-five degrees, and not infrequently going to eighty degrees; while outside, the temperature is down among the thirties, the twenties, and, in some sections, is at times below zero — thus making a contrast of from forty to eighty degrees or more between the out-door and the in-door temperature.

In connection with this fact, and as a part of it, an American in visiting Europe observes the out-doorness of the life of the people as compared with American life.

In the Northern, Eastern, and Western portions of the United States, there are so many days in winter and spring when, from extremity of cold, depth of snow, slush or mud, going out of doors is positive punishment to any but the most hardy, or those whose lives compel them to be out; and in midsummer, also, so many days when, extremity of heat and danger of exposing one's self to the direct rays of the sun are great, that the habit of staying in the house becomes fixed, not with women alone, but with men also, and with children of both sexes, and this habit of keeping us in-doors is formed and is kept up at those delightful seasons of our summer and early fall when the temptation to go out and stay out is stronger, perhaps, than in any other civilized country. Even in our perfect Octobers, on days that are pictures of beauty and ideals of climate — just warm enough to be agreeable and stimulating enough not to be depressing, we yet remain in the house far more than Europeans are wont to do even in rainy or ugly seasons.

Not only the British themselves, but all people who visit Great Britain during their sad seasons, unite in cursing the English climate; but against all these impatient criticisms should be kept in remembrance this partially redeeming fact that, there is not, probably, on earth, another great country in which, taking all the year round, there are so few days when one cannot go out of doors and, if need be, spend a good portion of the time there. The English know nothing of summer, as we know of it — they have no days when it is dangerous, and scarcely any days when it is painful to walk or ride in the direct rays of the sun; and in winter, spring, and fall there are few hours when one cannot by proper clothing keep warm while moderately exercising.

So little accustomed are the English to warm weather, and so little do they know of summer or of summer heat, that they have no standard of heat as we have; and when, as very often happens, in July, August, or September, there appears a succession of days very much like our October weather, they say they are having a hot spell.

This past summer (1880), I spent a week in Cambridge, attending a meeting of the British Medical Association. After a long period of wet and cold there came a few days of our October or early November weather — when it was safe even for an American to lay by the overcoat, save in the early morning or in the evening, and perchance to even run the risk of changing from thick to somewhat thin underclothing. It was a perfect week, as judged by the American standard — the only flaw being the chilliness of the nights and the danger of taking cold in the early morning hours; but all the British, Scotch, and Irish whom we met when referring to the weather spoke of it as being "excessively warm.

In Paris and in Southern France, in Spain, Italy, and even in the southern portions of Germany, now and then, are days which the inhabitants call hot, but which we call comfortable, and only comfortable when we are clothed more warmly than is our custom when in our own country, at the same season.

During that week at Cambridge there were held a number of garden parties, mostly out-doors, in the grounds attached to the colleges, and mostly in the afternoon, at an hour when, in America at the same season, there would have been danger of sunstroke, or, at least, the heat would have been so intense that there would have been no chance of pleasure —whereas, there it was delightful.

The contrast between the English and American climates can also be well studied this very year; within the present season (1880–81) at the time that we have been suffering so much in America, there has been a snow-storm in Great Britain, with cold which for that climate is regarded as extraordinary if not unprecedented; and yet, neither the depth of snow nor temperature were at all unusual for America in any winter and would not excite attention or comment. Trustworthy accounts from London inform us, however, that the business and pleasure of that metropolis and vicinity were paralyzed by a slight fall of snow and the severity of the cold. Even the cabmen, who in this city never retreat in the lowest temperature or in the hardest storm, in London ran to their homes, and it was difficult to get conveyance except by the underground road.

Last year Paris was visited somewhat in the same way, and was in a similar state of want of preparation as in London; the horses were not shod for ice and snow, laborers and the travellers were not qualified for extremes of temperature, and were frightened by a move in the thermometer which we in America expect any time during the winter.

The way, indeed, the Englishman met, or rather refused to meet, this cold wave and storm that burst
upon him, is the best of all proof that he knows
nothing of cold, as he knows nothing of heat, as
cold and heat are experienced every year in America.

The chorographic map of the United States
which is appended, represents by the different degrees of shading, the relative nervousness of the
North and South, and with as much accuracy as
we are justified in attempting with our present
knowledge, and sufficient also, to give a clear and
just idea of what is here stated.

It will be noticed that the lines are thick and
dark all through New England and the Middle
States, and to the west as far as the Mississippi,
and that even north as far as Minnesota and Wis-
consin the lines are not as far apart as in the Gulf
States. In the distant west the population is not
yet thick enough to make data for us to form a
conclusion as to the comparative nervousness of
that region and the South; and in regard to California, also, it is impossible for us to get information
accurate enough to represent it fairly on this map;
it is probable, however, that nervousness is not so
prevalent in California as in the East and North,
the climate there being more uniform all the year
round, with less frequent and less violent changes,
and is more moist than in the East.

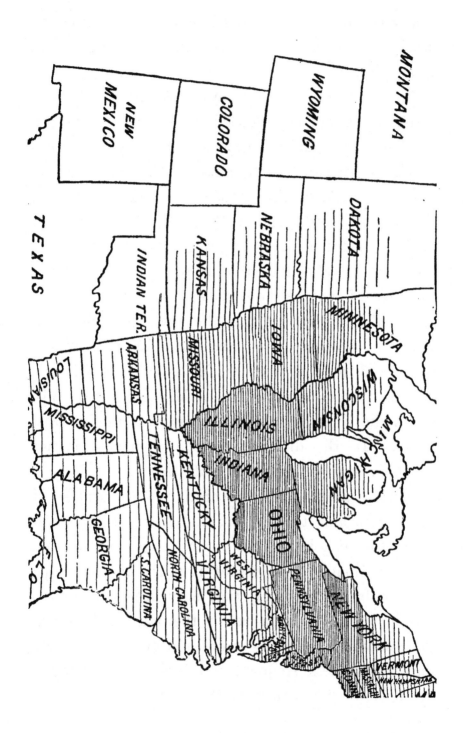

Our habits and institutions, so far as they are distinctively American — rapid eating, eager quest for gold, exciting revivals and elections — are the products of a dry atmosphere and extremes of temperature combined with the needs of a new country and a pioneer life. We are nervous, because the rapid evaporation in our dry, out-door air and in our overheated rooms, for reasons above given, heightens the rapidity of the processes of waste and repair in the brain and nervous system, and because of the exhausting stimulation of alternations of torrid heat and polar cold; and, this nervousness is enhanced by the stress of poverty, the urgency of finding and holding means of living, the scarcity of inherited wealth, and the just desire of making and maintaining fortunes. We cannot afford to be calm · for those to whom the last question is whether they shall exist or die there is no time or force for acquiring plumpness of the body. Not How shall we live? but Can we live at all? is the problem that almost every American is all his life compelled to face.

The neuroses, or functional nervous diseases — of which sick-headache, neurasthenia (nervous exhaustion), neuralgia, spinal irritation, and hay-fever are types — are vastly more frequent and more complex in the Northern and Eastern part of the United States than in all the world besides. These maladies are 'an evolution, a differentiation of the nervous exhaustion produced by our climate and institutions. They have increased *pari passu* with the increase of activity and the complexity and friction of our civilization. They did not appear in the first century of the republic, for time must elapse before climatic peculiarities could show, on a wide scale, their special effects on the organization; furthermore, in the last half century the stress and friction of civilization, under the influence of the railway, the newspaper, and the telegraph, have increased to a degree unparalleled in modern or ancient times. From this same cause— civilization—the European as well as the American nerves have been affected, though on account of differences of climate and institutions far less than in our own country.

All of the above reasonings apply to the Northern and Eastern portions of the United States far more than to the Southern States or to Canada. In the South, particularly in the Gulf States, there are not the extremes of heat and cold, nor the peculiar dryness of the air, that have been described. The Southern winters are mild, with little or no snow and abundance of rain and dampness, while the summers are never as intensely hot as in the latitude of Boston and New York. Throughout the year the Southern climate is both more equable and more moist than that of the North. Herein is explained the most interesting and suggestive fact that *functional nervous diseases of all kinds regularly diminish in frequency and variety as we go South.* Canada has extremes of temperature, but more of steady cold than the States, while the air is kept moist by numerous rivers, lakes, and the wide extent of forest; partly for this reason and partly on account of differences of institutions it does not share, to any very marked degree, in the nervousness of the Northern United States.

Climate of America compared with that of Japan.

The climates of the coasts of the Old and New World have certain resemblances, though they are not precisely alike. The isothermal line of 51° Fahrenheit passes through New York, Paris, and Kanagawa. The climates of coasts are to a considerable degree determined by the ocean currents. The Pacific Ocean, like the Atlantic, has its Gulf Stream. The Kuro Siwo stream of the Pacific, with its circuit of 18,000 miles, carries the warm water of the tropics towards the poles, and regulates in a manner the climate of Japan. Mr. Croll estimates that if the Gulf Stream were to stop, the annual temperature of London would fall thirty degrees, and England would become as cold as Nova Zembla. It is the influence of the Gulf Stream that causes

London, that is eleven degrees farther north than New York, to have an annual mean temperature but two degrees lower.

The best analogue to the American climate is that of Japan, which lies on the eastern coast of Asia, as America lies on the eastern coast of America. A portion of Japan which lies on the Pacific Ocean and receives the warmth which comes from the Gulf Stream of the Pacific, is considerably modified thereby in its temperature; but on the west side of the Islands the climate has something of the rigor of that of America. According to Miss Isabella Bird, who has recently published a work entitled, "Unbeaten Tracks in Japan," which is not only the very best work ever written on Japan, but one of the most remarkable works of travel ever written by man or woman, it seems that the Japanese suffer both from extremes of heat and cold, from deep snows and ice, and from the many weeks of sultriness such as oppress us in the United States. The atmosphere, however, of Japan, is all through far more moist than that of America, in that respect resembling some of the British Isles; there is more rain and more moisture without reference to rain, than in America. In the Japanese, however, we see suggestions of a fineness of type which is peculiarly American; and had the Japanese obtained civilization which, in institutions and in intensity had even approximated that of America and Europe, it is not improbable that they might have developed a nervous susceptibility which, in their present condition, does not exist.

This is certain; — that the Japanese, even of the lower orders, are of a far finer type than the Chinese, or any of the nations of the Orient, and that the Japanese woman of the higher classes, according to Miss Bird and all authorities, is of a sensitiveness of organization and a grace and delicacy of manner that suggest the highest types, as we meet them in the very highest civilization.

Differences in American Climate.

The mountain climate of the United States, or the territorial climate, somewhat resembles that of Central Asia; it is both very dry and very severe in heat or cold in Colorado, in Arizona, in Nevada, in Utah, and in Idaho. The atmosphere is thin and dry, and is subject to frequent, sudden, and furious changes; it is the brewery or pathway of storms for a whole continent. Our Meteorological Bureau has justified its existence and labors by demonstrating and popularizing the fact that our waves of extreme heat and of extreme cold and severe climatic perturbations of various kinds are born in or pass from the Pacific through these mountains and travel eastward, and hence their paths can be followed and their coming can be predicted with a measure of certainty. These storms and waves of heat and cold are the results of extremes of temperature in these mountain districts. In Northern Montana the mean temperature at 4.35 P. M., the hottest week in 1872, was 90° and the coldest week in the same year at 7.35 A. M., 12° below zero, which is a difference of 102°. At Denver, Colorado, the annual mean temperature is 48°; at this place, in January, 1873, the extreme temperatures were 62° above and 17° below zero, a difference of 79°. In October there was a difference of 81°—between 5 and 86.

Not only is this mountain climate noted for extremes of temperature, but, from the elevation, the air is very much rarified and is exceedingly dry—all the elements requisite for producing nervousness. It is not strange, then, that new-comers lose weight, in some cases quite rapidly, an average loss of one-eighth being not unusual; a two hundred pound man losing twenty-five pounds and becoming a hundred and seventy-five pounder. This takes place at Denver, the queen city of the mountains, situated a mile above the sea, where the sun almost always shines, where the atmosphere is translucent and dry and the temperature is extreme, though the nights are usually cool. In higher regions, as at Leadville, two miles above the sea, the loss in weight goes as far as one-sixth or one-seventh of the weight of the body, and goes on much more rapidly. Travellers in those very elevated regions confirm the statement of Bayard Taylor, that new residents may be recognized by the spots of blood upon their handkerchiefs.

In this section and generally also in the very dry and elevated plateaus of the distant West, sexual desire and power in man are diminished to a very remarkable degree.

Coming eastward across the Mississippi, we find that the climate of Minnesota has a yearly mean of 42°; 15° for the winter, 41° for the spring, 68° for the summer, and 45° for the autumn — a range of 53, between the means of summer and winter; the winters being very severe and not uniform, and with sudden and frequent variations; the extremes of the year ranging from 39° below zero to 99° above zero—a clear break of 138 degrees.

The air of this region is also very dry, though much less rarified than that of Denver and of the mountains; and as the mountains are the birth-places of storms, so Minnesota and the northwest is the centre of nervous diseases; probably no young and newly-settled district in the world has, in so short a time, developed in proportion to the brain-working population, so much nervousness as this region. I form this judgment from the testimony of many physicians and others who have visited or resided there, and from many patients from that section who consulted me professionally.*

Tropical and Sub-Tropical Climate contrasted with the Climate of America.

There appears to be no climate on the globe, in all respects, and at all times, equable and agreeable for civilized beings.

The Sandwich Islands is, on the whole, perhaps, at all seasons, and for nearly all years, the most agreeable climate in the world; the temperature ranging nearly all months between 65° and 85°, with occasional fallings and risings. The extraordinary uniformity of the seasons in those islands is accounted for in part by the under-currents of the ocean; cold streams from the north flowing at the bottom of the ocean and coming up to the surface in that vicinity, thus tempering the climate—which otherwise would be excessively hot — and producing also, a uniformity and equability at all seasons of the year. There is evidence, also, that the climate of Southern California and Mexico are very agreeable, at least for a considerable portion of the year. The climate of California proper has

* For many facts in the above analysis of climate I am indebted to very valuable and well written articles on " Climates for Invalids," by Dr. T. M. Coan, in *Harper's Magazine,* and to Dr. Dennison's " Rocky Mountain Health Resorts."

many and serious drawbacks, such as fogs, winds, cold and heat. None of the famous health resorts of Europe or America have good climates; the famed places on the Mediterranean are liable at any time to be attacked by chilling, biting winds that are hard even for the sturdy to bear. Our own Florida is in the spring months, though superior to the Mediterranean coast, very far from being uniform or trustworthy like the Sandwich Islands, the changes there being not only excessive, but violent, sudden, almost instantaneous.

I started one morning from Palatka on the St. Johns River, on a fishing excursion. So great was the heat during the middle of the day, that I found it convenient—even absolutely necessary, to take off my coat and hold an umbrella over my head, while my guide rowed to our destination ; but on returning, late in the afternoon, the cold became so severe that the heaviest ulster would have been agreeable, and I was forced to row myself with all my strength, to avoid taking cold. The day following, going up the river on a steamer, a closely-buttoned overcoat was as much needed as in midwinter at the North. In a short trip, less than two weeks, I caught cold twice, although taking all possible care; and that season was not regarded as an unusually unpleasant one.

While visiting Florida that year (1880), I was

informed by 'a resident that the cold had been so intense in that region, years ago, as to destroy the orange trees. This year (1881) the same intense cold has prevailed; even on the St. Johns River oranges have frozen, trees have been injured, if not destroyed, and invalids fleeing from the savage North, have shivered and suffered in the hotels and on the lines of travel. On the sea islands between Charleston and Savannah, ice an inch thick has been formed, and oranges have been frozen on the trees; fires and closed windows have been as much needed as at the North, and days and weeks of rain and mud have made the lives even of the healthy miserable.

It is said that this is an exceptional season, but almost all our seasons are exceptional; all over our country, unusual heat and unusual cold, or what seems to be unusual because it represents our latest suffering, and is therefore nearest to us and best remembered, is experienced many times every year and in nearly all portions of the United States.

The present season of 1881 illustrates in the extreme one great cause for American nervousness.

As I write, the whole North and West is covered with snow, the accumulation of nearly twenty storms during the past two months; so little rain has there been that streams and wells that rarely give out are dry, and in various country places, as

I am told, one must go far away, and often use melted snow to obtain water.

Wave after wave of Arctic cold, starting from the great reservoir or aqueduct of climates, Manitoba Territory, has rolled over the country carrying immense suffering to all classes, wealthy and poor, and causing the death of thousands by pneumonias, pleurisies, and kindred disorders.

The streets of New York at this very moment are blockaded, and are destined for a long time to remain blockaded with banks of snow, which this rich metropolis cannot afford to remove; rivers packed with blocks of ice that makes navigation both hard and dangerous; on all lines of travel in the city and of the roads leading to it, there is obstruction of trade, and in some places absolute suspension; not only delicate women aud children, but even moderately strong and vigorous men, have been for weeks imprisoned with the cold, as closely and as cruelly as by a besieging army; all the appliances for easing the temperature, by furnaces fireplaces, and ranges, have but partially succeeded, and the homes even of the wealthiest citizens are, a part of the time, cheerless and disagreeable. A large percentage of our population has been, or is now prostrated by severe cold; many of those who are able are fleeing southward, where they hope, and perhaps a part of the time may find milder skies, and escape the exhaustion of our protracted springs.

But seven months ago, in this very city, the heat was so powerful that those who dressed after the manner of the tropics could find, night or day, no comfort, even when idle, except by resorting to the sea-side, where, when the wind came from the land, but little more relief was to be had than at home; the waves of the fiercest tropical heat coming from the regions of the mountains are now succeeded by waves of polar cold; a difference in the temperature of between 100 and 140 degrees.

No other civilized country, ancient or modern, has ever had such a climate as this. It is noticed in the seasons of extreme cold, that we do not become hardened, but weakened and made sensitive by exposure and attempts to endure it; the longer the cold persists the more we feel it, and the more liable we are to be prostrated and carried away by it; hence it is, that in the latter part of the winter and early spring—or what passes for spring, which is really a part of winter, and sometimes its worse part—there is more suffering from cold, more liability to disease, by taking cold, and more debility from long confinement in dry and overheated air than in early and midwinter; hence, the suffering of spring; hence, the desire to go southward; hence, the old-fashioned custom of bleeding at that time; hence, the prevalence of what are called bilious attacks in the months of March, April, and May. Similarly we are not hardened but weakened by extreme heat; the early days of midsummer we bear well, but become more and more impressible as the summer advances.

Recapitulation of Causes of Nervous Exhaustion.

The series of causes which result in a case of nervous exhaustion or general nervousness may be thus tabulated :

First, the predisposing causes. Under this head comes—

1. *Modern Civilization.*

This is placed at the head, because none of the predisposing or exciting causes that follow it are competent to produce functional nervous disease of the class described in this work unless civilization prepares the way. The nervous diseases from whicl savages suffer, and the lower orders of peasantry, are largely of a subjective, psychical character, being caused by the emotions, and assume very different phases, whatever their names be, from those herein described. Civilization is, then, the one constant factor, the foundation of all these neuroses, wherever they exist. Other factors are inconstant; climate varies, special occupations vary ; hygienic habits vary, but civilization of some form, with its attendant brain-work and worry, with its in-door life, is an inevitable factor in the causation of all these neuroses.

2. *Climate.*

That climate must take a secondary, not a primary place among predisposing causes of nervous exhaustion, the history of our country alone proves. The American aborigines were the least nervous of all people; but the climate in which they lived was not much different from that in which are now living the most nervous people in the world.

3. *Race.*

In limited, historic time, race is, in some sociological aspects, more potent than climate, since the strong races, like the Hebrews and Anglo-Saxons, succeed in nearly all climates, and are dominant wherever they go; but in unlimited or very extended time, race is a result of climate and environment. We have seen already that these neuroses may be developed in almost any race, in two or three generations, as is proved almost constantly in our climate, under which are gathered so many different races.

The two great factors in climate which are of most import in their relation to the nervous system are, dryness and moisture, heat and cold. But there had been extremes of temperature and dryness of the atmosphere for ages before modern nervousness appeared.

4. *The Nervous Diathesis.*

The nervous diathesis can only be developed to its full expression under the combined influences of race and climate. That this is a predisposing, more perhaps than an exciting cause, is proved by the fact that very many persons have this nervous diathesis without developing to any very great extent nervous diseases.

Among the *exciting* causes are the following ·

First, *functional excess* of any kind, as of the brain, the spine, the digestive, the muscular, and the reproductive systems.

Under this head must be classed all excesses in eating or drinking, the use of stimulants and narcoties, financial and domestic trouble.

None of these factors are competent to produce these neuroses, unless the way is prepared by the predisposing causes. Savages may go to the most furious excesses without developing any nervous disease; they may gorge themselves, or they may go without eating for a week, they may rest in camp or they may go upon laborious campaigns, and yet never have nervous dyspepsia, sick-headache, hay-fever, or neuralgia. These exciting causes have usually been regarded as the sole causes of nervous diseases; although a philosophical study of this subject shows that of themselves they have but little power. They can only sow a crop of nervous diseases in a soil that has been prepared by civilization.

No people in the world are so careful of their diet, the quality and quantity of their food, and in regard to their habits of drinking, as the very class of Americans who suffer most from these neuroses.

At this point a query may be raised : Did not the eating, drinking, and smoking of our ancestors prepare the way for our nervousness? Is not modern nervousness the remote effect of ancient dissipation?

The answer is, that where there is no civilization there is no nervousness, no matter what the personal habits may be, even though the experiment be made, as in Africa, for centuries.

It would be impossible for an American Indian by any degree of recklessness or excess to make himself nervous. Alcohol only produces inebriety when it acts on a nervous system previously made sensitive. Alcoholism and inebriety are the products not of alcohol, but of alcohol plus a certain grade of nerve degeneration.

When a nervous American is shut up in bad and overheated air, he becomes more nervous; his face perhaps flushes, his head aches, there is a sensation of suffocation and vague misery that finds quick relief on getting into the open air, and in all directions there is an unshaken belief in the injuriousness of breathing bad air; and injunctions to live as much as possible out of doors, and to get away from cities and city-life are among the truisms of sanitary science. But bad air, that is, air simply made impure by the presence of human beings, without any special contagion, seems powerless to produce disease of any kind, unless the system be prepared for it. Not only bad air, but bad air and filth combined, the Chinese of the lower orders endure both in this country and their own, and are not demonstrably harmed thereby—certainly not in their nervous systems; but impure air, plus a constitution drawn upon and weakened by civilization, is an exciting cause of nervous disease of immense force. The Chinese huddled and herded together like sheep, of course breathe, by day as well as by night, an atmosphere as vile as it can be made by human breathing and human emanations, but seem to develop therefrom no form of nervous disease, and not always, any form of acute and inflammatory disease; and the savage tribes of the extreme North, and in cold regions everywhere, imprison themselves in their filthy houses without receiving any injury that can be easily traced, and if injury does result it is manifested otherwise than through the nervous system.

It cannot be too strongly enforced in all our thoughts, and controversies, and arguments on this complex theme of the causation of nervous disease,

that not tobacco, nor alcohol, nor digestive, nor
sexual excess, nor foul air, nor deprivation, nor in
dulgence in any form, can produce nervous disease
unless they act upon a constitution predisposed by
civilization. *American nervousness is the product
of American civilization.* All the other influences
—climate, nervous diathesis, evil habits, worry and
overtoil — are either secondary or tertiary. The
philosophy of the causation of American nervousness may be expressed in algebraic formula as
follows : civilization in general + American civilization in particular (young and rapidly growing
nation, with civil, religious, and social liberty) + exhausting climate (extremes of heat and cold, and
dryness) + the nervous diathesis (itself a result of
previously named factors) + overwork or over-
worry, or excessive indulgence of appetites or passions = an attack of neurasthenia or nervous exhaustion. A philosophic study of this question
requires us to consider the whole equation, and not
portions of it. To look exclusively to the bad
habits or excesses, whether in use of food or alcohol or tobacco, or to special worry or excitement,
or to any severe drafts on the nervous system that
come from parturition or lactation in women, or to
puberty or change of life, is as illogical, in the
study of this subject, as it would be in the study
of algebra. Climate is powerless without civiliza-

tion; the nervous diathesis can only exist in civilization and excesses of the most extreme kind, excitements of the most violent nature, of themselves, without the addition of civilization, cannot equal a case of nervousness.

The study of the eye on account of the great precision of modern ophthalmoscopes, helps us in the solution of many severe problems.

Dr. Brudenell Carter, of London, in his work on "Diseases of the Eye," quotes a letter of Dr. Dixon, from Constantinople, in which it is stated that the consumption of tobacco in that city averaged about three pounds a month for each individual, but that amaurosis was there a rare affection. Dr. Habseh, the chief oculist in Constantineple, says that the effect of tobacco upon the eyes is very problematical; that everybody smokes from morning to night, the men a great deal, the women a little less than the men, and the children smoke from the age of seven and eight years. He states that the number of cases of amaurosis is very limited. If expert oculists would examine the eyes of the Chinese, who smoke quite as much as the Turks, if not more, and smoke opium as well as tobacco, they would unquestionably confirm the conclusion of Dr. Habseh among the Turks. Dr. Habseh believes that in persons with a very delicate skin and conjunctiva among the Turks, smoking frequently causes chronic irritation, local congestion, profuse lachrymation, *blepharitis ciliaris*, and more or less intense redness of the eyelids.*

Dr. K. Hekimian Sewny, of the Central Turkish College, at Aintab, in a private letter to Dr. Roosa, recently published in the *Medical Record*, confirms what is here claimed. He says that in an extensive practice of four years and a half in various large cities of Asia Minor, he does not recollect ever seeing a single case of amblyopia or amaurosis due solely to the use of tobacco. He says that he thinks that in some rare cases these conditions may result from the use of alcohol and tobacco at the same time. He also states, what is known everywhere, that the Turks are great smokers, and that they use strong tobacco.

Dr. Sewny is endorsed by Dr. Roosa as an expert on diseases of the eye, and when he makes the above statements we may accept them as authoritative.

The Hollanders, according to a most expert traveller, Edmondo De Amicis, are the greatest smokers of Europe; on entering a house, with the

---

* For this reference I am indebted to a letter to the *Medical Record*, of December 1, 1880, from Dr. Roosa. The letter was called forth by the paper of Dr. Webster on " Amblyopia from the Use of Tobacco," read before the New York County Medical Association. Smoking acting on the savage or barbarian or semi-civilized constitution, can no more cause nervous disease than an acid can make soap without an alkali.

first greeting you are offered a cigar, and when you leave another is handed to you; many retire with a pipe in their mouth, re-light it if they awake during the night; they measure distances by smoke; to such a place by not so many miles but by so many pipes. Says one Hollander, smoke is our second breath; says another, the cigar is the sixth finger of the hand.

And yet by the accepted reasoning of the world amblyopia, and amaurosis, and neurasthenia, and hay-fever, and sick-headache, and sleeplessness, and insanity, and hysteria, would be proved to be just as common among these people as in America, if there were but experts on hand to make the observations. The method in which subjects of this kind have been discussed are most discreditable to our science and our logic. This method of reasoning I have been obliged to meet from the time when I first inaugurated the public discussion of this subject in accordance with the philosophy of this work, and it must be met even now, although with a higher evolution of ideas, and improved training among scientific men, it is slowly passing away. The need of our age, the need of all ages, of our country and of all countries, is a reconstruction of logic and the principles of evidence, so that we shall know how to reason justly—shall know what to reject, and what to believe.

Opium Eating not always Injurious to the Chinese.

Opium eating in China does not work in the way that the same habit does in the white races. Mr. Gardner, one of Her Majesty's consuls at Che Fooe, estimates that half the adult population of China are smokers of opium, some being occasional smokers, others habitual, and others still who smoke to great excess. He further observes that when it is said of a Chinaman that he smokes opium, it is meant that he smokes to excess and has a morbid craving for it, just as with us the expression a man drinks, means that he drinks too much — not that he drinks occasionally or moderately; and that it is really nothing against anyone to be an occasional user of opium, any more than it is against one here to be an occasional user of tobacco or alcohol. The same observer estimates that 17,000,000 pounds of opium are annually consumed in China, and as the most excessive smoker does not consume more than four pounds, it is safe to calculate that half a pound is the general average consumption of all classes. It is clear that the habit of taking opium does not necessarily impair fertility, since large families are known among those who use opium, even to excess. It is clear, also, that thousands of hard-toiling people in China find, in opium smoking, the same consolation that thousands of hard-toiling people in Europe and America find in tobacco smoking, and with no more demonstrably injurious effects. Among my nervous patients I find very many who cannot digest vegetables, but must use them with much caution; but all China lives on vegetables, and indigestion is not a national disease. Many of the Chinese live in undrained grounds, in conditions favorable to ague and various fevers, but they do not suffer from these diseases, nor from diseases of the lungs and bronchial tubes, to the same extent as foreign residents there who do not use opium. There is reason for the belief that the smoking of opium has an antiseptic power, and even if that fact be disproved or doubted, the general fact that the majority of those who use opium in China are not injured by it, cannot be questioned.

Health and Habits of North American Indians.

There was recently published in the *Maryland Medical Journal,* a very interesting paper on " The Peculiarities of American Indians, from a Physiological and Pathological Standpoint," by W. C. Boteler, M.D., I.U.S.S.S., Otoe Agency, Gage Co., Nebraska. Since the publication of this paper I have had some correspondence with Dr. Boteler, and I find from his paper and from the letters which he has written me, that his observations there, on the ground, are in entire harmony with all the conclusions that I have derived from a thorough study of the subject, extending over many years, and through all sources of information—literature, individual observations, and conversations, and correspondence with men who have passed their lives among the Indians.

Succinctly stated, his observations are these: *First.* The Indian does not need pure air in order to be healthy; the Indian's home, in his language, is his wigwam; instead of 3,000 feet of cubic air per individual, which, according to best estimates, the white man requires, his house will scarcely contain 1,000 cubic feet, and this is rendered impure also by emanations from the cookery, and contains in the average about six human beings; there are no windows or doors, and no ventilation; every crevice is closed, except for the door-drop occasionally opened, and a place for the exit of smoke at the top. *Secondly.* Food of any kind seems to be digested with equal ease, without regard to the method of its preparation. The Indian in his original state subsisted largely on beef, when he could get it—on the whole, the best single food for man; but now that buffalo are scarce, the Indian depends largely on Indian corn, and on one meal a day of corn will work at the plough from morning until night. The water is sometimes as bad as the food, and is taken, Dr. Boteler says, usually from streams and sloughs filled with germs and miserable impurities. *Third.* The Indian has less sickness than the white, and is, as a rule, in perfect health and well developed. This bad air, bad water, and bad food do not have any provably injurious effect on his constitution. Granted that the future generations may suffer from these unfortunate surroundings of their ancestors, this one fact is an entirety —that the present generation can endure this bad hygiene; whereas the whites, their contemporaries in the same climate, are affected in their own generation, not only in a year or month or day, but instantly, since there are those who cannot go into a crowded theatre, or into a hovel where the air is close and impure, without being at once unpleasantly affected, and, if they long remain, seriously so. Moreover, we know that the Kamschatkans may spend a good portion of their time in badly ventilated huts without any apparent injury to the nervous system.

All these facts impress upon us the important generalization that food and diet and exercise and air and drinks and modes of life are relative and not absolute; that their injuriousness or innocuousness depends on the subjective character of the individual; and that man in his original state, before the coming of civilization, could stand ex-

tremes of diet and extremes of exposure, and extremes of deprivation, and excess of almost every
form, just as he can stand extremes of temperature,
without demonstrable injury ; the amount of reserve
force in the normal constitution being so great, that
scarcely any conceivable extravagance can produce
bankruptcy.

Fourth. That the illnesses of the Indian are
more readily managed than the same illnesses of the
white people.   Their fevers are more readily
treated, their rheumatisms and bronchial affections
and lung fevers and pleurisies respond more quickly
and pleasantly to the usual treatment that we give
these troubles, than the same diseases in the whites.
Malaria, which is found among them, gives away
better to the bark treatment or quinine, than malaria in the whites ; and Dr. Boteler observed that the
whites who marry among the Indians and share their
wigwams, sometimes appear for treatment with the
Indians at the same time with the same symptoms,
and it is observed that after several days of medication the Indian will be well and the white man still
an invalid, and so remain for weeks.

Physique of Woman in the Savage State.

Woman in the savage state is not delicate, sensitive, or weak.   Like man, she is strong, well developed, and muscular, with capacity for enduring

toil, as well as child-bearing. The weakness of woman is all modern, and it is pre-eminently American. Among the Indians the girls, like the boys, are brought up to toil and out-door life; they are expected to tear limbs and boughs from trees and break sticks for fires. So different are the squaws from the tender and beautiful women of the white races, that they seem to belong to another order of creatures. The young wife of an Indian, having quarrelled one day with her husband, seized him by both ears and the hair, as he was raising his hand to strike her, threw him on the ground, as one would throw a child, and raising his head with her hands, beat it upon the hard ground until he begged for his life. In the same tribe (the Apaches) there was a young wife who prepared a meal for her husband and his friend, cooking the food and bringing it on the table. While they were eating, she went away, and in less than an hour returned, dressed in the finest apparel and ornaments and apparently very pleased and happy about something. Pressed for an explanation, she took her husband away down to the spring in a thicket near by, and there in a bed of moss, wrapped in finest skins, was a beautiful new-born child. Within the short period of less than an hour all this had been accomplished, and the mother was as lively and strong as though nothing had happened.

The problem can be solved by studying this Continent alone.

It is not necessary to go off the continent of North America, it is not necessary to leave the United States, in order to study the relation of civilization to the nervous system, and in order to demonstrate out of all dispute the proposition, that nervousness is a result and accompaniment and barometer of civilization.

As the Indian comes in contact with civilization there is a slight increase of insanity among them; as the negro obtains his freedom and uses it, there is likewise a slight increase of insanity, but not as yet perceptible as other forms of disease; but the insanity of the negro, if not of the Indian, so far as I can understand and learn, is of a more hopeful sort and has a better prognosis than the insanity of the whites.

Contrasting the North and the South, we not only find that nervous diseases of all kinds steadily diminish as we go towards the Gulf; but with this diminution of nervous diseases, we find, as a cause and explanation, a moister and less exciting climate, and institutions that favor conservatism more than radicalism. A Northerner worships the new, the Southerner the old. A Southern manufacturer successfully managing a cotton manufactory in Georgia, told me that he had always great difficulty in introducing any new machinery or devices or methods in his establishments; far more opposition was made than in the West, among the same class of people; they opposed the innovations not because they were bad, but because they were new. In the West the new is always preferred to the old, and if the old be accepted it must have a battle to gain that acceptance; and in the West also there is great and increasing nervousness.

I suspect, but am not able to prove, that since the war there has been among the whites of the South an increase of functional diseases. This is sure, that some of the most severe cases of this character have come under my care from the Gulf States; and I have found that in a number of these cases, over anxiety and toil have been the exciting causes. The Southerners have had their fortunes to re-make; old modes of business have been revived under different conditions, and new businesses and new interests have developed with a swiftness and complexity which before the war was impossible, or at least impracticable. Riding the other day through the streets and along the wharves of Savannah, I observed a commercial activity greater than were found in almost any Northern city except the very largest. Since the war, also, the Northerners have visited the South, for health and amusement, in large numbers, during the winter especially, and by the law of mental contagion, they are, no doubt, acting upon and influencing the Southern character.

A Study of Southern Negroes.

It is not necessary to read books of travel in order to know that nervous diseases do not exist, or exist but very rarely among savages or semi-savages, or even among barbarians, and that indulgence in passions and excess in narcotics and stimulants, as alcohol and tobacco and bad diet, are powerless of themselves to produce nervous diseases in any great frequency; on our own soil, barbarism can be well investigated. I have been twice favored with the chance to study Africa in America. On the sea islands of the South, between Charleston and Savannah, there are thousands of negroes, once slaves, most of whom were born on those islands, and there will die, and who at no time have been brought into relation with our civilization, except so far as it is exhibited in a very few white inhabitants in the vicinity. Intellectually, they can be not very much in advance of their African ancestors; in looks and manners they remind me of the Zulus now exhibiting in America; for although since emancipation they have been taught by philanthropists, part of the time under governmental supervision, some of the elements of common school teaching, yet none of them have made, or are soon likely to make, any very important ·progress beyond those elements, and few, if any of them, even care to exercise the art of reading after it is taught them. Here, then, is a bit of barbarism at our door-steps; here, with our own eyes, and with the aid of those who live near them and employ them, I have sought for the facts of comparative neurology. There is almost no insanity among these negroes; there is no functional nervous disease or symptoms among them of any name or phase; to suggest spinal irritation, or hysteria of the physical form, or hay-fever, or nervous dyspepsia among these people, is but to joke. Inflammatory diseases they have as frequently, perhaps more frequently, than the whites; colds and rheumatisms, and pneumonias are common, and of these diseases they die; but of nervousness and of nervous diseases, from insanity down through all the grades, they know little more, or no more than their distant relatives on the banks of the Congo. All the exciting causes which philosophers have assigned as explanations of nervous diseases and of their increase in civilized countries, are operating there with constant and tremendous power. These primitive people can go, when required, for weeks and months sleeping but one or two hours out of the twenty-four; they can labor for all day or for two days, eating nothing or but little; hog and hominy and fish, all the year round, they can eat without getting dyspepsia; indulgence of passions several-fold greater, at least, than is the habit of the whites, either there or here, never injures them either permanently or temporarily; if you would find a virgin among them, it is said you must go to the cradle; alcohol, when they can get it, they drink with freedom, and become intoxicated like the whites, but rarely, indeed, manifest the symptoms of delirium-tremens, and never of chronic alcoholism; some of them are drunkards, but none are inebriates. Although in the great cities, especially since emancipation, insanity has, perhaps, somewhat increased, these thousands of negroes are types of negroes all over the South; they are types of all Central Africa; they are types of South America· they are types of Australia; they are types of our not so very distant ancestors in Europe.

These blacks cannot summon as much energy for a moment in an emergency as the whites, since they have less control over their energies, but in holding-on power, in sustained, continuous, unbroken muscular endurance, for hours and days, they surpass the whites. One of my friends seeing a negro attempting unsuccessfully to lift a trunk, seized hold of it himself and with ease carried it up stairs. The negro said, "You can lift a heavier trunk than I can, but I can work longer than you, I can tire you out."

My friend Dr. Tonner, formerly of the United States Army, tells me that the Indians of Arizona exhibit a similar endurance. For a reward of fifty cents and a little sugar, he could at any time hire a young Indian to take a journey of over one hundred miles in twenty-four hours, going all the time at a dog-trot, and with no rest and no refreshment except sugar and water.

All this freedom from nervousness and nervous diseases we have sacrificed for civilization: we cannot, indeed, have civilization and have anything else; as we advance we lose sight and possession of the region through which we have passed.

Comparative Physique of the East and West.

West of the Alleghanies, particularly west of the Mississippi, the state of civilization is much like that of the country east of the Alleghanies twenty-five or thirty years ago—showing the same haste, anxiety, resolution, and eagerness for quick and positive results that English travellers of the last generation observed in New England. While survivals of this Puritan character in the East are even now passing away, the Westerners exhibit, in cases not a few, a feverishness, an eagerness, a fremescence, an expectancy, a constant and ever present conviction of the tremendous importance of things, such as characterized our immediate ancestors. The whole physical character is in the face, if we can only read it; and in the Easterners and Westerners these differential characteristics are easily read. In New York and vicinity there is probably less of impatience, solemnity and a sense of the all importance of getting somewhere instantly, than in the last generation. The West is where the East was a quarter of a century ago—passing more rapidly, as it would appear, through the same successive stages of development.

On the other side of the world, in Australia and New Zealand, the new settlements are passing —though more slowly, and in a minor degree—through somewhat the same experience as the United States. There is less mental activity in those regions; there is less of fury and drive, and there is smaller population and a smaller rate of increase; but yet, as travellers aver, there is a nervousness of manner and in the style of living and doing, that in many ways suggests America.

Australian institutions—both religious and political—are more like those of Canada than the United States; and the climate is considerably different from ours.

CHAPTER IV.

WITHOUT civilization there can be no nervousness; there is no race, no climate, no environment
that can make nervousness and nervous disease
possible and common save when re-enforced by
brain-work and worry and in-door life. This is the
dark and, so far as it goes, truthful side of our
theme; the brighter side is to be drawn in the
present chapter.

Thomas Hughes, in his life of "Alfred the
Great," makes a statement that "the world's hardest
workers and noblest benefactors have rarely been
long-lived." That any intelligent writer of the
present day should make a statement so absolutely
untrue, shows how hard it is to destroy an old
superstition.

The remark is based on the belief which —
against the clearest evidence of general observation
— has been held for centuries, that the mind can
be used only at the injurious expense of the body.

This belief has been something more than a mere popular prejudice; it has been a professional dogma, and has inspired nearly all the writers on hygiene since medicine has been a science; and intellectual and promising youth have thereby been dissuaded from entering brain-working professions; and thus, much of the choicest genius has been lost to civilization; students in college have abandoned plans of life to which their tastes inclined, and gone to the farm or workshop; authors, scientists, and investigators in the several professions have thrown away the accumulated experience of the better half of life, and retired to pursuits as uncongenial as they were profitless. The delusion has, therefore, in two ways wrought evil, specifically by depriving the world of the services of some of its best endowed natures, and generally by fostering a habit of accepting statement for demonstration.

Between 1864 and 1866 I obtained statistics on the general subject of the relation of occupation to health and longevity that convinced me of the error of the accepted teachings in regard to the effect of mental labor. These statistics, which were derived from the registration reports of this country and of England, and from a study of the lives of many prominent brain-workers, were incorporated in an essay on the subject, that was delivered before an association of army and navy surgeons, in New

Orleans, in 1863, and afterwards published in the *Hours at Home* magazine. The views I then advocated, and which I enforced by statistical evidence, were :—

1st. That the brain-working classes—clergymen, lawyers, physicians, merchants, scientists, and men of letters, lived much longer than the muscle-working classes.

2d. That those who followed occupations that called both muscle and brain into exercise, were longer lived than those who lived in occupations that were purely manual.

3d. That the greatest and hardest brain-workers of history have lived longer on the average than brain-workers of ordinary ability and industry.

4th. That clergymen were longer lived than any other great class of brain-workers.

5th. That longevity increased very greatly with the advance of civilization; and that this increase was too marked to be explained merely by improved sanitary knowledge.

6th. That although nervous diseases increased with the increase of culture, and although the unequal and excessive excitements and anxieties attendant on mental occupations of a high civilization, were so far both prejudicial to health and longevity, yet these incidental evils were more than counterbalanced by the fact that fatal inflammatory diseases have diminished in frequency and violence in proportion as nervous diseases have increased; and also that brain-work is, *per se*, healthful and conducive to longevity.

Many of these views have since received various and powerful confirmation, and by a number of independent observers. The statistics on this subject I have endeavored to use without abusing them; to draw from them only those lessons that they are really capable of teaching. Among those classes who live mainly by routine and muscular toil (mechanics, artisans, laborers, etc.), change of occupation is the rule rather than the exception, especially in this country; and any statistics of mortality derived from the registration reports, are, so far as these classes are concerned, of but little value in the study of the relative effects of the different occupations on health and longevity. Another important complication arises from the fact that certain occupations, as clerkships, positions in factories, teaching, etc., are followed almost exclusively by the young and middle-aged; while other callings, as judgeships, are filled only by those in middle and advanced life. Another difficulty arises from the fact that some important occupations, as journalism, for example, are adopted only by a limited number; and the number in them who annually die is too small to afford any basis for

comparison. But this generalization is, I am persuaded, admissible, that the greater majority of
those who die in any one of the three great professions — law, theology, and medicine — have, all
their lives, from twenty-one upwards, followed that
profession in which they died. The converse generalization, that the great majority of those who
die in the muscle-working avocations, have all their
lives followed some kind of muscle-working employment, however frequently they may have changed
from one to another at different periods, is also
true. Very few who once fairly enter theology,
medicine, or law, ever permanently change to a
purely physical calling; and, on the other hand, the
number of those who begin life as farmers, laborers,
and mechanics, and end it as lawyers, physicians, or
clergymen, is quite limited, even in the United
States, where every man has a better chance to
follow the bent of his genius than in any other
country.

A comparison, therefore, of the longevity of the
professional and of the muscle-working classes, as
derived from registration reports, such as I have
made, is quite justifiable. The value of this comparison would be vitiated if it could be proved that
those who enter the professions are originally
healthier and stronger, and come from better stock
than those who enter physical avocations; but in

this country, the practice has been to allow the more delicate members of a family to enter a profession, whilst the tough and hardy work on the farm or learn a trade. Here, as in Europe, there is growing up a distinctively intellectual class who live solely by brain-work; it is, however, not from this class alone, but from the farming, mercantile, and artisan class that the ranks of the professions are filled.

Great Longevity of Great Men.

I have ascertained the longevity of five hun dred of the greatest men in history. The list I prepared includes a large proportion of the most eminent names in all the departments of thought and activity.

It would be difficult to find many illustrious poets, philosophers, authors, scientists, lawyers, statesmen, generals, physicians, inventors, musicians, actors, orators, or philanthropists, of world-wide and immortal fame, and whose lives are known in sufficient detail for such an investigation, that are not represented in the list. My list was prepared, not for the average longevity, but in order to determine at what time of life men do their best work. It was, therefore, prepared with absolute impartiality; and includes of course, those who, like Byron, Raphael, Pascal, Mozart, Keats, etc., died comparatively young.

Now the average age of those I have mentioned, I found to be 64.20.

The average age at death at the present time, of all classes of those who live over, twenty years, is *about fifty-one*. (See Drawing). Therefore, the greatest men of the world have lived longer on the average than men of ordinary ability in the different occupations by fourteen years; six years longer than physicians and lawyers; nineteen or twenty years longer than mechanics and day laborers; from two to three years longer than farmers and clergymen, who are the longest-lived class in our modern society. The value of this comparison is enforced by the consideration that longevity has increased with the progress of civilization, while the list I prepared represents every age of recorded history. A few years since I arranged a select list of one hundred names, comprising the most eminent personages, and found that the average longevity was *over seventy years*. Such an investigation any one can pursue; and I am sure that any chronology comprising from one to five hundred of the most eminent personages in history, at any cycle, will furnish an average longevity of from sixty-four to seventy years. Madden, in his very interesting work, " The Infirmities of Genius," gives a list of two hundred and forty illustrious names, with their ages at death.

COMPARATIVE LONGEVITY OF BRAIN-WORKERS.

Category	Longevity
One Hundred Gates Men of the World.	75
One Hundred and Fifty Precocious Great Men.	66-50
Five Hundred Great Men.	64-20
Clergymen.	64
Farmers.	64
Lawyers.	58
Physicians.	57

Average Longevity.... ..... . 51-20... ....

In view of these facts, it may be regarded as established that "the world's hardest workers and noblest benefactors" have usually been very long-lived.

Causes of the Great Longevity of Brain-Workers.

The full explanation of the superior longevity of the brain-working classes would require a treatise on the science of sociology, and particularly of the relation of civilization to health. The leading factors, accounting for the long life of those who live by brain-labor, are:—

1. *The inherent and essential healthfulness of brain-work, when unaccompanied by worry.* To work is to grow; and growth, except it be forced, is always healthful. It is as much the function of the brain to cerebrate, as of the stomach to digest; and cerebration, like digestion, is normal, physiological, and healthful. In all bodily functions the exercise of force develops more force; work evolves strength for work. A plant that is suffered to bud and bloom, is more sturdy and longer lived than the plant that is kept from the light, or trimmed of all its blossoms. By thinking, we gain the power to think; functional activity, within limits, tends to vigor and the self-preservation of an organ and of the body to which the organ belongs. The world has been taught that the brain can be developed only at the expense of the other organs

of the body; granting that brain-work strengthens the brain itself, the rest of the body is impoverished thereby — hence disease, and early death; but it is certain that the very best of the brain-working classes are, on the average, well developed muscularly; and in size and weight of body are superior to the purely muscle-working classes, although their muscles may not be as large or hard or powerful as they would be if more used.

2. *Brain-workers have less worry and more positive comfort and happiness than muscle-workers.* Worry is the converse of work; the one develops force, the other checks its development, and wastes what already exists. Work is growth; worry is interference with growth. Worry is to work what the chafing of a plant against the walls of a greenhouse is to limitless expansion in the free air. In the successful brain-worker worry is transferred into work; in the muscle-worker work too often degrades into worry. Brain-work is the highest of all antidotes to worry; and the brain-working classes are therefore less distressed about many things, less apprehensive of indefinite evil, and less disposed to magnify minute trials than those who live by the labor of the hands. To the happy brain-worker life is a long vacation; while the muscle-worker often finds no joy in his daily toil, and very little in the intervals. Scientists, physicians, lawyers, clergymen,

orators, statesmen, literati, and merchants, when successful, are happy in their work, without reference
to the reward; and continue to labor in their special
callings long after the necessity has ceased. Where
is the hod-carrier that finds joy in going up and
down a ladder? and from the foundation of the
globe until now, how many have been known to
persist in ditch-digging, or sewer-laying, or in any
mechanical or manual calling whatsoever, after the
attainment of independence? Good fortune gives
good health. Nearly all the money of the world is
in the hands of brain-workers; to many, in moderate amounts, it is essential to life, and in large or
comfortable amount it favors long life. Longevity
is the daughter of comfort. Of the many elements
that make up happiness, mental organization, physical health, fancy, friends,* and money — the last is,
for the average man, greater than any other, except
the first. Loss of money costs more lives than the
loss of friends, for it is easier to find a friend than
a fortune. Almost all muscle-workers are born, live,
and die poor. To live on the slippery path that
lies between extreme poverty on one side, and the

---

* I do not here refer to accumulated wealth exclusively,
but to income or sufficient amount to purchase comforts and
luxuries. Many persons (and notably successful professional
men), live out their days in comfort and luxury, although they
never succeed in accumulating fortunes; to them, their reputation is capital and wealth.

gulf of starvation on the other; to take continual thought of to-morrow, without any good result of such thought; to feel each anxious hour that the dreary treadmill by which we secure the means of sustenance for a hungry household may, without warning, be closed by any number of forces, over which one has no control, to double and triple all the horrors of want and pain, by anticipation and rumination,—such is the life of the muscle-working classes of modern civilized society; and when we add to this the cankering annoyance that arises from the envying of the fortunate brain-worker who lives in ease before his eyes, we marvel not that he dies young, but rather that he lives at all.*

3. *Brain-workers live under better sanitary conditions than muscle-workers.* They have better food and drink, warmer clothing, breathe purer air, and are less exposed to fatal accident and the poison of disease. None of the occupations are ideal; none fulfil all the laws of health; but the muscle-working callings are all more or less unhealthy; tradesmen, artisans, common laborers, and even farmers (who combine muscle with brain

---

* Those who question the truth of the above picture are referred to any of the recently published essays and treatises on the condition of the peasantry of England. Observations show that in our own country, not only in large cities, but in all manufacturing towns, and even in farming districts, the laboring classes are as badly circumstanced as I have stated.

work), all are forced to violate sanitary law, every hour and moment; not one out of ten have enough good food; many are driven by passion and hunger to excess in the worst forms of alcoholic liquors; for a large number, sleep is a luxury of which they never have sufficient for real recuperation; healthful air is but rarely breathed by the laboring classes of any large city; exposure to weather, that brings on fatal inflammatory diseases; accidents that cripple or kill;—in all these respects, the muscle-worker, as compared with the brain-worker, is at stupendous disadvantage.

4. *The nervous temperament, which usually predominates in brain-workers, is antagonistic to fatal, acute, inflammatory disease, and favorable to long life.* Comparative statistics have shown that those in whom the nervous temperament prevails, live longer than those in whom any one of the other temperaments prevail, and common observation confirms the statement. Nervous people, if not too feeble, may die every day. They do not die; they talk of death, and each day expect it, and yet they live. Many of the most annoying nervous diseases, especially of the functional, and some even of the structural varieties, do not rapidly destroy life, and are, indeed, consistent with great longevity. I have known a number of men and women who were nervous invalids for half a century or more, and

died at an advanced age. It is one of the compensations of nervousness that it protects the system
against those febrile and inflammatory diseases that
are so rapidly fatal to the sanguine and the phlegmatic; the nervous man can expose himself to
malaria, to cold and dampness, with less danger of
disease, and with less danger of death if he should
contract disease, than his tough and hardy brother.
This was shown in our late war, when delicate, en-
sanguined youth, followed by the fears of friends,
went forth to camp and battle, and not only survived, but grew stout amid exposures that prostrated by thousands the lumbermen of Maine and
the sons of the plough and the anvil. In the conflict with fevers and inflammations, strength is
often weakness, and weakness becomes strength—
we are saved through debility. Still further, my
studies have shown that, of distinctively nervous
diseases, those which have the worst pathology and
are the most hopeless, such as locomotor ataxia,
progressive muscular atrophy, apoplexy with hemi-
plegia, and so on, are more common and more severe, and more fatal among the comparatively vigorous and strong, than among the most delicate and
finely organized. Cancer, even, goes hardest with
the hardy, and is most relievable in the nervous.

The incidental and important proof of the correlation of nervousness and longevity is afforded in

those statistics of the comparative longevity of the sexes.

Women, with all their nervousness—and in civilized lands, women are more nervous, immeasurably than men, and suffer more from general and special nervous diseases—yet live quite as long as men, if not somewhat longer; their greater nervousness and far greater liability to functional diseases of the nervous system being compensated for by their smaller liability to certain acute and inflammatory disorders, and various organic nervous diseases, likewise, such as the general paralysis of insanity.

There is evidence that Americans, on the average, live longer than Europeans, and American insurance companies that have used the English life-tables as a basis for policies have gained thereby at the expense of the policy-holder.

5. *Brain-workers can adapt their labor to their moods and hours and periods of greatest capacity for labor better than muscle-workers.* In nearly all intellectual employments there is large liberty; literary and professional men especially, are so far masters of their time that they can select the hours and days for their most exacting and important work; and when from any cause indisposed to hard thinking, can rest and recreate, or limit themselves to mechanical details. Thus, there is less of the dreadful in their lives; they work when work is

easy, when the desire and the power are in harmony; and, unlike their less fortunate brother in the mill or shop, or diggings, need not waste their force in urging themselves to work. Forced labor, against the grain of one's nature, is always as expensive as it is unsatisfactory; it tells on the health and happiness and on life. Even coarser natures have their moods, and the choicest spirits are governed by them; and they who worship their moods do most wisely; and those who are able to do so are the fortunate ones of the earth.

Again, brain-workers do their best work between the ages of twenty-five and forty-five; before that period they are preparing to work; after that period, work, however extensive it may be, becomes largely accumulation and routine. Lawyers and physicians do much of their practice after forty; but to practice is easy, to learn is hard — and the learning is done before forty or forty-five. In all directions the French motto holds true: "It is the first step that costs." Successful merchants lay the foundations of fortune in youth and middle life, to accumulate, and recreate, and take one's ease in old age; thus they make the most when they are doing the least, and only become rich after they have ceased trying to be so. With muscle-workers, there is but little accumulation, and only a limited increase of reward; and in old age, after their

strength has begun to decline, they must, with increasing expense, work even harder than before.

To this should be added the fact that manual
employments cost nearly as much force after they
are learned as before; they can never, like many
intellectual callings, become so far forth spontaneous
as to require little effort. It is as hard to lay a
stone wall after one has been laying it fifty years,
as during the first year. The range of muscular
growth and development is narrow, compared with
the range of mental growth; the day laborer soon
reaches the maximum of his strength. The literary
or scientific worker goes on from strength to
strength, until what at twenty-five was impossible,
and at thirty difficult, at thirty-five becomes easy,
and at forty a pastime; and besides he has the
satisfaction that the work done so easily at thirty-
five and forty is incomparably better than the work
done with so much difficulty at twenty-five.

Relation of Age to Work, Reputation, and Ability.

The true and only way by which the subject
of the relation of age to work can be approached
is by studying the history of the original work of
the world, and noting the time of life at which it
was done.

Reputation is, on the whole, as approximately

correct, as it is the only test of ability of men who have long been before the world. Fame rightly analyzed is, on the positive side, as truly a measure of cerebral force, as is the thermometer of heat or the barometer of atmospheric pressure.

In differentiating the various classes of merit we should aim to represent, it is hardly necessary to say, not the opinion of any one, but the settled opinion of mankind. The number of illustrious names of history is by no means so great as is currently believed; for, as the visible stars of the firmament, which at a glance appear infinite in number, on careful estimate are reduced to a few thousands, so the galaxy of genius, which appears interminable on a comprehensive estimate, presents but few lights of immortal fame. Mr. Galton, in his "Hereditary Genius," states that there have not been more than four hundred great men in history. I should be inclined to make an estimate more liberal and bring four hundred and fifty, or perhaps five hundred into the catalogue. I do not forget that Goethe has said that "fame is no sure test of merit, but only a probability of such;" but the converse of this statement, that obscurity is no sure evidence of demerit, but only a probability of such, would more nearly approach truth. Brain-force, like all other great forces—light, heat, and electricity —is evolved in enormous excess of the apparent and immediate need of the world, and but a fraction is ever directly and especially utilized. Only in rare instances is special or general talent so allied with influence, or favor, or fortune, or energy that commands circumstances, that it can develop its full functions; "things are in the saddle and ride mankind;" environment commands the environed. If, however, through circumstances, or in spite of circumstances, the power of any man becomes permanently felt in the world, we may be sure that it is a reality and not a sham; we are not sure but that near him live in permanent obscurity a thousand men who, through ill favor or ill health, shall keep their colossal forces forever in reserve. The stars we see in the sky are but mites compared with the infinite orbs that shall never be seen; but no star is a delusion — each one means a world, the light of which very well corresponds to its size and distance from the earth and sun. In the galaxy of history, sham reputations go out in darkness like the meteors that flame across the heavens; but every abiding reputation — every name that shines along the ages — must have great deeds, or great thoughts to feed it. Routine and imitation work can no more confer the fame that comes from work · that is original and creative, than the moon can take the place of the sun.

Distinction between Force and the Results of Force.

In all our studies of this problem we must rigidly keep apart our ideas of force and the results of force. Just as heat in a room is the result of the combustion of the coal in the grate; just as the movement of a cannon-ball is the result of explosion in the cannon; just so fame is the result of mental work. It follows it, oftentimes, at a long distance — years or centuries — as the room remains warm after the fire is extinguished, and the cannon-ball speeds on its course after the gases — by the explosion of which it was discharged — have been dissipated.

It is this confounding of force with the results of force, of fame with the work by which fame is attained that causes philosophers to dispute, deny, or doubt, or to puzzle over the law of the relation of age to work, as here announced.

When the lightning flashes along the sky, we expect a discharge will soon follow, since light travels faster than sound; so some kinds of fame are more rapidly diffused than others, and are more nearly contemporaneous with their origin; but as a law, there is an interval — varying from years to hundreds of years — between the doing of any original work and the appreciation of that work by any considerable number of mankind that we call fame.

The great men that we know are old men; but they did the work that has made them great, when they were young; in loneliness, in poverty, often, as well as under discouragement, and in neglected or despised youth has been achieved all that has advanced, all that is likely to advance mankind. The psychological distinction between original and routine work is in the complete analysis of degree, rather than of kind; since the operations of the brain — as of all organic nature — are processes rather than creations; but practically, the distinction between original work of the highest kind and original work of a lower or ordinary kind — that is, between what we call genius and what we call imitation — we may consider as amounting almost to a difference in kind. The difference between an original man and a routine man is like that between a very fruitful tree and one that is comparatively barren; both produce, and of the same kind of fruit, but the one of more and incomparably better than the other; more in quantity, larger, more luscious, exquisite and inviting in quality. In the brain of a genius ideas evolve as in the brain of a dullard, and by the same laws, but more easily and more rapidly, with higher, more extended, more complex, and more interesting branches and a more fragrant and extensive blossoming. In the man of genius, the idea starts where, in the man of routine, it leaves off, and it keeps on growing and growing; each unit of force or combination of units corresponding to the thoughts or combination of thoughts that the routinist or imitator could never have conceived; this is the work that men call genius, which — in the language of evolution — is but a higher and richer growth of ideas in some one direction, or in many directions.

Original work—that done by geniuses who have thereby attained immortal fame, is the only kind of work that can be used as the measure of cerebral force in all our search for this law of the relation of work to the time of life at which work is done; for the twofold reason — *first,* that it is the highest and best measure of cerebral force; and, *secondly,* because it is the only kind of work that gives earthly immortality. As we estimate the strength of an engine or an electrical machine by so many horse-power, so we judge the strength of the brain by the original work that it can do; but between the engine and the brain there is this difference — that, whereas, in the case of the former we are able to estimate what it can do, whether it does it or not; in the case of the brain, we are only able to judge inductively by what it has done; and therefore, must refer to the biography of genius for the data out of which we are to construct the law of the relation of age to work.

Men do not long remember, nor do they earnestly reverence those who have done only what everybody can do. We never look up, unless the object at which we look is higher than ourselves; the forces that control the rise and fall of reputation are as inevitable and as remorseless as heat, light, and gravity; if a great man looms up from afar, it is because he is taller than the average man; else, he would pass below the horizon as we receded from him; factitious fame is as impossible as factitious heat, light, or gravity; if there be force, there must have been, somewhere, and at some time, a source whence that force was evolved.

The strength of a bridge is the strength of its weakest point — what it will bear at that point, under pressure; the strength of a man is his strength at his strongest point — what he can do in any one direction, at his very best. However weak and even puerile, immature, and non-expert one may be in all other directions except one, he gains an immortality of fame if, in that one direction he develops a phenomenal power; weaknesses and wickednesses, serious immoralities and waywardnesses are soon forgotten by the world, which is, indeed, blinded to all these defects in the face of the strong illumination of genius. Judged by their defects, the non-expert side of their character, moral or intellectual, men like Burns, Shakespeare,

Socrates, Cicero, Cæsar, Napoleon, Beethoven, Mozart, Byron, Dickens, etc., are but as babes or lunatics, and far, very far below the standard of their fellows.

The above remarks are in part replies to the criticisms of the *London Spectator* and other journals on these researches. The suggestion of Mr. Proctor, the astronomer, as presented by him in his very beautiful and thoughtful essay on the growth and decay of mind — and which was called forth apparently by these researches when they were first published — is that the original work we do in youth keeps us from doing more original work in old age; since the latter years of life are required to develop and perfect that which youth has conceived. That there is a truth in this suggestion all biography demonstrates; but it also, at the same time demonstrates with equal clearness, that when the old are brought to positions of emergency or crises where there is a demand for creative power they are usually wanting, even though they have originated nothing before; even though they be men of intellectual force, they do not originate then, but must give way in battles, and campaigns, and inventions to the brazen and golden decade.

Men to whom these truths are repelling, put their eyes on those in high positions and in the decline of life, like Disraeli or Gladstone, forgetting that we have no proof that either of these men have ever originated a new thought during the past twenty-five years, and that in all their contributions to letters during that time there is nothing to survive, or worthy to survive, their authors. They point to Darwin the occupation of whose old age has been to gather into form the thoughts and labors of his manhood and youth, and whose only immortal book was the product of his silver and golden decade. They point to I cannot well number how many philosophers and scholars who in their old age acquired, or are said to have acquired, ages ago, when there was little else to do, a certain knowledge of certain languages — the poorest, and thinnest, and least to be respected test of cerebral force.

Method of Investigation.

The method by which I sought to learn the law of the relation of age to work was to study in detail the biographies of distinguished men and women of every age.

I have prepared a list embracing nearly all of the greatest names of history, whose lives are recorded in sufficient detail to be of value in such an investigation, and have noted the age at which they did the original work by which they have gained their fame. I have noted the ages at which phi-

losophers have founded and announced their systems; at which divines and religious teachers have
originated their creeds, and have been most effec-
tive as preachers; at which statesmen have un-
folded their highest acts of legislation, of diplomacy
and reform; at which men of science have made
their greatest discoveries and written their best
works; at which generals and admirals have gained
their greatest victories, and carried on their most
successful campaigns; at which lawyers have led
the bar, and physicians made their explorations in
medicine, and artists have painted their masterpieces; at which musicians have composed and
performed their most illustrious creations; at which
architects and engineers have planned and executed
the greatest monuments to their memories; at
which actors and orators have been at the zenith
of their power, and at which teachers and professors
have led eras in the service of education. From
these data, which, though not absolutely exhaustive,
are sufficiently so for a final and convincing settle-
ment of the questions involved, I have derived the
period, the decade, and year of maximum productiveness, and the various grades between this and
the period, the decade, and the years of the least
productiveness.

I have not overlooked the difficulties, the complications, and the various forms of error involved

in such an investigation, and have endeavored, so far as possible, to calculate and provide for them.

The lives of some great men are not sufficiently defined to differentiate the period, much less the decade or the year of their greatest productive force. Such lives are either rejected, or only the time of death and the time of first becoming famous are noted; very many authors have never told the world when they thought out or even wrote their masterpieces, and the season of publication is the only date that we can employ. These classes of facts, it will be seen, tell in favor of old rather than of young men, and will make the year of maximum production later rather than earlier, and cannot, therefore, be objected to by those who may doubt my conclusions. In an investigation so wide, and in the arrangement of facts gathered from so many sources, there is room for many numerical errors in regard to the dates of births, of deaths, and of special performances; but it is believed that these errors, though they may be numerous, are yet slight, and will, in the main, counterbalance each other.

In a number of instances the honors that have been accorded to distinguished men — as knighthoods, baronetcies, memberships of learned societies, or of legislative bodies — have been noted, and inasmuch as public honors, especially those which

depend on kings and queens, princes and politi-
eiaus, come late, and are in time very far behind
the true deserts, the dates represented by them will
be against young men rather than for them. For
those who have died young, and have worked in
original lines up to the year of their death, the date
of death has sometimes been regarded as sufficient.
Great difficulty has been found in proving the
dates of the labors of the great names of antiquity,
and, therefore, many of them are necessarily ex-
cluded from consideration, but in an extended comparison between ancient and modern brain-workers,
so far as history makes possible, there was but little
or no difference.

Number and Quality of Biographies consulted.

 ˙ After analyzing the lives of seven hundred and
fifty of the most eminent among the names of history, including eighteen hundred dates from which I
derived the law of the relation of age to work, as
here described, and as represented in the aecom-
panying engraving, it seemed that it might be well
to take an equal number of lives of less eminent
persons; the second, third, and fourth grades of
distinction — those who are known only in limited
lines, or in their lifetimes, whose lives are only
recorded in special biographies, or to whom very
slight space is given.

The names in this second or supplementary list would be mostly unknown, except to specialists, whereas the names of the first list are known to all persons of general intelligence. This second or supplementary list was analyzed in the same way as the primary list, and it was found that the law was true of these, as of those of greater distinction. The conclusion is just, scientific, and inevitable, that if we should go down through all the grades of cerebral force, we should find this law prevailing among medium and inferior natures, that the obscure, the dull, and the unaspiring accomplished the little they did in the direction of relatively original work—laid the foundation of small fortunes — in the brazen and golden decades.

To give the names in these lists is needless; since in them is included every famous person in any department of human activity where fame is achieved.

These researches were originally made as far back as 1870, and were first made public in lectures delivered by me before the Long Island Historical Society. The titles of the lectures were, "Young Men in History, and the Decline of Moral Principle in Old Age."

Subsequently, and more elaborately, the subject was discussed in its medico-legal relations, in a paper read before the New York Medico-Legal

Society. At a still later date I employed a mathematician, Mr. David R. Alden, to go over the subjcet anew, and independently; he confirmed in all respect my conclusions.

Finally, it should be remarked that the list has been prepared with absolute impartiality, and no name and no date has been included or omitted to prove any theory. The men who have done original or important work in advanced age, such as Dryden, Radetzky, Moltke, Thiers, De Foe, have all been noted, and are embraced in the average.

GENERAL RESULTS OF THE INVESTIGATION.

The golden decade is between 30 and 40.
The silver   "   "   40 "   50.
The brazen   "   "   20 "   30.
The iron   "   "   50 "   60.
The tin   "   60 "   70.
The wooden   "   "   70 "   80.

Seventy per cent. of the work of the world is done before 45, and eighty per cent. before 50. The golden decade represents about twenty-five per cent. more dates than the silver. The difference between the first and second half of the golden decade is but slight. The golden decade alone represents nearly one-third of the original work of the world. (See Drawing.)

The best period of fifteen years is been 30 and 45. The advantage of the brazen over the iron

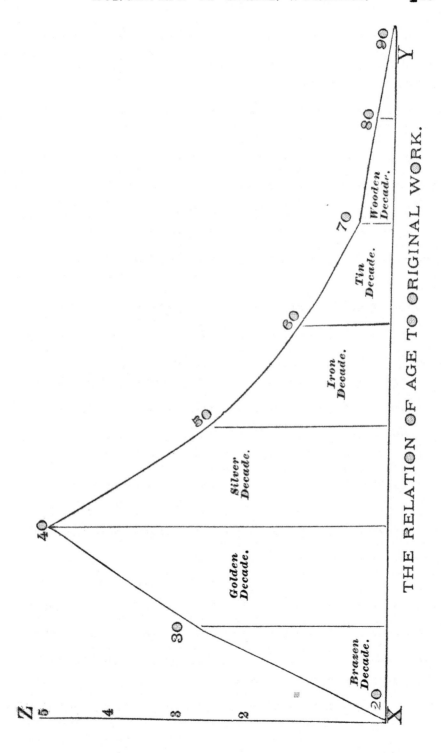

THE RELATION OF AGE TO ORIGINAL WORK.

decade — of 20 and 30 over 50 and 60 — is very striking, and will cause surprise. There is considerably more work done between 35 and 40 than between 40 and 45. The year of maximum productiveness is *thirty-nine.*

The average age of the great personages from whose lives the law is derived is not far from *sixty-six years.* A very large number of them lived to be over seventy. On the average the last *twenty* years in the lives of original geniuses are unproductive.

The broad fact, then, to which these statistics lead us is, that the brain follows the same line of growth, maturity, and decay as the rest of the body; that the nervous, muscular, and osseous systems rise, remain, and fall together, and that the received opinion that the mind, of which the brain is the organ, develops and matures later than the power of motion or of physical labor and endurance, is not sustained by the facts of history. The capacity for production is greatest in the latter part of the first half of the full life of man.

If in the same way, and in obedience to the same principles, we analyze the labors of those who are eminent for muscular force, the famous athletes, prize-fighters, the stroke-oarsman, and the pedestrians who win the belts — those who are leaders in trials of force on shipboard, in camp, in armies and in

all sports, we shall find that here, also, youth conquers. In comparing muscle-workers with brain-
workers in this respect, we must take those who,
all their lives, live by muscle, or mainly by it, just
as brain-workers live by brain. A comparison of
this kind cannot fail to make clear this fact — that
muscle-workers very early reach their maximum,
and that the capacity for work and for endurance
of work is either stationary or on the decline after
35 or 40. All the athletes with whom I have conversed on this subject, the guides and lumbermen
in the woods, — those who have always lived solely
by muscle — agree substantially to this; that their
staying power is better between the ages of 35
and 45, than either before or after. To get the
best soldiers, we must rob neither the cradle nor
the grave; but select from those decades when the
best brain-work of the world is done.

The result of my researches has been to demonstrate that mind, instead of being outside of law, is
itself obedient to law, and that we are at our best
mentally, just as we are at our best physically, in
youth rather than in old age.

Distinction between Original and Routine Work.
The quantity of work done by the aged is
greater than that done by the young; in quality
the advantage is on the side of youth. Original

work requires enthusiasm; routine work experience. In society both' forces are needed — one makes the world move, the other keeps it steady. Men are their best at the time when enthusiasm and expericuce are most evenly balanced. This period, on the average, is from 38 to 40. After this period the law is that experience increases but enthusiasm declines; like buckets in old-fashioned wells, as one goes up the other goes down. Unconsciously the people recognize this distinction between the work that demands enthusiasm and that which demands experience, for they prefer old doctors and lawyers, while in the clerical profession, where success depends on the ability to constantly originate and express thought, young men are the more popular, and old men, even of great ability, passed by. In the editorial profession original work is demanded, and most of the editorials of our daily press are written by young men. In the life of every old man there comes a point, sooner or later, when experience ceases to have any educating power; and when, in the language of Wall St, he becomes a bear, in the language of politics a Bourbon.

Apparent and Real Exceptions to the Average.

The most marked apparent exceptions to the law are found in the realm of imagination; some of the greatest poets, painters, and sculptors, such as Dryden, Richardson, Cowper, Young, De Foe, Titian, Christopher Wren, and Michael Angelo, have done a part of their very best work in advanced life. The imagery both of Bacon and of Burke seemed to increase in richness as they grew older.

In the realm of reason, philosophic thought, invention and discovery, the exceptions are very rare. Nearly all the great systems of theology, metaphysics, and philosophy are the result of work done between 20 and 50. The exceptions are both ways, and there are some who, like Napoleon, though they may die after 50, reach their prime long before 38.

The apparent exceptions to the law that original work is done chiefly in youth and early maturity are in the arts — painting, architecture, and acting; but physchologically analyzed, the artist in these realms, like the conversationalist, simply tests his work in his productions; the work itself having been done, it may be, years before; the painter speaks through his paintings, the sculptor through his statues, the orator and actor in their orations and readings as truly as the artist in conversation; and in their several arts they but pour out the gathered treasures of a life.

Michael Angelo and Sir Christopher Wren could wait for a quarter or even half a century before expressing their thoughts in St. Peter's or

St. Paul's; but the time of the conception of
those thoughts — long delayed in their artistic expression — was the time when their cerebral force
touched its highest mark.

In the old age of literary artists, as Carlyle,
Dickens, George Elliot, or Tennyson, the form may
be most excellent; but from the purely scientific side
the work though it may be good, is old; a repetition oftentimes, in a new form, of what they have
said many times before. Whence it is that none
of the great thinkers or philosophers in any age,
or in any domain of thought, have done good work
in old age; for thought once uttered becomes old;
whereas art, appealing only to the senses and emotions, may with its infinite permutations and com-
binations continue to give pleasure after copyings
without number. The philosophy of Bacon can
never be written but once; to re-write it, to present it a second time, in a different dress, would
indicate weakness, would seem almost grotesque;
but to statuary and painting we return again
and again; we allow the artist to re-portray his
thought, no matter how many times; we visit in
succession a hundred cathedrals, all very much
alike; and a delicious melody grows more pleasing
with repetition; whence it is that in poetry — the
queen of the arts — old age has wrought little, or
not at all, since the essence of poetry is creative

thought, and old age is unable to think; whence, also, in acting — the oldest of all the arts, the servant of all — the best experts are often at their best, or not far below their best, save for the acquisition of new characters, in the iron and wooden decades.

No art when once acquired is readily lost, even in advanced life; but on the contrary, most of the arts may be refined and developed in age. Most strikingly is this illustrated in painting and sculpture, in which realms, as we have seen, quite old men have succeeded. Similarly with the art of writing—the style, the dress, the use of words, the art of expressing thoughts, and not of *thinking.* Men who have done their best thinking before 40 have done their best writing after that period. This would appear to have been the experience of Dr. Johnson, Rousseau, and Voltaire. But the art of writing—the mere style of expressing thought— noble as it is—must and does in the estimation of men, rank far below the art of thinking: it is thought, and not the language of thought, that best tests the creative faculties. In every form of art — painting, sculpture, architecture—it is the conception that tells, although conception needs execution to make it available. It is wise, therefore, for young philosophers to do their thinking while young and in middle life, and to delay the permanent and final publication of their thoughts until they have also perfected the inferior but not unimportant art of clothing ideas in language.

The conversation of old men of ability, before they have passed into the stage of imbecility, is usually richer and more instructive than the conversation of the young; for in conversation we simply distribute the treasures of memory, as a store hoarded during long years of thought and experience. He who thinks as he converses is a poor companion, as he who must earn his money before he spends any is a poor man. When an aged millionnaire makes a liberal donation it costs him nothing; he but gives out of abundance that has resulted by natural accumulation from the labors of his youth and middle life. When an old man utters great thoughts, it is not age, but youth that speaks through the lips of age; his ideas which, in their inception and birth, drew heavily on the productive powers of the brain, are refined, revolved, and disseminated almost without effort.

Childhood and Old Age but Imitators.

The creative period of life. it will be observed, is limited to fifteen years, between 25 and 40. An amount of work not inconsiderable is done before 25 and a vast amount is done after 40; but at neither period is it usually of the *original* or *creative* sort that best measures the mental forces. The work done before 20 and after 40 is usually work of imitation or routine. In early youth we follow others; in old age we follow ourselves. Boys in school and college copy, commit, repeat, and but rarely think. Collegians who, in this country, graduate at the age of twenty-two or three, rarely give themselves to fresh research, and almost never make any invention or discovery; hence the barrenness of even the best prize essays and orations. Commencement orations are dull because the authors tell us nothing new; even their language is copied with slight variations from the authors whom they have most read and studied. Only the most precocious minds create thoughts before 20; from 25 to 30 the majority of thinkers begin to develop new ideas; from 40 and upwards they develop perfect and repeat the conceptions of the period between 25 and 40; they copy themselves as in early youth they copied others.

Application of the Law to Animals and Plants.

The same law applies to animals. Horses live to be about 25, and are at their best from 8 to 14; this corresponds to the golden decade of man. Dogs live nine or ten years, and are fittest for the hunt between 2 and 6. Plants also appear to be subject to the same law. Fruit-bearing trees, so far as I can learn, are most prolific at a time of their average life corresponding pretty nearly to the golden and silver decade of man. Children born of parents one or both of whom are between 25 and 40, are, on the average, stronger and smarter than those born of parents one or both of whom are very much younger or older than this. The same fact applies to the breeding of horses, dogs, and probably of other animals. It should be noted also, that in women, the procreative function ceases between 40 and 50 just the time when the physical and mental powers begin to decline, as though nature had foreseen this law and provided that the world should not be peopled by those whose powers had fallen from their maximum; we are most productive when we are most reproductive.

The law of the relation of age to work is very well illustrated by the egg-laying power of the hen. It has been estimated that in an average lifetime of nine years a hen will lay from 500 to 700 eggs, thus distributed: first year, 16 to 20; second year, 100 to 120; third year, 120 to 135 (the golden period); fourth year, 100 to 113; fifth year, 60 to 80; sixth year, 50 to 60; seventh year, 35 to 40; eighth year, 15 to 20; ninth year, 1 to 10.

Man is but a higher animal, subject to the same laws, cabined by the same limitations, and illustrative of the same processes of growth and decay as the lowliest organisms in nature. The hen is a type of humanity.

When Women are most Attractive.

In an interesting paper entitled "When Women Grow Old," Mrs. Blake has brought facts to show that the fascinating power of the sex is oftentimes retained much longer than is generally assumed.

She tells us of Aspasia, who, between the ages of 30 and 50 was the strongest intellectual force in Athens; of Cleopatra, whose golden decade for power and beauty was between 30 and 40; of Livia, who was not far from 30 when she gained the heart of Octavius; of Anne of Austria, who at 38 was thought to be the most beautiful queen in Europe; of Catherine II. of Russia, who, even at the silver decade was both beautiful and imposing; of Mademoiselle Mars, the actress, whose beauty increased with years, and culminated between 30 and 45; of Madame Récamier, who, between 25 and 40, and even later, was the reigning beauty in Europe; of Ninon de l'Enclos, whose own son — brought up without knowledge of his parentage — fell passionately in love with her when she was at the age of 37, and who even on her sixtieth birthday received an adorer young enough to be her grandson.

These facts, the representatives of many others, establish that the golden decade of fascination is the same as the golden decade of thought; that woman is most attractive to, and most influential over man at that period when both man and woman are nearest the maximum of their cerebral force. The voice of our great prima donnas is at its very best between 27 and 35; but still some retains, in a degree, its strength and sweetness even in the silver decade. The voice is an index of the body in all its functions, but the decay of other functions is not so readily noted.

A gentleman, being asked his age, replied as follows: "I am 27; not that it matters much, for it has always seemed to me that a man's age was not of the least consequence between 25 and 40. I should not like to be less than 20, nor more than 40: between these periods, I am indifferent to the progress of time." The name of the philosopher who made the above remark I do not know; but whoever he may be, he forestalled the law of the relation of age to work, as derived from these elaborately detailed researches.

Mr. J. Appleton Morgan, in a private letter, calls my attention to the following:

"In a 'Code of Gentes Laws, or Ordinations of the Pundits,' from a Persian translation made from the original in the Sanscrit language (London, 1777), Pootee Chapter III., Section 8, of Proper and Improper Evidence (p. 111), it is enacted that 'a devotee who becomes very infirm shall not be a witness.'"

Illustrative Cases.

Under this head I append a few representative biographical facts, which are taken impartially at random without reference to specialties, or classification or to their bearing on the theory here advanced, from the collection of nearly two thousand names that I have analyzed. They are given merely to show the method of investigation.

As a lad of 16, Lord Bacon began to think independently on great matters; at 44, published his great work on "The Advancement of Learning; at 36, published twelve of his Essays; and at 60 collected the thoughts of his life in his "Organum." His old age was devoted to scientific investigation.

At the early age of 29, Descartes began to map out his system of philosophy, and at 41 began its publication, and at 54 he died.

Schelling, as a boy, studied philosophy, and at 24 was a brilliant and independent lecturer, and at 27 had published many important works; at 28 was professor of philosophy and arts, and wrote his best works before 50.

Dryden, one of the exceptions to the average, did his best work when comparatively old; his "Absalom" was written at 50, and his "Alexander's Feast" when he was nearly 70.

Dean Swift wrote his "Tale of a Tub" at 35, and his "Gulliver's Travels" at 59.

Ruskin wrote the first part of the principal work of his life, " Modern Painters," at 28, though it was not completed until seventeen years afterward, when he was 45. " Seven Lamps of Architecture " appeared at 30, and " Stones of Venice " at 33. None of his latter works have taken as deep a hold of the popular heart, and are so sure of being remembered by posterity as those which were composed before he was 35.

Thackeray, after an unsuccessful youth, wrote " Vanity Fair " at 36 and 37, and " Esmond," which he regarded as his best work, at 41. But though he matured so late, he was but 51 when he sadly remarked to a friend: " Dickens and myself have worked out our vein, and what is more, the people have found it out." The judgment of the literary world would now accord with that of Thackeray.

Charles Dickens wrote " Pickwick " at 25, " Oliver Twist " and " Nicholas Nickleby " before 27, " Christmas Chimes " at 31, " David Copperfield " at 38, and " Dombey and Son " at 35. Thus we see that nearly all his greatest works were written before he was 40 ; and it is amazing how little all the writings of the last twenty years of his life took hold of the popular heart, in comparison with " Pickwick " and " David Copperfield," and how little effect the most enormous advertising and the cumulative power of a great reputation really have to give a permanent popularity to writings that do not deserve it. If Dickens had died at 40 his claim to immortality would have been as great as now, and the world of letters would have been little, if any, the loser. The excessive methodical activity of his mature and advanced life could turn off works with fair rapidity; but all his vast experience and all his earnest striving failed utterly to reach the standard of his reckless boyhood. His later works were more perfect, perhaps, judged by some canons, but the genius of " Pickwick " was not in them.

Emerson published the first series of his essays at 38, and the second at 41; and that these essays had been in his thoughts for years is evident from his statement that from his boyhood he had desired to write an essay on " Compensation." " Representative Men " appeared at 46; " English Notes " at 53; " Conduct of Life " at 56, and " Society and Solitude " at 67. It is, I believe, the view of many of his critics that the essence of his thought is embraced in his earlier essays, which were written between 25 and 40, and that none of his subsequent writings are so sure of immortality as these.

I find no record of any very important invention conceived and developed after the age of 60. Edison with his three hundred patents, is not the only young inventor. All inventors are young.

Colt was à boy of 21 when he invented the famous weapon that bears his name; and Goodyear began his experiments in rubber while a young man of 24, and made his first success at 38, and at 43 had brought his discovery to approximate perfection.

Eli Whitney invented the "cotton gin" at 27, and between 33 and 41 discovered and perfected his method of making fire-arms.

Fulton at 28 had begun to study steam navigation, and was 42 when he made his first success on the Hudson.

Dreyse, the inventor of the needle-gun at 42, had, after various experimenting, at 49 constructed his first breach-loader.

The name of Bichat is one of the greatest in science, and he died at 32.

Graefe, the greatest of ophthalmologists, and one of the greatest men of history, was famous at 25; at 31 had a world-wide fame, and died at 42.

Pinel at 35 had made an important investigation in science: at 40 took charge of an insane asylum and introduced his humane method; at 46 he gained a prize for an essay on the subject, and at 47 was appointed to the Bicetre, where he introduced a great reform in the treatment of the insane.

Turner at 15 exhibited to the Royal Academy, at 27 was an academician — painted his best works, "the Middle Period," in the years between 39 and 45. The works of the last twenty years of his life are inferior.

Handel at 19 was director of the opera at Hamburg; at 20 composed his first opera; at 35 was appointed manager of the Royal Theatre at London; at 25 composed "Messiah," and at 66 "Jephtha," and in old age and blindness his intellect was clear and his power of performance remarkable.

Luther early displayed eloquence, and at 20 began to study Aristotle; at 29 was doctor of divinity, and when he would refuse it, it was said to him that "he must suffer himself to be dignified, for that God intended to bring about great things in the church by his name;" at 34 he opposed the "Indulgencies," and set up his ninety-five propositions; at 37 he publicly burned the Pope's bull; at 47 he had completed his great task.

Von Moltke between 66 and 70 directed the operation of the great war of Prussia against Austria and France But that war was but a conclusion and consummation of military study and organization that had been going on for a quarter of a century.

Nelson at 39 was distinguished at the battle of St. Vincent, and was knighted and made rear admiral. At the age of 40 he had been actually and personally engaged with the enemy one hundred and twenty times and had gained the battle of the Nile, and was 47 at Trafalgar, where he was killed in action.

It is a fact of very great interest that the experiments and speculations that have led to the pretty generally adopted theory of the correlation of forces were made by young men. Thus:

Rumford at 31 was a very successful administrator in Bavaria; at 45 published the experiments on what he had been engaged, on heat, etc. Grove at 31 set forth his views on the correlation of forces, and at 41 was queen's counsel.

Harvey at 40 made the discovery of the circulation of blood, and made it public at 49.

Jenner at 21 began his investigation into the difference between cow-pox and small-pox. His attention was called to the subject by the remark of a country girl, who said in his hearing that she could not have the small-pox, because she had had the cow-pox. At 47 he had perfected his great discovery.

If Carlyle had died at 45, the loss to literature would have been but slight; all that is best in his writings, all that has given him his renown, all for which he is to be remembered, was originated and mostly published before that date. During the last forty years of his life he went, mostly, on the momentum acquired in the first forty years;

and it is one of the proofs of his insight that he himself suspected, if he did not quite know this fact, and when urged to write, replied, "I have nothing more to say to the world, beyond what I have already said." The discoursings of this Titanian rhapsodist were perhaps never so rich, impressive, and amazing as in his old age; but, like the conversations of all old people, they were historical and biographical; new, it may be, to the listener, but to the speaker very old; accumulated treasures of a lifetime brought out for exhibition and refreshment, like old and rare wines from well-stocked cellars; even fifteen years before his death a keen reporter describes his conversation — to which he listened for hours, as mostly a recital of "Sartor Resartus," and Characteristics of Past, Present, and latter day pamphlets.

Not Mr. Peabody at the age of 70, going up and down the land distributing his millions; but Mr. Peabody young, unknown, laying the foundation for those millions, represents the highest and strongest capacity of the man; the time when they gained materials for conversation, when they prospected, mined for, and analyzed their jewels which now, when well set and polished, they display to every visitor, was the time when they were at their maximum, for old men, like nations, can show their treasures of art long after they have begun to die; this, indeed, is one of the sweetest and most refreshing compensations for age; but we err, from a scientific point of view, if we confound exhibiting with originating.

A contemporary leader in science (Huxley) has asserted that it would be well if all men of science could be strangled at the age of 60, since after that age their disposition — with possible exceptions here and there — is to become re-actionary and obstructionists; but such a course would be as unwise as it would be cruel, since it would deprive us of the accumulations of thought which are only possible in old age. Killing off our millionnaires at that age would not be more unscientific and disastrous; the thought, like the wealth of the world, is organized in youth, but multiplied, concentrated, diffused, and made practical in old age.

The lives of some individuals are typical illustrations of the law. I may mention as especially worthy of study in this regard the lives of Goethe, Humboldt, Wordsworth, Carlyle, Newton, and Liebig. A minute study of the intellectual history of these six men alone will illustrate the law of the relation of age to work, though it will not demonstrate it.

Death is a process more than an event; even while we live we die; living itself is but a mode of dying. We die, not in wholes, but in fractions, branch after branch falling away, until the tree is utterly bare. Those who long survive, are called upon to attend the funerals of their own forces, as they slowly perish, one by one, We are to bury Carlyle to-morrow, but he had been dying for a quarter of a century.

Suggestions of Previous Thinkers.

Although I have been the first to *make the discovery of the Law of the Relation of Age to Work* and organize this subject in science as well as to point out its various practical applications, yet the general fact has been more or less anticipated by a number of illustrious thinkers.

Thus Goethe, whose rich and powerful brain saw farther into almost every subject than any of his contemporaries — soaring high on the wings of science and of song — in his conversations over and over again sings the praises of youth. Says he to Eckermann: "Yes, yes, my good friend, we must be young to do great things." And in another place, speaking of government, he said with emphasis: "If I were a premier I would never place in the highest offices people who have risen gradually by mere birth and seniority, and who, in their old age, move on leisurely in their accustomed tracks; for in this way but little talent is brought to light. I would have young men."

Luther is reported to have said that: "If a man

is not handsome at 20, strong at 30, learned at 40 and rich at 50, he will never be handsome, strong, learned or rich in this world." In the light of these statistics this statement becomes a prophecy with a most remarkable fulfilment. Says Sterne "at sixty years of age the tenement gets fast out of repair, and the lodger, with anxiety, thinks of a discharge." Mr. Emerson, even in his excellent plea for old age, makes this admission: "We do not count our years until there is nothing else to count;" and of literary inactivity in old age he says, with high wisdom: "We postpone our literary work until we have more experience and skill to write, and we one day discover that our literary talent was a youthful effervescence which we have now lost."

Schiller has expressed the same idea as his friend Goethe in the maxim: "Denn der Lebende hat Recht"—"For he who lives is in the right." The French have a motto that must have been originated by some one who thought of these things, "Qui n'a point de sens a trente ans, n'en aura jamais," "He who has no sense at thirty years of age will never have any," and the words of Louis XIV., written with his own hand in the palace at Versailles: "En il faut de la jeunesse"—"In everything youth is indispensible," are probably the best he ever uttered. Dr. Oliver Wendell Holmes, used this language: "New ideas build their nests in young brains; revolutions are not made by men in spectacles, as I have heard it remarked; and the whisperings of new truths are not caught by those who begin to feel the need of an ear trumpet."

The late General Halleck, in his book on "Military Science and Art," has a very interesting chapter on the age of the generals of the world; in that he shows, by a powerful and convincing array of statistics, that, with a few exceptions, nearly all the successful campaigns of history have been fought by young men. The history of the campaigns of Napoleon illustrates this point most astonishingly; his early successes were gained over old and worn-out generals, on whom great hopes had been centered; but he was finally overthrown by the young and middle-aged; at Waterloo he and Wellington were about the same age.

In our recent civil war, the North began with old generals, and failed ignominiously at nearly every point, the average age of the generals and admirals (including Farragut) who put the war through was between 35 and 39.

One of the most striking passages on this subject is the following from Montaigne's Essay on Age:

For my part, I believe our souls are adult at 20 as much as they are ever likely to be, and as capable then as ever. A soul that has not by that

time given evident earnest of its force and virtue
will never after come to proof. Natural parts and
excellences produce what they have fine and vigorous within that term or never:

> ' Si l'espine non picque quand nai,
> A peur que picque jamais,'

as they say in Dauphiny. Of all the great human
actions I ever heard or read of, of what sort soever,
I have observed, both in former ages and our own,
more were performed before 30 than after, and oftentimes in the lives of the same men. May I not
confidently instance in those of Hannibal and his
great competitor, Scipo? The better half of their
lives they lived upon the glory they had acquired
in their youth; great men after, 'tis true, in comparison of others, but by no means in comparison of
themselves. As to myself, I am certain that since
that age both my understanding and my constitution
have rather decayed than improved, retired rather
than advanced.* 'Tis possible that with those who
make the best use of their knowledge and experience may grow up and increase with their years;
but the vivacity, quickness, steadiness, and other
qualities, more our own, of much greater importance and much more essential, languish and decay.

---

* This confession is all the more remarkable from the fact
that the immortal essays of Montaigne were not written down
until he had passed the golden decade.

'Ubi jam validis quassatum est viribus aeVi
Corpus, et obtusis ceciderunt viribus artus,
Claudicat ingenium, deli rat linguaque mensque.

When once the body's shaken by time's rage,
The blood and Vigor ebbing into age,
No more the mind its former strength displays,
But eVery strength and faculty decays.'"

The same author in his own old age, thus writes:
"Two of my acquaintances, great men in this faculty, have in my opinion lost half in refusing to
publish at forty years old that they might stay till
threescore " . . . "Maturity has its defects as well as
greenness, and worse;" . . . "our wits grow costive
and thick in growing old."

Unpopularity of these Truths.

These truths, unlike new truths in general, are
acceptable to the old, but most unacceptable to the
young and middle-aged. A former instructor of
mine—a broad-minded and liberally cultured man, a
well known professor—once remarked to me: " You
can hardly expect any one about 38 or 40 to accept
your theory." The reason for this is that not one
of ten thousand ambitious men who have reached
their fortieth year have at all fulfilled their ideal;
those who have failed hope to succeed, and those
who have somewhat succeeded aspire to nobler success in the future. The harvest is passing, the summer over, and they are neither as rich or famous

as they hoped to become. It is not in ambitious human nature to be content with what we have been enabled to achieve up to the age of forty. Twice I have been told by men of ability, and culture, and achievement: "If your theory is true I ought to commit suicide." My reply in both cases was in substance this: The best of your original, pioneering, radical work is in all probability already accomplished. The chances are tens of thousands to one that you will originate less in the future than you have in the past; for, just as we know by statistics that a man at 40 has a certain average expectation of life, so do we know that he has a certain average expectation of original work. There is a chance in many, many thousands that he will live to be a hundred years old; there is about the same chance that he will make some phenomenal discovery or invention, or conceive and execute some original production in art. Fame and wealth may come to him far exceeding your wildest dreams; but they will be the result and the reward of the work already done. Happiness may augment with years, because of better external conditions; and yet the highest happiness is obtained through work itself more than through the reward of work; earth has no joy like that which comes from the birth of a new thought in a young brain.

It is now ten years since this reply was made

to the criticisms of these young men, and neither of them have accomplished as much since that time as they had accomplished before.

Moral Decline and Happiness in Old Age.

The time of life at which men are happiest is a question that is germain to the one here discussed. Says Chateaubriand, "The wind that blows on a hoary head never comes from a happy shore."

The pleasure of doing original work to him who is organized for ideas is surely of a higher order than the pleasure of recognition and reward. Of the three motives to activity—wealth, fame, and satisfaction—the most potent to the strongest natures, in the highest realms, is surely satisfaction; he who declared that he would like to be forever 35, and he who on being asked his age replied that it was of little account provided that it was anywhere between 25 and 40, but expressed the fact which these researches have formulated. Wealth is an element in happiness, the potency of which is both under and over rated, and almost all the wealth of the world is in the hands of age since very few either by acquisition or by inheritance obtain large means, before the passing away of the golden and silver decade; the world's work is done by youth and poverty. Capacity for original work age does not have, but in compensation it has almost everything else.

The querulousness of age, the irritability, the avarice are the resultants partly of habit and partly of organic and functional changes in the brain.

Increasing avarice is at once the tragedy and the comedy of age; as we near the end of our voyage we become more chary of our provisions, as though the ocean and not the harbor were before us. Avarice is indeed the offspring not of poverty or uncertainty, but of opulence and security; those are chiefly avaricious who are most above the need of being so; our intellectual ruin very often dates from the hour when we begin to save money.

Moral courage is rare in old age; sensitiveness to criticism, fear of opposition, take the place, in the iron and wooden decades, of delight in criticism and love of opposition of the brazen and golden decades; hostility is best borne by those whose reputation is yet to be made; fame like wealth makes us cautious, conservative, cowardly, since it implies the possibility of loss.

Intellectual decline sometimes favors the development of a kind of negative morality, for positive vice requires intellectual force as much as positive virtue, and when the intellect declines the man is obliged to be virtuous. Physical health is also needed for indulgence in many of the vices; in Bulwer's language, " it requires a strong constitution to be dissipated." Probably on the whole men are happiest neither in youth nor extreme age, but in the silver and golden decades, about equally distant from the morning and evening shadows.

As the moral and reasoning faculties are the highest, most complex, and most delicate developments of human nature, they are the first to show signs of cerebral disease; when they begin to decay in advanced life we are generally safe in predicting that, if neglected, other faculties will, sooner or later, be impaired. When conscience is gone the constitution may soon follow.

The decline of the moral faculties in old age may be illustrated by studying the lives of the following historic characters: Demosthenes, Cicero, Sylla, Charles V., Louis XIV., Frederic of Prussia Napoleon (prematurely old), Voltaire, Jeffries, Dr. Johnson, Cromwell, Burke, Sheridan, Pope, Newton, Ruskin, Carlyle, Dean Swift, Chateaubriand, Rousseau, Milton, Lord Bacon, Earl Russell, Marlborough and Daniel Webster. In some of these cases the decline was purely physiological, in others pathological; in the majority it was a combination of both.

Very few decline in all the moral faculties. One becomes peevish, another avaricious, another misanthropic, another mean and tyrannical, another exacting and ugly, another sensual, another cold and cruelly conservative, another excessively vain and ambitious, others simply lose their moral enthusiasm and their capacity for resisting disappointment and temptation. Prof. Tyndall, in his address on the scientific use of the imagination, admits these claims of the unproductiveness of age, but explains it by loss of enthusiasm more than of insight.

There are not a few who are exceptions to the law of the decline of the intellectual and moral nature, just as there are exceptions to the universally accepted law of the decline of the physical nature. There are men who in extreme age preserve their teeth sound, their hair unchanged, their complexion fresh, their appetite sharp and digestion strong and sure, and their repose sweet and refreshing, and who can walk and work to a degree that makes their children and grandchildren feel very humble; but these observed exceptions in no way invalidate the general law, which no one will dispute, that the physical powers reach their maximum between 30 and 40, and that the average man at 70 is less muscular and less capable of endurance than the average man at 40. Just so there are men who, for several decades, preserve their reason clear, their imagination rich and strong, their memory faithful, their conscience sensitive, their moral courage heroic, and their temper sweet and pure. There are those who sail into the harbor of old age freighted with well preserved treasures of virtue gathered during a voyage crowded with adventure, and difficulty, and peril.

Compensations of Age.

Longfellow, writing a class poem in his own old age, closes with these lines :

> " For age hath opportunity no less
>   Than youth itself, though in another dress ;
>   And as the evening twilight fades away,
>   The sky is filled with stars invisible by day."

Subjecting these lines to psychological analysis it can be counted among the compensations of age that it obtains the reward denied it in maturity and youth; that the appreciation of the work done in the silver, golden, and brazen decades is substituted for the pleasure of the work itself.

The same author, after enumerating the familiar and doubtful catalogue of those who in life's decline have yet acquired new knowledge, presents this consolation :

> " These are indeed exceptions, but they show
>   How far the gulf-stream of our youth may flow
>   Into the Arctic region of our lives,
>   'Till little else than life itself surVives."

To age is granted in increasing richness the treasures of memory and the delights of recognition which most usually come from those who, at the time of the deeds whose value they recognize, were infants or unborn; only those who bury their contemporaries, can obtain, during their own lifetime, the supremacy of fame. Mrs. Carlyle, when congratulated on the honors given to her husband on the delivery of his Edinburgh address, replied with a certain disdain, as though he should have been honored before; but only by a reversal of the laws of the evolution of fame shall the manifestation of genius and the recognition of genius be simultaneous.

The high praise of contemporaries is almost insulting, since it implies that he whom they honor is but little better than themselves. Permanent fame, even in this rapid age, is a plant of slow growth—first the blade; then, after a time, the ear; then, after many, many years, the full corn in the ear; we have most reputation when we least deserve it. Single acts, however brilliant and important, rarely insure immortality; the heights of glory are not scaled at a bound, but only by long climbing and many wearisome and painful steps.

But the highest compensation of age in brain-workers, before the coming of the last childhood, is, as indicated above, that work grows easier and more automatic; while the higher power of creating is disappearing, the lower, but for many the more needful, and with contemporaries more quickly appreciated, power of imitation, repetition, and routine, is increasing; we can work without working, and enjoy without striving for the means of enjoyment.

Comparative Longevity of the Professions.

Inasmuch as professional men do not usually change their callings, but die in the special profession in which they have lived, the vital statistics, at least of lawyers, physicians, and clergymen, become of value in determining their comparative longevity. I found in my researches, made several years ago, that lawyers and physicians lived to be about 57 or 58. The difference in the longevity of lawyers and physicians is but trifling. My observations in this respect have since been variously confirmed by other statisticians.* (See Drawing p. 200).

Longevity of the Precocious.

That precocity predicts short life, and is therefore a symptom greatly to be feared by parents, has, I believe, never been questioned. In poetry and in science the idea has been variously incorporated that early brilliancy is a sure indication of

---

* An investigation made more recently by a Berlin physician into the facts and data relating to human longevity shows the average age of clergymen to be 65 ; of merchants, 62 ; clerks and farmers, 61 ; military men, 59 ; lawyers, 58 ; artists, 57 ; and medical men, 56. Statistics are given showing that medical men in England stand high in the scale of longevity. Thus, the united ages of twenty-eight physicians who died there last year, amount to 2,354 years, giving an average of more the 84 years to each. The youngest of the number was 80 ; the oldest, 93 ; two others were 92 and 89, respectively ; three were 87, and four were 8C each ; and there were also more than fifty who averaged from 74 to 75 years.

a feeble constitution and an early death. This view is apparently sustained by analogy, and by facts of observation; plants that are soon to bloom are soon to fade; those which grow slowly live long and decline slowly. Observing these facts we naturally adhere to the opinion that the same principle should hold as regards men, but in making the analogy we forget that it loses its pertinency unless the objects implicated start in life with the same potential force and are surrounded by the same external conditions. It is probable that, of two individuals with precisely similar organizations and under similar circumstances, the one that develops earlier will be the first to die; but we are not born equally endowed and similarly environed. Not only are men unlike in organization, but they are very widely unlike; between the brain of Shakespeare and the brain of an idiot is a measureless gulf, and we may believe that difference of degrees may be found between the greatest and simply great men; we may believe that some are born with far more potential nervous force than others; millionnaires in intellect as well as in money, who can afford to expend enormous means without becoming impoverished. An outlay of one hundred dollars may ruin the mechanic, working for his daily wages, while the royal merchant may spend a thousand, and barely know it. There are those who can begin their life-work earlier, toil harder and longer, than the multitude, and yet attain a very great age.

The average age of 500 illustrious men, including those who did not exhibit any special precocity, was about 64.20. Of these 500 individuals, among whom there were 25 women, 150 were decidedly precocious, and their average age was 66.50, or more than two years higher than that of the list of 500, that included the precocious and non-precocious. So far as I could ascertain, the instances of extraordinary longevity were as great among the precocious as among those who were not.* My investigations in this department fully confirm the remark of Wieland, that "an almost irresistible impulse to the art in which they are destined to excel manifests itself in future *virtuosi* — in poets, painters, etc., from their earliest youth." Not only in poetry and painting, but also in philosophy, in science, and in invention — indeed, in every great department in which human nature has displayed itself, it is true, as Milton beautifully remarks, "Childhood shows the man, as morning shows the

---

* A contributor to the *Galaxy* for August (G. W. Winterburn) thus discourses concerning musical prodigies. Investigating the records of the past two centuries, he finds 213 recorded cases of acknowledged prodigies. None of them died before their fifteenth year, some attained the age of 103 — and the average duration of life was 58 — showing that, with all their abnormal precocity, they exceed the ordinary longevity by about six per cent.

day." Madden, in his "Infirmities of Genius," says, that "Johnson is indeed of the opinion that the early years of distinguished men, when minutely ·traced, furnish evidence of the same vigor or originality of mind by which they are celebrated in after-life.

The more closely I study biography, the more strongly I become convinced that the number of really illustrious geniuses who did not give early manifestations of their genius, is very limited. I do not forget that some of the currently reported exceptions are very striking; thus we are told that Chalmers at school was stupid and mischievous; that Adam Clark, as a boy, could do nothing but roll huge stones about; that of Sir Walter Scott, his teacher, Professor Dalzell, frankly said : " Dunce he was and dunce he would remain ; " that Burns, though a good athlete, showed in his boyhood no unusual gifts; that Goldsmith was "a plant that flowered late ;" that John Howard, and Napoleon, and Wellington, were, to say the least, but little remarkable at school; and that the father of Isaac Barrow is reported to have said that "if it pleased God to take away any of his sons, he prayed that it might be his son Isaac, as being the least promising of them all."

These exceptions, apparent and real, may be explained in two ways :—

First. The stupidity attributed to men of genius may be really the stupidity of their parents, guardians, and biographers.

Men are precocious, if they are precocious at all, in the line of their genius. It is observed, as Wieland has stated, that almost all artists and musicians are recorded as precocious, the exceptions being very rare. Music and drawing appeal to the senses, attract attention, and are therefore appreciated, or at least observed by the most stupid parents, and noted even in the most superficial biographies. Philosophic and scientific thought, on the contrary, does not at once, perhaps may never, reveal itself to the senses—it is locked up in the cerebral cells ; in the brain of that dull, pale youth, who is kicked for his stupidity and laughed at for his absent-mindedness, grand thoughts may be silently growing ; the plant which to-day looks stunted and dwarfed may hereafter quicken into life, rise into strength and beauty—to give fruit and shade to many generations. Scott, for example, though he stood low in his class at school, yet very early exhibited genius as an inventor and narrator of " tales of knight-errantry, and battle, and enchantments ; " and Newton, according to his own account, was very inattentive to his studies and low in his class, but a great adept at kite-flying, with paper lanterns attached to them, to terrify the country people, of a dark night, with the appearance of comets; and when sent to market with the produce of his mother's farm, was apt to neglect his business, and to ruminate at an inn, over the laws of Kepler.

It is fair to infer that the slowness attributed to many other distinguished geniuses may be similarly explained. This belief is strengthened by the consideration that many, perhaps the majority, of the greatest thinkers of the world seemed dull, inane, and stupid to their neighbors, not only in childhood but through their whole lives. The brains as well as the muscles of men differ in the times of their growth; of a dozen individuals of the same endowments and external conditions, some will ripen early, others late. This is observed in colleges, where some who take the lead in everything, make no farther progress in after life; they "strike twelve the first time;" others who, between 15 and 25 are dullards, between 25 and 40 develop genius.

It is probable, however, that nearly all cases of apparent stupidity in young geniuses are to be explained by the want of circumstances favorable to the display of their peculiar powers, or to a lack of appreciation or discernment on the part of their friends. It is very difficult to find any college graduate of remarkable ability who did not, during his collegiate course, in some way manifest the germs of that ability, but there are many who fail in the proscribed routine of studies in the race for literary honors, who yet, in some department or other, do attain distinction. As compared with the world, the most liberal curriculum is narrow; to one avenue of distinction that college opens, the world opens ten. In order to learn the material of which a college class is made, it is necessary not only to look at the marks on the tutor's book and scan the prize lists of the societies, but also to go out on the ball-ground and down the river—we must mingle in the evening carousal and study the social life of the students in their rooms, or their walks, in vacation, and at home.

Whether we regard those general considerations or not, the statistical fact remains, that in spite of the incompleteness of biographies and the ignorance of parents and teachers, *a very considerable proportion of the greatest geniuses of the world are known to have been as remarkable in their precocity as in their genius; and in spite of this precocity were exceedingly long-lived.*

Normal vs. *Morbid Precocity.*

Great precocity, like great genius, is rare. Although I have known but few children whom fond parents did not at some time believe to be more or less superior to the average, yet I do not remember that I ever saw a very precocious child. There is in some children a petty and morbid smartness that is sometimes mistaken for precocity, but which in truth does not deserve that distinction. The manifestation of genius in childhood is as normal and as healthful as its manifestation in maturity; but in childhood, as in extreme old age, the effects of overtaxing the powers are more severely felt than in middle life. Petty smartness is oftentimes a morbid symptom; it comes from a diseased brain, or from a brain in which a grave predisposition to disease exists; such children may die young, whether they do or do not early exhibit unusual quickness.

The morbidly precocious soon wear themselves out, early find their level, and in after life are stupid or ordinary; the normally, physiologically precocious go on from strength to strength, and do not reach their maximum until between 30 and 40; and live longer and are capable of working harder than those of average gifts. There have been noted and oft-quoted instances where the precocious geniuses have died in early manhood, or just at reaching the maximum of their strength, between 30 and 40. The names of Pascal, Mozart, Keats, will be at once recalled; but we forget the infinite number who have died at the same age or earlier, and of the same diseases; but who neither in childhood nor in manhood exhibited any superior genius. The only method of arriving at the truth on the question is the one here adopted; that is, to obtain the average longevity of a large number who were known to have been greatly precocious, and compare it with the average longevity of other able men in the same departments.

M. D. Delaunay has addressed to the French Société de Biologie a communication in which he takes the ground that precocity indicates biological inferiority. To prove this he states that the lower species develop more rapidly than those of a higher order; man is the slowest of all in developing and reaching maturity, and the lower orders are more precocious than the higher. As proof of this he speaks of the children of the Esquimaux, negroes, Cochin Chinese, Japanese, Arabs, etc.

Advance in civilization reduces precociousness, as is proved by the lowering of the standard for recruits in France, which has been made necessary twice during the present century. He also states that women are more precocious than men; and that from eight to twelve years of age, girls gain one pound a year over boys. Inferior tissues develop faster than higher ones — the brain being the last and slowest of all in reaching maturity. He also says that precocity of organs is in inverse ratio to the extent of their evolution.

There is truth in all this reasoning, and it is in harmony with the instincts of mankind; but it is not inconsistent with the absolutely demonstrated fact that the very precocious may be very long lived. The highest genius, as here and elsewhere seen, never repeats itself; very great men never have very great children; and in biological analysis, geniuses who are very precocious may be looked upon as the last of their race or of their branch—from them degeneracy is developed; and this precocity, despite their genius, may be regarded as the forerunner of that degeneracy.

Those who have not given special thought to this theme will be surprised to learn how early and how strikingly the genius of some of the greatest and longest lived heroes was displayed. Leibnitz, at 12 understood Latin authors well, and wrote a remarkable production; Gassendi, "the little doctor," preached at 4; and at 10 wrote an important discourse; Goethe, before 10, wrote in several languages; Meyerbeer, at 5, played remarkably well on the piano; Niebuhr, at 7, was a prodigy, and at 12 had mastered eighteen languages; Michael Angelo at 19 had attained a very high reputation; at 20 Calvin was a fully-fledged reformer, and at 24 published great works on theology that have changed the destiny of the world; Jonathan Edwards, at 10, wrote a paper refuting the materiality of the soul, and at 12 was so amazingly precocious that it was predicted of him that he would become another

Aristotle; at 20 Melanchthon was so learned that Erasmus exclaimed: "My God! What expectations does not Philip Melanchthon create!"

Causes of the Exceptional Longevity of Great Brain-Workers.

The explanation of the surprising longevity of great brain-workers is quite complex. The readiest answer to the problem would be that brain-work is healthful; and that, therefore, the better the brain and the harder it is worked, the longer the life of its possessor. Such a solution would not be entirely true; and if it were true unqualifiedly, it would clear up but one side of the question.

The answer is to be found, not in any single consideration, but in many considerations, as follows:—

1. *Great men usually come from healthy, long-lived ancestors.* Longevity is a correlated inheritance of genius. In order that a great man shall appear, a double line of more or less vigorous fathers and mothers must fight through the battles for existence and come out triumphant. However feeble the genius may be, his parents or grandparents are usually strong; or if not especially strong, are long lived. Great men may have nervous if not insane relatives; but the nervous temperament holds to life longer than any other temperament. The great man may himself be incapable of producing other great

men; in him, indeed, the branch of the race to which he belongs· may reach its consummation but the stock out of which he is evolved must be vigorous, and usually contains latent if not active genius. Longevity is hereditary, like all qualities or tendencies of organized life; and if great men come from long-lived stock, this fact is a most potent explanation of their exceptional longevity.*

2. *A good constitution usually accompanies a good brain.* The cerebral and muscular forces are often correlated; the brain is a part of the body. This view, though hostile to the popular faith, is yet sound and supportable; a large and powerful brain in a small and feeble body is a monstrosity. When a specially small and delicate frame sustains a specially large and potent brain, men wonder, as at a tree bowed to the earth by the weight of its overabundant fruit. Everywhere nature is a slave to the necessity of correlation or correspondence of parts and organs with each other; and unless she heeds it, all organized life would become awry and misshapen. In all the animal realm, there is a general though

---

* I haVe had an opportunity to confirm the conclusion of Mr. Galton by obserVations made in the States. This is a young country to study the inheritance of anything ; but out of a list of three hundred Americans, who in science, in inVention, in literature, in statesmanship, in commerce, in art, and in war, haVe been more or less illustrious, more than two-thirds had distinguished relatiVes; oVer one hundred were fathers and sons, or grandfathers and grandsons.

not unvarying relation between the brain and the
body of which it is a part and to which it ministers; a hundred great geniuses, chosen by chance,
will be larger than a hundred dunces anywhere —
will be broader, taller, and more weighty. In all
lands, savage, semi-civilized, and enlightened — the
ruling orders, chiefs, sheiks, princes by might and
mind, scientists, authors, orators, and merchants of
renown weigh more than the slaves, peasants, and
riffraff over whom they rule; and bear the evi-
deuces of their superiority so clearly that they
need no other insignia. In any band of workmen
on a railway, you shall pick out the "boss," by his
size alone: and be right four times out of five.
"In monstrosities Nature reveals her secrets," says
Goethe. Those monstrosities where genius is cabined in a small body, show the law by their very
rarity.

3. *Great men who are permanently successful
have correspondingly greater will than common men;
and force of will is a potent element in determining longevity.* The one requisite for great success
is *grit;* and, more uniformily than any other single
quality or combination of qualities, it is found in
those who attain high distinction. In the grand
struggle for life it is everywhere the stiff upper lip
that conquers; the timid and the yielding are cowed
and crushed, and over them rise the courageous and

the strong.   In certain of the arts extraordinary gifts
may lift their possessor into fame with but little
effort of his own, but the choicest seats in the tem-
ples of art are given only to those who have earned
them by the excellence that comes from consecutive
effort, which everywhere test the vital power of the
man.   That longevity depends not a little on the
will, no one will dispute.   The whole subject of the
relation of mental character to longevity is one of
vast interest, and is too far-reaching to be here discussed; but this single point must be granted without argument, that of two men every way alike and
similarly circumstanced, the one who has the greater
courage and staying force will be the longer-lived.
One does not need to practice medicine long to
learn that men die that might just as well live if
they had resolved to live and that many who are
invalids, could become strong if they had the native or acquired will to vow that they would do so.
Those who have no other quality favorable to life,
whose bodily organs are nearly all diseased, to whom
each day is a day of pain, who are beset by life-
shortening influences, yet do live by the determina-
tion to live alone.   Races and the sexes illustrate this;
the pluck of the Anglo-Saxon is shown as much on
the sick-bed as in Wall Street or on the battle-field.
During the late war I had chances enough to see
how thoroughly the black man wilted under light

sickness, and **was** slain by disease over which his white brother would have easily triumphed. When the negro feels the hand of disease pressing upon him, however gently, all his spirit leaves him. The great men of history are as much superior in their will-power to the average of their fellows, as are the races to which they belong to the inferior and uncivilized races; they live, for the same reason that they become famous; they obtain fame because they will not be obscure; they live because they will not die.

4. *Great men work more easily than ordinary men.* Their expenditure of force to accomplish great things is less plenteous than the expenditure of ordinary men to accomplish small things. A Liverpool draft-horse draws with ease a load at which a delicate racer might tug and strain without moving it. The greatest work is done easily; the best action is the unconscious; it is the essence of genius to be automatic and spontaneous. Many a huckster or corner tradesman expends each day more force in work or fretting than a Stewart or a Vanderbilt. "As small print most tires the eyes, so do little affairs the most disturb us;" the nearer our cares come to us the greater the friction; it is easier to govern an empire than to train a family. It is notorious that Beecher's sermons cost him only an hour's musing or so, while many speakers

grind for a week over "efforts" that suggest no thought, except sorrow for the composer. Great genius is usually industrious, for it is its nature to be active; but its movements are easy, frictionless, melodious. There are probably many school-boys who have exhausted themselves more over a prize composition than Shakespeare over "Hamlet," or Milton over the noblest passages in "Paradise Lost." At one time I acted as surgeon on a gun-boat of the United States Navy on the blockade, which was under the command of a man who, I am sure, worried and distressed himself more over that little craft than did Admiral Farragut over the entire squadron. When he died, shortly after the close of the war, I was requested by his widow to use my influence in procuring a pension for her. This I was able to do most conscientiously, for I knew that he had worn himself out in the service, although the vessel under his charge, while I was on board at least, never went into action, chased no blockade runner, and experienced not one moment of real or suspected peril.

The Great Longevity of Clergymen.

When, in 1867, I first called attention to the fact that clergymen were longer-lived than any other large class of brain-workers, serious doubt was expressed whether there might not be some error in

my statistics. So much has been said of the pernicious effects of mental labor, of the ill-health of
brain-workers of all classes, and especially of clergymen, that very few were prepared to accept the
statement that the clergy of this country and of
England lived longer than any other class, except
farmers; and very naturally a lurking fallacy was
suspected. Other observers, who have since given
special attention to the subject, have more than
confirmed this conclusion, and have shown that
clergymen are longer lived than farmers.

The Rev. Josiah F. Tuttle, D.D., President of
Wabash College, Indiana, has ascertained the ages
of 2,442 clergymen — 600 Trinitarian Congregation-
alists, 317 Presbyterians, 231 Episcopalians, 268
Baptists, 208 Methodists, 166 Unitarians, etc.,— and
found that the average was "a little over 61 years."
"Considerably over one-half of the whole were
over 60 years of age at their death; three-fourths
of the whole were over 50 years old at death; and
seven-eighths of the whole were over 40 years of age
at death." Dr. Tuttle found that the average age
at death of 408 individuals (not clergymen), and
who had died over 21 years of age, was a little over
51 years. This result pretty nearly corresponds
with mine.

But by far the more thorough investigation on
this subject, and one that must fully settle the ques-

tion for all minds over whom facts have any influence has been made by Rev. J. M. Sherwood, formerly editor of "Hours at Home" (in which my paper on longevity was originally published), and now Secretary of the "Society for Promoting Life Insurance among Clergymen." This gentleman has labored long and patiently in this department, and has ascertained that the average age of our ministers at death is 64.

These conclusions differ slightly from mine, but the difference is in favor of clergymen. Mr. Sherwood informs me that he had obtained the average from a list of ten thousand clergymen, whose ages at death he ascertained at great labor by consulting "the minutes of ecclesiastical bodies for thirty years past, the catalogues of theological seminaries, Wilson's 'Historical Almanac,' Dr. Sprague's 'Annals of the American Pulpit,' biographical dictionaries, the files of religious journals, etc." A list of ten thousand is sufficient and more than sufficient for a generalization; for the second five thousand did nothing more than confirm the result obtained by the first. It is fair and necessary to infer that if the list were extended to ten, twenty, or even one hundred thousand, the average would be found about the same.

In England, also, clergymen live to a greater age than any other class. According to the report of the Secretary of the Clerical Mutual Life Assurance Society, the mortality is less than that in twenty other companies by a very important percentage.

Causes of the Exceptional Longevity of Clergymen.

The reasons why clergymen are longer lived than any other class of brain-workers are these :—

1. *Their callings admit of a wide variety of toil.*— In their manifold duties their whole nature is exercised — not only brain and muscle in general, but all, or nearly all, the faculties of the brain — the religious, moral, and emotional nature, as well as the reason. Public speaking, when not carried to the extreme of exhaustion, is the best form of gymnastics that is known; it exercises every inch of a man, from the highest regions of the brain to the smallest muscle. In his public ministrations, in his pastoral calls, in his study, in his business arrangements, in his general reading, the pastor exercises more widely and variously than any other calling.

2. *Comparative freedom from financial anxiety.*— The average income of the clergymen of the leading denominations of this country in active service as pastors of churches (including salary, house rent, wedding fees, donations, etc.), is between $800 and $1,000, which is probably not very much smaller

than the net income of all other professional classes. Furthermore, the income of clergymen in active service is collected and paid with greater certainty and regularity, and less labor of collection on their part, than the income of any other class except, perhaps, government officials; then, again, their earnings, whether small or great, come at once, as soon as they enter their profession, and is not, as with other callings, built up by slow growth.

Worry is the one great shortener of life under civilization; and of all forms of worry, financial is the most frequent, and for ordinary minds, the most distressing. Merchants now make, always have made, and probably always will make, most of the money of the world; but business is attended with so much risk and uncertainty, and consequent anxiety, that merchants die sooner than clergymen, and several years sooner than physicians and lawyers.

The average income of families of all classes in this country is small — about $700 a year — and for the laboring classes, not more than half that sum; and if the same efforts were made to obtain the details of the financial history of every family in the land, as has been done in the case of clergymen, there would be some very dreary reading indeed.

3. *Their superior mental endowments.* — I speak calmly and discriminately, and from a careful comparison of biographical data, when I say that clergy-

men—as represented by the Congregational, Presbyterian, Unitarian, and other leading denominations —have presented a higher average of the higher, though not, perhaps, of the very highest kinds of ability, than any other equally large class in modern history.

During the past fifteen years, there has been a tendency, which is now rapidly increasing, for the best endowed and best cultured minds of our colleges to enter other professions, and the ministry has been losing, while medicine, business, and science have been gaining.

4. *Their superior temperance and morality.*— Clergymen are more regular in their sleep, meals, and exercise, than any other intellectual class; and are less exposed to injurious influences and contagions diseases than some other occupations.

Consolation for the Nervous.

Persons nervously organized are unquestionably cheated somewhat in the game of life. shorn of at least a portion of their possible happiness and usefulness, prisoners of their own feebleness, with no certain hope of perfect and permanent liberation. There are those who come into life thus weighted down, not by disease, not by transmitted poison in the blood, but by the tendency to disease, by a sensitiveness to evil and enfeebling forces that seems to make almost every external influence a means of torture; as soon as they are born, debility puts its terrible bond upon them, and will not let them go, but plays the tyrant with them until they die. Such persons in infancy are often on the point of dying, though they may not die; in childhood numberless physical ills attack them and hold them down, and, though not confining them to home, yet deprive them, perhaps, of many childish delights; in early maturity an army of abnormal nervous sensations is waiting for them the gauntlet of which they must run if they can; and throughout life every function seems to be an enemy.

The compensations of this type of organization are quite important and suggestive, and are most consolatory to sufferers. Among these compensations, this perhaps is worthy of first mention — that this very fineness of temperament, which is the source of nervousness, is also the source of exquisite pleasure. Highly sensitive natures respond to good as well as evil factors in their environment, salutary as well as pernicious stimuli are ever operating upon them, and their capacity for receiving, for retaining, and for multiplying the pleasures derived from external stimuli is proportionally greater than that of cold and stolid organizations: if they are plunged into a deeper hell, they also rise to a brighter heaven; their delicately-strung nerves make music to the slightest breeze ; art, literature, travel, social life, and solitude, pour out on them their selected treasures· they live not one life but many lives, and all joy is for them variously multiplied. To such tempera-ments the bare consciousness of living, when life is not attended by excessive exhaustion or by pain, or when one's capacity for mental or muscular toil is not too closely tethered, is oftentimes a supreme felicity. The true psychology of happiness is grati-fication of faculties, and when the nervous are able to indulge even moderately and with studied cau-tion and watchful anxiety their controlling desires of the nobler order, they may experience an exquis-iteness of enjoyment that serves, in a measure, to reward them for their frequent distresses. In the human system, as in all nature, everything is in motion, and all motion is rhythmical, and movement in any one direction is the more forcible and spon-taneous when it follows movement in another di-rection ; the motions that constitute what we call health are most delicious and satisfying when fol-lowing quickly after debility or pain. Perfect health of itself is not a condition of positive hap-piness, and is not at all essential to 'happiness. The happiest persons I have seen, or expect to see, were partial invalids—not those who were racked and tor-tured with nameless agonies, or kept prostrate by absolute exhaustion, but who were so far under bondage to susceptible nerves as never to realize even approximate health; even in their slavery they were sufficiently free to indulge some, at least, of their higher faculties, and to that degree were capable of enjoyment all the more intense from contrast with the restrictions that disease imposed on the rest of their organization. I recall the case of a lady who, as an effect of severe functional nervous disorder, had become temporarily paralyzed, so that none of the limbs had power of self-motion, and yet she was apparently and really more joyous than the majority of those who have full physical liberty.

The mystery, long noted by physicians, that patients who are half cured of a severe malady are more grateful than even those fully cured, is explained by the fact that we need a certain degree of debility, a limited and bearable amount of pain or discomfort, to keep us constantly mindful by contrast of the pleasantness of our present state as compared with what it has been or might be. The physician who collects his fee before his patient has quite recovered, does a wise thing, since it will be paid more promptly and more gratefully than after the recovery is complete. Nervous organizations are rarely without reminders of trouble that they escape —their occasional wakefulness and indigestion, their headaches and backaches and neuralgias, their disagreeable susceptibility to all evil influences that may act on the constitution, keep them ever in sight of the possibility of what they might have been, and suggest to them sufferings that others endure, but from which they are spared.

The most exquisite physical pleasure, it has been said, is sudden relief from violent pain. This pleasure is quite often the experience of the nervous : alternations of depression and vigor, of pain and the relief of pain, of wakefulness and sound sleep, mark the lives of thousands. While it is true that pain is more painful than its absence is agreeable, so that we think more of what is evil than of what is good in our environment, and dwell longer on the curses than the blessings of our lot, and fancy all others happier than ourselves, yet it is true likewise that our curses make the blessings more blissful by contrast ; the bright colors of the picture seem all the lighter against the dark and stormy background.

I have heard of a prominent public man who, when governor of his State, once remarked to an acquaintance that he was suffering from a slight pain in his hand, and that it was the first real pain he had ever felt in his life. This statement was probably, in scientific strictness, untrue ; he had no doubt experienced pains, perhaps many of them, that had been forgotten, but his life must have been, up to that time, unusually free from physical evils. A freedom from disease so absolute as that can be a source of negative pleasure only; it is not of necessity any positive mental possession; it may not be thought of from year to year, any more than the existence of sunlight or of oxygen in the air, save when we are shut out from them, and therefore can be but an uncertain element of consolation amid the struggles and disappointments of life

In contrast with this painless life there are in this land immense numbers who pass no day free from pain; who are ever conscious, unless diverted by mental or other employment, of disagreeable if not distressing sensations; and who, notwithstanding, are cheerful and, to a degree, in love with life.

There are those who though never well are yet never sick, always in bondage to debility and pain, from which absolute escape is impossible, yet not without large liberty of labor and of thought; held by a long tether which gives them, within certain limits, free play, but never condemned to utter confinement; ignorant alike of perfect health and perfect prostration. Such persons may be exposed to every manner of poison, may travel far and carelessly with recklessness, even may disregard many of the prized rules of health; may wait upon and mingle with the sick, and breathe for long periods the air of hospitals or of fever-infested dwellings, and come out apparently unharmed.

When the poison of fever enters the strong,

phlegmatic constitution, it at once intrenches itself and finds protection in its solid walls, and then is driven out only with difficulty; but in the nervous constitution there are no such means of defence — it is vulnerable on every side, and the intruder having no means of holding his position, may be expelled with slight effort.

Natural History of Nervousness.

The nervous may also find consolation in the fact of medical observation that nervousness, like other physical evils, tends to cure itself. After remedies, and even hygiene, have done their best, and have been foiled — after the wisest physicians have found their Waterloos or Sedans — time, cooperating with the natural growth of the constitution, may bring deliverance. This recuperative tendency of the nervous system is stronger, oftentimes, than the accumulating poison of disease, and overmasters the baneful effects of unwise medication and hygiene. Between the ages of 25 and 35, especially, the constitution often consolidates as well as grows, acquires power as well as size, and throws off, by a slow and invisible evolution, the subtile habits of nervous disease, over which treatment the most judicious and persistent seems to have little or no influence. There would appear to be organizations which at certain times of life must needs pass through the dark valley of nervous depression, and who cannot be saved therefrom by any manner of skill or prevision; who must not only enter into this valley, but, having once entered, cannot turn back: the painful, and treacherous, and agonizing horror, wisdom can but little shorten, and ordinary misdoing cannot make perpetual; they are as sure to come out as to go in; health and disease move in rhythm; the tides in the constitution are as demonstrable as the tides of the ocean, and are sometimes but little more under human control. I call up here the experience of a gentleman once under my care for profound and protracted disease of the nervous system, and whose life, mainly through his own fault, was but a series of alternations of ups and downs, which, though modified by treatment, could not be, at least were not, entirely broken up. One day, as I called to see him, he was much better than usual, and was clearly mending, and I made a remark to that effect. "Yes," said he, "I'm getting ready for another relapse."

It is an important consolation for those who are in the midst of an attack of sick-headache, for example, that the natural history of the disease is in their favor. In a few days at the utmost, in a few hours frequently, the storm will be spent, and again the sky will be clear, and perhaps far clearer than before the storm arose.

Cycles of Debility.

The capacity of the system for bearing pain, like its capacity for pleasure, is limited: it is only possible to suffer, as it is only possible to enjoy, a certain measure of sensation; the power to appreciate disagreeable sensations is and must be restricted by the forces in the organism, and can no more exceed them than the drawing-power of the locomotive can exceed the measure of the latent force of the consumed fuel. Thus it is that nearly all severe pain is periodic, intermittent, rhythmical: the violent neuralgias are never constant, but come and go by throbs, and spasms, and fiercely-darting agonies, the intervals of which are absolute relief. After the exertion expended in attacks of pain, the tired nerve-atoms must need repose. Sometimes the cycles of debility, alternating with strength, extend through long years — a decade of exhaustion being followed by a decade of vigor. There are those also who pass entirely and permanently out of the stage of depression; whose constitutions, originally sensitive, capricious, untrustworthy, slowly acquire strength and endurance, and are able to transmit these acquired qualities to their children and children's children. There are those who pass through an infancy of weakness and suffering and much pain, and through a childhood and early manhood in which the game of life seems to be a losing one,

to a healthy and happy maturity; all that is best in
their organizations seems to be kept in reserve, as
though to test their faith, and make the boon of
strength more grateful when it comes.   The early
life of some of the world's best heroes was passed
in debility and strife with maladies over which, in
time, they became victorious.   Not a few of the
most useful and most honored names in history
were scarcely thought worth the raising — the question being, not whether they should be famous and
laborious, but whether they could live at all;
whether they must not early go down in the struggle for being.   The fineness, the delicacy, the complexity of the highest organizations render them
liable to manifold disturbance, to be more easily dis-
ordered in the play of the various machinery than
those of coarser and simpler fibre; but, when once
they have succeeded in adapting themselves to their
environment, when the initial battle of the campaign
of life has been won, they seem to be stronger
for the oppositions and difficulties they have met
and overcome, and may endure and achieve far
more, and last all the longer.   Changes in the constitution of the kind here described take place, as
it sometimes appears, not through any regimen or
care, but in obedience to inevitable development;
they are signs of growth, which may, indeed, be
modified but not radically changed by any degree

of medical skill or practical wisdom, and only the most atrocious and persistent violation of the laws of life can avail to absolutely arrest their progress.

Nervousness a Constant Warning.

Perfect health is by no means the necessary condition of long life; in many ways, indeed, it may shorten life; grave febrile and inflammatory diseases are invited and fostered by it, and made fatal, and the self-guarding care, without which great longevity is almost impossible, is not enforced or even suggested. "The only fault with my constitution," said a friend to me, "is that I have nothing to make me cautious." Headaches, and backaches, and neuralgias, are safety-valves through which nerve-perturbations escape, and which otherwise might become centres of accumulated force, and break forth with destruction beyond remedy. The liability to sudden attacks of any form of pain, or distress, or discomfort, under overtoil or from disregard of natural law, is, so far forth, a blessing to its possessor, making imperative the need of foresight and practical wisdom in the management of health, and warning us in time to avoid irreparable disaster. The nervous man hears the roar of the breakers from afar, while the strong and phlegmatic steers boldly, blindly on, until he is cast upon the shore, oftentimes a hopeless wreck.

The familiar malady called writer's cramp,* for example does not in its worst form usually attack the weak, but the comparatively strong; it is. in fact, in its severer phase, the penalty for having a good constitution. Those who are sensitive, and nervous, and delicate, whom every external or internal irritation injures, and who appreciate physical injury instantly, as soon as the exciting cause begins to act, cannot write long enough to get writer's cramp; they are warned by uneasiness or pain, by weariness, local or general, and are forced to interrupt their labors before there has been time to receive a fixed or persistent disease. Hence it is that those who suffer from this disorder are surprised when the symptoms come upon them; they declare that they have always been well, and wonder that they do not continue so: had they been feeble they would have been unable to persevere in the use of the pen so as to invite permanent nervous disorder. As with this malady of writers, so with other affections not a few, some of which are of a more serious and directly fatal character. The nervous are frequently saved from incurable disturbances of the brain by a constant succession of symptoms that individually are trifling, but by their recurrence cause at first

---

* See my paper entitled " Conclusions from the Study of One Hundred and Twenty-five Cases of Writer's Cramp and Allied Affections: also Neurasthenia." Second edition, p. 128.

annoyance, then uneasiness, and then positive distress, and finally compel a moderation in labor, perhaps a suspension of employment, which at this stage is all that the system needs for complete recuperation. Without such warnings they might have continued in a life of excessive friction and exhausting worry, and never have suspected that permanent invalidism was in waiting for them, until too late to save themselves either by hygiene or medication. When a man is prostrated nervously, all the forces of nature rush to his rescue; but the strong man, once fully fallen, rallies with difficulty, and the health-evolving powers may find a task to which, aided or unaided, they are inadequate.

The history of the world's progress from savagery to barbarism, from barbarism to civilization, and, in civilization, from the lower degrees towards the higher, is the history of increase in average longevity, corresponding to and accompanied by increase of nervousness. Mankind has grown to be at once more delicate and more enduring, more sensitive to weariness and yet more patient of toil, impressible but capable of bearing powerful irritation: we are woven of finer fibre, which, though apparently frail, yet outlasts the coarser, as rich and costly garments oftentimes wear better than those of rougher workmanship.

The tendency to live long runs in families; mental discipline also the result of opportunities for education and intellectual · society, becomes a family inheritance, and thus favors family longevity. Even in this young country there are not a few well-known families in which longevity is an heirloom, many of whose members have passed by a number of years the highest average age of brain-workers.

Healthy Old Age.

Among our educated classes there are nervous invalids in large numbers, who have never known by experience what it is to be perfectly well or severely ill, whose lives have been not unlike a march through a land infested by hostile tribes, that ceaselessly annoy in front and on flank, without ever coming to a decisive conflict, and who, in advanced age, seem to have gained wiriness, and toughness, and elasticity, by the long discipline of caution, of courage, and of endurance; and, after having seen nearly all their companions, whose strength they envied, struck down by disease, are themselves spared to enjoy, it may be, their best days, at a time when, to the majority, the grasshopper becomes a burden, and life each day a visibly losing conflict with death.

I have known many who have survived a youth

and manhood of wearisome nervous invalidism, to an old age of comparative vigor and freedom from physical vexation; until past fifty, or even sixty, they have never known what it is to have no sense of weariness or pain; the irritability, the sensitiveness, the capriciousness of the constitution, between the ages of 15 and 45, have, in a degree, disappeared, and the system has acquired a certain solidity, steadiness, and power; and thus, after a long voyage against opposing winds and fretting currents, they enter the harbor in calmness and peace.

Recent Progress in the Treatment of Nervous Diseases.

The nervous, likewise, have the consolation that progress of the most important character, indeed, unprecedented in its rapidity, has been made, and is now being made in the medical treatment of functional diseases of the nervous system. It may be doubted whether, in the history of disease of any kind, there has been made so decided and so satisfactory an advance as has been made within the last quarter of a century, in the treatment of nervousness in its various manifestations. This new treatment does not consist only in the use of medicines alone, although many new medicines have been introduced, and new modes of administering medicines, and new ideas in regard to doses—smaller doses in some cases, and very much larger in other cases; but, also, in the scientific study of diet, of exercise, of sleep, of rest; in the application of such agencies as electricity, water, cold and hot, in various forms, and by methods adapted to the nervous and sensitive constitution. One great factor in the modern treatment of these functional nervous diseases is individualization, no two cases being treated precisely alike, but each one being studied by itself alone. Among wise physicians, the day for wholesale treatment of nervous diseases can never return. The result of all this progress is, that thousands who formerly would have suffered all their lives, and with no other relief except that which comes from the habitual addiction to narcotics, can now be cured, or permanently relieved, or at least put into working order where they are most useful and happy. If, in the future, as in the past, nervous diseases are to be a measure of our civilization,—if every increase in the illuminating power of the mind is but an increase of surface to be eclipsed,— if all new modes of action of nerve-force are to be so many added pathways to sorrow,—if each fresh discovery or invention is to be matched by some new malady of the nerves —if insanity and epilepsy and neurasthenia, with their retinue of neuroses, through the cruel law of inheritance, are to be organized in families, descending in fiery streams through **the** generations, we yet have this assurance,—that science, with keen eyes and steps that are not slow, is seeking and is finding means of prevention and of relief.

CHAPTER V.

FROM the vantage-ground of the above facts and philosophy, and with the light afforded by the past and present experience of races and nations, it becomes possible to see, though dimly and for a limited period, into the physical future of the American people. In the twentieth century, as now, America will be inhabited by all the leading races of modern civilization, although by that time there will have been an enormous advance towards unity. At the present time it is observed that the process of Americanization among our recent foreigners, goes on with great rapidity; the peculiarities of our climate being so decided, universal, and determinate, that even the second generation of stolid and plethoric Germans, often acquires the sharpness of features, delicacy of skin, and dryness of hair, that everywhere, and for a long period, have been rightly looked upon as American characteristics. I have seen highly nervous Englishmen and Irishmen, who early emigrated to this country and engaged in severe mercantile or professional pursuits; such persons are sometimes so changed, even in a half or quarter of a century, as to become, in their physique, thoroughly Americanized.

This increase of neuroses cannot be arrested suddenly; it must yet go on for at least twenty-five or fifty years, when all of these disorders shall be both more numerous and more heterogenous than at present. But side by side with these are already developing signs of improved health and vigor that cannot be mistaken; and the time must come — not unlikely in the first half of the twentieth century — when there will be a halt or retrograde movement in the march of nervous diseases, and while the absolute number of them may be great, relatively to the population, they will be less frequent than now; the evolution of health, and the evolution of nervousness, shall go on side by side.

Relation of Health to Wealth and Poverty.

Accumulated and transmitted wealth is to be in this, as in other countries, one of the safeguards of national health. Health is the offspring of relative wealth. In civilization, abject and oppressed poverty is sickly, or liable to sickness, and on the average is short-lived; febrile and inflammatory disorders, plagues, epidemics, great accidents and catastrophes even, visit first and last and remain longest with those who have no money. The anxiety that

is almost always born of poverty; the fear of still
greater poverty, of distressing want, of sickness that
is sure to come; the positive deprivation of food
that is convenient, of clothing that is comfortable,
of dwellings that are sightly and healthful; the constant and hopeless association with misery, discomfort, and despair; the lack of education through books,
schools, or travel; the absence of all but forced
vacations — the result, and one of the worst results,
of poverty — added to the corroding force of envy,
and the friction of useless struggle, — all these factors that make up or attend upon simple want of
money, are in every feature antagonistic to health
and longevity. Only when the poor become absolute paupers, and the burden of life is taken from
them and put upon the State or public charity, are
they in a condition of assured health and long life.
For the majority of the poor, and for many of the
rich, the one dread is to come upon the town; but
as compared with many a home the poorhouse is a
sanitarium. The inmates of our public institutions
of charity of the modern kind, are often the happiest of men, blessed with an environment, on the
whole, far more salubrious than that to which they
have been accustomed, and favorably settled for a
serene longevity. Here, in a sanitary point of view,
the extremes of wealth and poverty meet; both
conditions being similar in this — that they remove

the friction which is the main cause of ill-health and short life. For the same reasons, well-regulated jails are healthier than many homes, and one of the best prescriptions for the broken-down and distressed, is for them to commit some crime.

The augmenting wealth of the American people during the last quarter of a century is already making its impress on the national constitution, and in a variety of ways. A fat bank account tends to make a fat man; in all countries, amid all stages of civilization and semi-barbarism, the wealthy classes have been larger and heavier than the poor. Wealth, indeed, if it be abundant and permanent, supplies all the external conditions possible to humanity that are friendly to those qualities of the physique — plumpness, roundness, size — that are rightly believed to indicate well-balanced health: providing in liberal variety agreeable and nourishing food and drink, tasteful and commodious homes. and comfortable clothing; bringing within ready and tempting access, education, and the nameless and powerful diversions for muscle and mind, that only a reasonable degree of enlightenment can obtain or appreciate; inviting and fortifying calmness, steadiness, repose in thought and action; inspiring and maintaining in all the relations of existence, a spirit of self-confidence, independence, and self-esteem, which, from a psychological point of view, are, in the fight for life, qualities of the highest sanitary importance; in a word, minifying, along all the line of the physical functions, the processes of waste and magnifying the processes of repair. So insalubrious are the hygienic surroundings of the abjectly poor that only a slow adaptation to those conditions makes it possible for them to retain either the power or the desire to live. In India this coincidence of corpulence and opulence has been so long observed that it is instinctively assumed; and certain Brahmins, it is said, in order to obtain the reputation of wealth, studiously cultivate a diet adapted to make them fat.

Poverty has, it is true, its good side from a hygienic as well as from other points of view; for, practically, good and evil are but relative terms, the upper and nether sides of the same substance, and constantly tending to change places. The chief advantage of poverty as a sanitary or hygienic force is that, in some exceptional natures, it inspires the wish and supplies the capacity to escape from it, and in the long struggle for liberty we acquire the power and the ambition for something higher and nobler than wealth; the impulse of the rebound sends us farther than we had dreamed; stung by early deprivation to the painful search for gold, we often find treasures that gold cannot buy. But for one whom poverty stimulates and strengthens, there are thousands whom it subjugates and destroys, entailing disease and an early death from generation to generation. The majority of our Pilgrim Fathers in New England, and of the primitive settlers in the Southern and Middle States, really knew but little of poverty in the sense in which the term is here used. They were an eminently thrifty people, and brought with them both the habits and the results of thrift to their homes in the New World. Poverty as here described is of a later evolution, following in this country, as in all others, the pathway of a high civilization.

In the centuries to come there will probably be found in America, not only in our large cities, but in every town and village, orders of financial nobility, above the need but not above the capacity or the disposition to work: strong at once in inherited wealth and inherited character; using their vast and easy resources for the upbuilding of manhood, physical and mental; and maintaining a just pride in transmitting these high ideals, and the means for realizing them, to their descendants. Families thus favored can live without physical discomfort, and work without worrying. Their healthy and well-adjusted forces can be concentrated at will, and in the beginning of life, on those objects best adapted to their tastes and talents; thus economizing and utilizing so much that those who are born poor and sickly and ignorant are compelled to waste in oftentimes fruitless struggle. The moral influence of such a class scattered through our society must be, on the whole, with various and obvious exceptions and qualifications, salutary and beneficent. By keeping constantly before the public high ideals of culture, for which wealth affords the means; by elevating the now dishonored qualities of serenity and placidity to the rank of virtues, where they justly belong, and by discriminatingly co-operating with those who are less favored in their toils and conflicts, they cannot help diffusing, by the laws of psychical contagion, a reverence for those same ideals in those who are able but most imperfectly to live according to them. Thus they may help to bring about that state of society where men shall no more boast of being overworked than of any other misfortune, and shall no longer be ashamed to admit that they have both the leisure and the desire for thought; and the throne of honor so long held by the practical man shall be filled, for the first time in the history of this nation, by the man of ideas. The germs of such a class have even now begun to appear, and already their power is clearly perceptible on American society. The essence of barbarism is equality, as the essence of civilization is inequality; but the increasing inequality of civilization may be in a degree corrected by scientific philanthropy.

Comparative Healthfulness of Different Orders of Brain-Work.

While all brain-work is so far forth healthful and conducive to longevity, yet the different orders of mental activity differ very widely in the degree of their health-giving power; the law is invariable that the exercise of the higher faculties is more salutary and more energizing than the exercise of the lower. The higher we rise in the atmosphere of thought the more we escape the strifes, the competitions, the worryings and exhausting disappointments — in short, all the infinite frictions that inevitably attend the struggle for bread that all must have, and the more we are stimulated and sustained by those lofty truths for which so few aspire. The search for truth is more healthful as well as more noble than the search for gold, and the best of all antidotes and means of relief for nervous disease is found in philosophy. Thus it is in part that Germany, which in scientific and philosophic discovery does the thinking for all nations, and which has added more to the world's stock of purely original ideas than any other country, Greece alone excepted, is less nervous than any other nation; thus it is also that America, which in the same department has but fed on the crumbs that fall from Germany's table, has developed a larger variety and number of functional nervous diseases than all other nations combined.

Evolution in Relation to National Health.

The commanding law of evolution — the highest generalization that the human mind has yet reached — affords indispensable aid in solving the problem we are here discussing. This law, when rightly understood, in all its manifold dependencies, developments, complications, ramifications, divergencies, sheds light on numberless questions of sociology which formerly were in hopeless darkness. It is a part of this law that growth or development in any one direction, or along any one line of a race, family, or tribe, in time reaches its limit, beyond which it cannot pass, and where, unless re-enforced by some new or different impression or influence — a supply of vital force from some centre outside of itself to take the place of that which is expended in the exhausting processes of reproduction and expansion — it dies utterly away. Not more surely does a branch of a tree subdivide into numerous twigs, all of which must sooner or later reach their respective terminations, than do the various families of any people tend to their own elimination. The capacity for growth in any given direction, physical or mental, is always limited; no special gift of body or mind can be cultivated beyond a certain point, however great the tenderness and care bestowed upon it. The more rapid and luxurious the growth the sooner the supply of potential force is exhausted ; and the faculty or gift, whatever it may be, is lost, only to be renewed in an entirely distinct family, or by the injection of the blood and nerve of a radically different race. The infinity of nature is not in the endurance or permanency of any of its elements — everything is changing, everything is dying — but in the exhaustlessness of the supply. In horses only a certain rate of speed, in cows only a limited milk-forming power, in fowls but a moderate fertility, can be reached in anv line of stock by any degree of mortal prevision and skill. The dying is as natural and as inevitable as the living ; deelension is as normal as ascension as truly a part of exceptionless law. In man, that higher operation of the faculties which we call genius is hereditary, transmissible, running through and in families as demonstrably as pride or hay-fever, the gifts as well as the sins of the fathers being visited upon the children and the children's children ; general talent, or some special talent, in one or both parents rises and expands in immediate or remote offspring, and ultimately flowers out into a Socrates, a Shakespeare, a Napoleon, and then falls to the ground ; a very great man can never be the father of a very great man. In accordance with this law, it is inevitable that many of the strong and great families of America at the present day must perish, and their places be supplied by the descendants of those who are now ignorant and obscure. This does not mean, as many have fancied, the dying out of the American people: the race lives while tribes and families perish: the periodical crops ripen and decay while the tree that produces them is every year adding to its growth.

It is also a part of this law of evolution that the lower must minister to the higher. The strength of the strong must come, in part, from the weakness of the weak; millions perish that hundreds may survive. That a single family may rise to enduring prominence and power, it is needful that through long generations scores of families shall endure poverty and pain and struggle with cruel surroundings; shall vainly desire and perhaps strive for wealth and fame and position and ease, and sink at last in the conflict. For every brain-worker there must be ten muscle-workers. Even in Greece, the flower of all the civilizations, the majority of the population were slaves; that a few thousand might cultivate the intellect, hundreds of thousands must cultivate the soil. One cannot imagine a nation in which all should be rich and intelligent; for a people composed wholly of educated millionnaires, intelligence would be a curse and wealth the worst form of poverty. For America, as for all people, this law is as remorseless as gravity, and will not go out of its way at the beck either of philanthropy or philosophy. The America of the future, as the America of the present, must be a nation where riches and culture are restricted to the few — to a body, however, the *personnel* of which is constantly changing. But although the distance between the extremes of society will still be great, perhaps even greater than in the past, the poor will have comforts and luxuries which now they cannot even picture, and correspondingly their health and comeliness should improve. The conserving and regenerating force of a large body of muscle-workers in society is enormous, and for the physical well-being of a nation indispensable, since it not only preserves itself, but supplies the material to be engrafted on branches whose productive power is tending to decay; our cities would perish but for the country, our country would perish but for other countries.

Yet further, it is a part of the law of evolution that nations, as well as the individuals of which nations are composed, can in time so fit themselves to unfavorable external conditions as practically to reverse them and make them favorable This moulding of the internal to the external, with its accompanying disappearance of weak elements and persistence of the strong, is a process that never halts or wearies, but goes on without ceasing so long as there is any want of harmony between the internal and the external in the individual or the nation. A nation thrust into an unusual and hostile environment tends, with all the might of its subjective forces, to fit itself to that environment, and to make itself at home there; old habits are dropped, new habits take their places; instinctively or rationally, there is constant sacrifice and study and deprivation, and correspondingly, friction of the internal against the external diminishes. Young America finds itself contending with the combined disadvantages of youth, an exhausting climate, and the heightened activity, common to all civilization, made necessary by the introduction of the railroad, the telegraph, and the periodical press. In the process of moulding itself to these conditions, it has been found necessary to seek out and develop numberless modes of physical exercise, and reduce the philosophy of enjoyment and recreation to a science and art. Habits of the ages have been shifted, medicine and medical practice revolutionized, while inventive skill everywhere exhausts itself in the constant effort to supply mechanical devices for senses and faculties bankrupted through over-confinement, over-excitement, and disproportionate use of the brain and nervous system. In this cruel process thousands have perished — are perishing to-day; but from the midst of this confusion, conflict, and positive destruction a powerful and stable race has been slowly, almost imperceptibly, evolving.

Prospective Increase of Nervous Diseases —
Inebriety a Type of all.

Before the redeeming forces that are in a measure to neutralize our nervousness shall be in full
operation, there must be a still greater, perhaps even
more rapid increase of nervousness and of functional nervous disease.

The inebriates of our day and country must be
counted already by tens and tens of thousands, and
by the twentieth century their numbers must be very
much greater; the law of inheritance, which, briefly
stated, is that we are parts of our parents, together
with the constant activity of the exciting causes of
nervousness, as heretofore described, cannot be neutralized in the next quarter of a century, by any of
the agencies suggested, to a sufficient degree to prevent rapid increase.

Inebriety being a type of the nervous diseases
of the family to which it belongs, may properly be
here defined and differentiated from the vice and
habit of drinking with which it is confounded.

The functional nervous disease inebriety, or dipsomania, differs from the simple vice of drinking to
excess in these respects :—

First. The disease inebriety is more irresistible
than the mere vice.   The simple habit of drinking
even to an extreme degree may be broken up by
pledges or by word promises or by quiet resolution,

but the disease inebriety can be no more cured in
this way than can neuralgia or sick-headache, or
neurasthenia, or hay-fever, or any of the family of
diseases to which it belongs.

Secondly. Inebriety is frequently or usually preceded, or accompanied, or followed by certain nervous symptoms, and it is powerfully hereditary like
all other nervous diseases. Of the nervous symptoms that precede, or accompany, or follow inebriety, are tremors, hallucinations, insomnia, mental
depressions, and attacks of trance, to which I give
the term alcoholic trance; striking cases of this form
of trance have been reported by Dr. T. D. Crothers.
Inebriates or those who have a tendency to inebriety—may go off for several days in states of un-
consciousness of what they do, and are consequently
irresponsible, and in this state may transact business
and commit crime. The details of these cases of
alcoholic trance are among the most interesting facts
of medical literature; and will be recorded in a
work on trance on which I have been many years
engaged. Among the nervous diseases there is no
one, not even hay-fever, which is more demonstrably
hereditary; even drunkenness in a parent or grand-
parent may develop in children epilepsy or insanity, or neurasthenia or inebriety.

Third. Inebriety is distinguished frequently by
the suddenness of its attacks. These attacks may

come on as suddenly as an attack of neuralgia of the face, with no more warning than cases of epilepsy; in some cases simply coming in contact with salt air will bring an attack of inebriety. Some attacks are of a subjective character quite independent of any external irritations, and in that respect differ from the forms of intoxication.

Fourth. The attacks of inebriety may be periodical; they may appear once a month, and with the same regularity as chills and fever or sick-headache, and far more regularly than epilepsy, and quite independent of any external temptation or invitation to drink, and oftentimes are as irresistible and beyond the control of will as spasms of epilepsy or the pains of neuralgia or the delusions of insanity. Inebriety is not so frequent among the classes that drink excessively as among those who drink but moderately, although their ancestors may have been intemperate; it is most frequent in the nervous and highly organized classes, among the brain-workers, those who have lived in-doors; there is more excessive drinking West and South than in the East, but more inebriety in the East. The habit of drinking may by insensible gradations develop into the disease inebriety; in some cases an attack of inebriety may appear without any previous habit of drinking.

While there is to be, probably, less and less

drinking in certain classes of American society during the next quarter of a century, there must, for the reason stated, be an increase of the disease inebriety, and there is little doubt that even the West, beyond the Mississippi, must in time suffer from this malady; already, indeed, our far-away States and Territories are enacting prohibitory laws, which are the combined products of our nervousness and our non-expertness.

The opium habit, likewise, is fated to increase during the next quarter of a century. Within twenty years the amount of opium imported into this country has increased five hundred per cent., being in 1859 seventy-one thousand eight hundred and fifty-nine pounds, in 1880, three hundred and seventy-two thousand pounds; probably no country outside of China uses, in proportion to population, so much opium as America, and as the pains and nervousness and debility that tempt to the opium habit are on the increase, the habit must inevitably develop more rapidly in the future than in the past; of hay-fever there must, in a not very distant time, be at least one hundred thousand cases in America, and in the twentieth century hundreds of thousands of insane and neurasthenics.

Women, though more nervous than men, are not so likely to suffer from inebriety, for two reasons:

First. Because they have on the negative side

less temptation to drink than men, while on the positive side they have socially more dissuasion from drinking; thus positively and negatively they are impelled and driven into temperance; but exceptions enough there are among the women of our land to make it necessary to erect a large building for the treatment of inebriety in females, as Dr. Turner is now doing.

Increased Susceptibility to Muscular Exercise.

There must be, also, an increasing number of people who cannot bear severe physical exercise. Few facts relating to this subject are more instructive than this — the way in which horseback-riding is borne by many in modern times. In our country, I meet with large numbers who cannot bear the fatigue of horseback-riding, which used to be looked upon — possibly is looked upon to-day — as one of the best forms of exercise, and one that is recommended as a routine by physicians who are not discriminating in dealing with nervously-exhausted patients. I find it is necessary to be very careful indeed in recommending this mode of pleasure which our fathers could indulge in freely without ever asking whether it was healthy or not.

I have been consulted by physicians whose nervous symptoms were brought on, or at least intensified by horseback-riding in country places, and I have seen attacks of spinal congestion induced in the same way, in persons who are accustomed to that mode of exercise, and who are reasonably strong and enduring. The greatest possible care and the best judgment are required in prescribing and adapting horseback-riding to nervous individuals of either sex; it is necessary to begin cautiously, to go on a walk for a few moments; and even after long training excess is followed by injury, in many cases.

Gymnastics, also, must be administered in small doses; the nervous weaken themselves by trying to make themselves strong by dumb-bells, Indian clubs, parallel bars, and imitations of rowing; not because these exercises have not a place in hygiene, but because where the quantity of nervous force is limited there is the greatest danger possible of drawing too heavily upon it; and especially is this true where there are classes and ambition of one to do what another can not do. If either extreme is to be chosen, it is well, on the whole, to err on the side of rest rather than on the side of excess of physical exertion. I can see that twenty-five years hence the number of those who, though they may be in reasonable health, yet can not ride, row, or exercise in gymnastics recklessly will be much larger than now, and probably much greater in proportion to the population. A few years ago it was pretty safe to advise a person who was somewhat broken down to ride, or row, or practise gymnastics; now, it is not safe to give that advice indiscriminately, especially to natives of the United States.

Reconstruction of Systems of Education demanded.

The systems of education in colleges and universities, and at home, are, in almost all respects, adapted to exhaust the nervous system — from their very cradles our children are trained to nervousness; our schools are too often on the road to the asylum.

In the philosophic analysis of any case of nervous disease or of nerve sensitiveness not yet developed into active disease, we are to go back to the ancestry, near or remote — then we are to go back to childhood — we are to follow the infant from the maternal arms through home-life, school and university, business and professional life, to the time when the symptoms of nervousness first appeared. For various reasons which can be traced and analyzed, if one should choose to attempt the task, the science and art of education are kept in the rear of the other sciences and arts; but during the last century, pre-eminently perhaps, during the last decade — most of all, indeed, during the last five years, and never more than during the past year, there has developed an inquiry in the scientific study of the problems of education. This inquiry is to extend until the existing modes of discipline and instruction shall have only an historic and antiquarian interest. •

Why Education is behind other Sciences and Arts.

Schools and colleges everywhere are the sanctuaries of mediævalism, since their aim and their powers are more for retaining what has been discovered than for making new discoveries; consequently we cannot look to institutions or organizations of education for the reconstruction of that system by which they enslave the world and are themselves enslaved. It is claimed by students of Chinese character, that that great nation has been kept stationary through its educational policy — anchored for centuries to competitive examinations which their strong nerves can bear while they make no progress. In a milder way, and in divers and fluctuating degrees, all civilized nations take their inspiration from China, since it is the office and life of teaching to look backward rather than forward ; in the relations of men as in physics, force answers to force, and as the first, like the second childhood is always reactionary, a class of youths tend by their col lective power to bring the teacher down more than he can lift them up. Only conservative natures are fond of teaching; organizations are always in the path of their own reconstruction; mediocrity begets mediocrity, attracts it, and is attracted by it. Whence all our institutions become undying centres of conservatism. The force that reconstructs an organization must come from outside the body that is to be reconstructed. To psychologists are we to look for the philosophy of education which in time is to give a new life to all the universities of the world.

The Gospel of Rest.

The gospel of work must make way for the gospel of rest. The children of the past generation were forced, driven, stimulated to work, and in forms most repulsive, the philosophy being, that utility is proportioned to pain; that to be happy is to be doing wrong, hence it is needful that studies should not only be useless but repelling, and should be pursued by those methods which, on trial, proved the most distressing, wearisome, and saddening. That this philosophy has its roots in a certain truth psychology allows, but the highest wisdom points also to another truth, the need of the agreeable; our children must be driven from study and all toil, and in many instances coaxed, petted, and hired to be idle; we must drive' them away from schools as our fathers ‹drove them towards the schools; one must be each moment awake and alive and active, to keep a child from stealthily learning to read; our cleverest offspring loves books more than play, and truancies and physical punishments are far rarer than half a century ago.

Dr. Pallen, of this city, has lately attempted to make some statistical study of the methods by which the schools, especially for girls, are conducted in this country.

Of a large number of circulars of inquiry which he sent out, satisfactory replies were received only to a few; but these were sufficient to clearly show that nearly everything about the conduct of the schools was wrong, unphysiological and unpsychological, and that they were conducted so as to make very sad and sorrowing the lives of those who were forced to attend them; it was clear that the teachers and managers of these schools knew nothing and cared nothing of those matters relating to education that are of the highest importance, and that the routine of the schools was such as would have been devised by some evil one who wished to take vengeance on the race and the nation. Scarcely anything taught that needs to be taught, almost everything that ought not to be taught, and which girls ought not to know, everything pushed in an unscientific and distressing manner; nature violated at every step; endless reciting and lecturing and striving to be first; such are the female schools in America at this hour; but this picture, dark as it is, is brightening in many features, at least in some respects they are less bad than they were a quarter of a century ago.*

* Dr. Treichler read before the sections of Psychiatry and Neurology, at the 52d meeting of the German Association of Natural Historians and Physicians, in Baden-Baden, in 1879, a very important paper on " Habitual Headache in Children."

From investigations at Darmstadt, Paris, and Neuremburg, he concludes that one-third of the pupils suffer more or less from some form of headache. It is not probable that these headaches in children, which are common enough in this country, are the result purely of intellectual exertion, but of intellectual exertion combined with bad air, with the annoyances and excitements and worries, the wasting and rasping anxieties of school life. If children would only study that which was well for them to study, and study only in a psychological way,—if their studies were conducted on sound psychological principles instead of in opposition to all psychological principles, as they are, and if the pupils lived in pure air instead of impure, headaches and other nerve symptoms would be far less frequent.

Even studies that are agreeable and in harmony with the organs, and to which tastes and talents are irresistibly inclined, are pursued at an expenditure of force which is far too great for many nervously organized temperaments. I have lately had under my care a newly married lady who for some years has been in a state of neurasthenia of a severe character, and of which the exciting cause was devotion to music at home; long hours at the piano, acting on a neurasthenic temperament given to her by inheritance, had developed morbid fears and all the array of nervous symptoms that cluster around them, so that despite her fondness for a favorite art she was forced to abandon it, and from that time was dated her improvement, though at the time that I was called in to see her she had yet a long way to travel before she would reach even approximate health.

It may be affirmed that the education of the future will differ from the education of the present and the past in these vital features ·

First. The recognition of the fact that there is very little in this world worth knowing. Nearly all that passes for, and is believed to be, knowledge, is but different expressions of ignorance ; and for these the interest is psychological only. The reconstruction of the principles of evidence, the primary need of all philosophy, which cannot ‚ much longer be delayed, is to turn nearly all that we call history into myth, and destroy and overthrow beyond chance of resurrection all but a microscopic fraction of the world's reasoning. Of the trifle that is saved, the higher wisdom of coming generations will know and act upon the knowledge that a still smaller fraction is worthy of being taught, or even remembered by any human being.

Secondly. A recognition of the fact that out of all real knowledge but a trifle, an infinitessimal portion, is to be acquired by any individual. The fact that anything is known, and true and important for some, is of itself no reason why all should know or attempt to know it; one might as well expect to devour every eatable substance, because it is eatable and nutritious, as to know every thing because it *is* known, and is of value to mankind.

In selecting ideas, as in selecting food, we are to consider relativity of individual capacity and the organic differences of taste and assimilative power in different individuals, and in the same individual at different times, and under diverse surroundings.

Ignorance is power as well as joy, as even our knowledge takes its roots in our lack of knowledge; to know one thing, we must needs be ignorant of many other things, a very general though accurate acquaintance with what is farthest from us in science, and exhaustive knowledge of what is nearest to us and most in the line of our tastes and duty — the harmonizing of these two aims is the true ideal of scholarship. The constant and unwavering admission of the fact that the human brain, in its very highest evolution, is an organ of very feeble capacity indeed, is the preliminary truth, by starting from which we shall reach other and more complex truths in the science and art of mental training. The brain can hold but little—it is more like a sieve than a target — allowing the majority of all external irritations to sweep over it, leaving no trace of their presence.

An army to make swift marches must dismiss its heavy baggage and take only what is imperative for a day; so the brain that is to do its best must forego or forget impedimental facts that have been

forced into it. In modern days an unschooled Edi
son, an unknown Bell or Gray, seize upon scientific
inventions or discoveries that the grand scholar in
universities, with all the appliances and all past
experiences at his hand, shall not even comprehend.
Thus even our sciences would seem to flourish best
in the soil of ignorance and non-expertness.

Our children are coaxed, cajoled, persuaded, en-
ticed, bluffed, bullied, and driven into the study of
ancient and modern tongues; though the greatest
men in all languages, whose writings are the inspiration to the study of languages, themselves knew
no language but their own; and, in all the loftiest
realms of human creative power the best work has
been done, and is done to-day, by those who are
mostly content with the language in which they
were cradled. A quart measure that is filled to the
brim with water has no room for wine, and the
brain that is packed with foreign words and dialects
is usually incapable of thinking, in any language;
of all accomplishments, the ability to speak and
write in many tongues is the poorest barometer of
intellectual force, and the least satisfactory for happiness and practical use; a hundred pennies a day
would buy for a lifetime the best couriers in
Europe.

Shakespeare, drilled in modern gymnasia and
universities, might have made a fair school-master,

but would have kept the world out of Hamlet and Othello; — the popular delusion that one cannot know his own language without first knowing others, being best of all refuted, so far as it is possible for a single case in illustration to do, by the fact that the chief creator of our language knew no language, not even his own, and thus was made free, bold, and powerful to originate and organize.

Of the sciences multiplying every day, but few are to be known by any one individual; he who has studied enough of the systematized knowledge of men, and looked far enough in various directions in which it leads to know which his tastes and environment best adapt him to follow, and who resolutely obeys his tastes, even in opposition to all teachers, philosophers, and scholars, has won the battle of life — success is his, even although he does nothing more; he has only to fold his arms, rest upon his oars, and float into victory.

Thirdly. The recognition of the fact that not knowledge, but the power to acquire and use knowledge, is the supreme need. The athlete in fencing, boxing, sparring, rowing, running, or acrobatics, develops the power, that he may use it when the time comes. In physical training, modern customs, with some exceptions and extremes, are mostly wise; in intellectual training, we have been mostly unwise; since our schools load us with baggage far beyond our strength, in the unscientific expectation that we will gain strength by carrying it.

It is of little concern how much or how little a man knows, but it is of all concern whether he knows how to know, and to concentrate, and vitalize his knowledge. He whose mental discipline is so perfect that all his faculties play together like perfect machinery, and with the least friction, and most economical expenditure of force, finds the acquisition of the knowledge necessary for his mental peace or for the acquirement of a livelihood, or glory, but trifling sport; and without conscious toil he rejects the useless and harmful, passes by all obstructions and goes straight and swift to the heart of truth. Mental discipline of this kind is secured in various ways; nearly all forms of self-culture in all the paths that lead to success, require a certain grade of intellectual control; the study of the art of thinking, of the philosophy of reasoning, in mathematics, poetry, science, literature, or language, is the best exercise for those who would gain this mental discipline; but the art of thinking is what the schools have never thought of teaching, save through the century-old formula of logic that lead more to error than to ideas, and are, to a vitalized system of reasoning, what a log hut is to the tree out of which it was constructed. The art of thinking, the study of the reconstructed principles of evidence can be made most fascinating as well as valuable, even to the immature mind, and mental discipline acquired by this process is far more complete, and attained at incomparably less cost of force, time, and money, than the methods of the schools.

Fourthly. A recognition of the fact that education is but evolution — a mental growth — and, like all else in nature, without leaps, breaks, or chasms, from the single and simple elements towards the complex and multiform. The brain grows — the whole nervous system grows, and the mind grows with it, like a tree of the field, and the processes of education should follow the same natural processes. The mind does grow in this way — despite all the organized attempts to prevent it—the child becomes an adult by the assimilation of food, no matter how unwholesome it may be or how ill-advisedly, stintingly or extravagantly it may be given — the mind grows by assimilating the assimilable products of the vast and unnutritious material that is cast upon it, just as the tree grows by absorbing and vitalizing the inorganic constituents of earth and air. We can stunt the mind, as we can stunt the tree; we can aid the progress of the tree by fertilization and care — so we can aid the growth and progress of the mind in analagous ways; but, whether stunted or highly developed, the mind, like the tree, grows;

so far as it makes any progress at all, it must grow; it cannot be fed by burying it in learning, any more than can the tree be nourished through the support of props and slabs.

Fifthly. A recognition of the fact that very much knowledge that may be acquired is for temporary use only, to be laid aside when the occasion for its use is past. The brain is so organized that it can take possession of a fact at order, through a short or a long time, as may be needed, to be surrendered at the end of that time, just as we give notes, for a month, six months, a year or more. This psychological fact all actors understand, and they commit their parts with the expectation which is always met, that they may forget them in a week or more, as may be needed. To them the brain is a hotel where the words make but a short stay, or perhaps, stop but for a night, then pass on; were they to become permanent guests, the space would be at once over-crowded, and there would be no room for new comers. In all spheres of thought, the most hospitable of intellects, the most generous in their welcome to new truths or dreams of truth, are those who have once learned the great secret of life—how to forget. He who wisely acquires and wisely forgets will be likely to use wisely what he needs.

Conscientious professors in colleges oftentimes

exhort their graduates to keep up some of the studies of college life during the activity of years — if those graduates are ever to do much in the world, it is by doing precisely *not* what they are thus advised to do. As well might they be urged to take with them their dumb-bells, their boxing-gloves, their Indian clubs, and bear them on their persons all their lives, and hang their boat shells and oars on their shoulders, because with these agencies they have gained strength of muscle, as to take with them in their brains, the mathematics, the philosophy, the logic through which their intellect has been trained. The details of geography, of mathematics, and of languages, ancient as well as modern, of most of the sciences, ought, and fortunately are, forgotten almost as soon as learned, save by those who become life-experts in these special branches; success in life of the highest order for the educated man, may oftentimes be measured by the rapidity and completeness with which he has forgotten what he has been taught in colleges and schools.

Sixth. The recognition of the fact that the truly psychological and most economical method of education is that which makes the most use of all the senses. The mind is a highly evolved sense, and it is to be fed and developed from the roots upward, as a tree draws its nourishment from the soil. The education of the schools has sought, so far as may be, to reverse the laws of nature, and to feed the tree through the leaves and branches. To put knowledge into the brain through other avenues than the senses, is like carrying food to a city and climbing over the walls or undermining them, instead of going through the open gates. The systems of Froebel and Pestalozzi, and the philosophy of Rousseau in his "Emile," analyzed and formulated in physiological language, is, in substance, that it costs less force and is more natural and easy to get into a house through the doors, than to break down the walls, or come through the roof, or climb up from the cellar. Modern education is burglary; we force ideas into the brain through any other pathway and every other way except the doors and windows, and then we are astonished that they are unwelcome and so quickly expelled. Fortunately nature is stronger than our system of education, and our children, in spite of all our efforts, do get their education through the senses, since all the knowledge they acquire is obtained and retained through processes of mental imagery; they see with the mind's eye, though we close their eyelids. When a child reads history or biography or geography, it must unconsciously form the mental image of that which it is reading; it must see the men, the battle, the country, the city, else it gains no fact. All education should be clinical. We should see the case at the bedside; indeed, a right understanding of what medical education is and 'what medical education ought to be, and what it is to be, unlocks the whole mystery of the general subject of education. Medicine has been taught in all our schools in a way the most unphilosophical, and despite all the modifications and improvements of late years, by bedside teaching and operations and demonstrations, the system of medical education is in need of reconstruction from the foundation; it begins where it should end; it feeds the tree through the leaves and branches instead of through the roots; physiology itself is taught unphysiologically; the conventional, hereditary, orthodox style is, for the student to take systematic text-books, go through them systematically from beginning to end, and attend systematic lectures, reserving study at the bedside for the middle and later years of his study; the didactic instruction coming first, and the practical instruction and individual observation coming last. Psychology and experience require that this should be reversed; the first years of the medical student's life should be given to the bedside, the laboratory and dissecting room, and the principles of systematic instruction should be kept for the last years, and then used very sparingly. The human mind does not work systematically, and all new truths enter most easily and are best retained when they enter in psychological order. System in text-books is a tax on the nerve-force, costly both of time and of energy, and it is only by forgetting what has been taught them in the schools, that men even attain eminence in the practice of medicine.

The first lesson and the first hour of medical study should be at the bedside of the sick man; before reading a book or hearing a lecture, or even knowing of the existence of a disease, the student should see the disease, and then, after having seen it and been instructed in reference to it, his reading will be a thousand-fold more profitable than it would had he read first and seen the case afterwards. Every practitioner with any power of analyzing his own mental operations, knows that his reading of disease is always more intelligent after he has had a case, or while he has a case under treatment under his own eyes, and he knows also that all his reading of abstract, systematic books is of but little worth to him when he meets his first case, unless he re-read, and if he do so, he will find that he has forgotten all he has read before, and he will find, also, that he never understood what he read, and perhaps thoroughly and accurately recited on examination. By this method one shall learn more what is worth learning of medicine in one month, than now we learn in a year, under the common system, and what is learned will be in hand and usable, and will be obtained at incommensurably less cost of energy, as well as of time. So-called "systematic instruction," is the most extravagant form of instruction, and is really no instruction, since the information which it professes to give does not enter the brain of the student, though the words in which it is expressed may be retained, and recited or written out on examination. I read the other day an opening lecture by a professor in one of our chief medical schools. I noticed that the professor apologized for being obliged to begin with what was dry and uninteresting, but stated that in a systematic course it was necessary to do so. It will not be his fault only, but rather the fault of the machinery of which he is one of the wheels, if the students who listen to and take notes of and worry over his lecture, never know what he means; five minutes study of a case of rheumatism or an inflamed joint, under the aid of an expert instructor, will give a person more knowledge of inflammation, in relation to the practice of medicine, than a year of lectures on that subject.

I make particular reference to medical education, not because it is the leading offender, but because it has made greater progress than, perhaps, almost any other kind of modern education. It is already half a convert to the extreme revolutionary view that I am here advocating, and the next generation it will be a whole convert to it; and the time will come when men shall read with amusement and horror of intelligent, human, and responsible young men beginning a medical course by listening to systematic abstract lectures. All the other systems of professional education need the same reconstruction. In theological seminaries, students are warned about preaching, or speaking, or lecturing during their first or second year, and tied and chained down to lectures and homiletics, and theology and history, just as medical students are warned about seeing the sick, to the study and relief of which their life is devoted. Aside from the study of language, which is a separate matter, the first day's work in a theological school should be the writing or preparing a sermon, and homiletics should follow —not precede.

All languages should be learned as we learn our own language — not through grammars or dictionaries, but through conversation and reading, the grammars and dictionaries being reserved for a more advanced stage of investigation and for reference, just as in the language in which we were born. Grammars, dictionaries, and didactic teaching are for experts; only those who are already scholars should use them. That the system of putting grammars and dictionaries last instead of first, is possible and practicable, has been and is now being demonstrated in our country. The best and cheapest method of studying geography is to travel, and it would be much cheaper than to spend years in school. When my little daughter asks me where a certain place is I reply, "Wait a little and perhaps we will go and see." Thus she has travelled with her parents a distance nearly equal to the circumference of the globe, and it costs less than to send her to a fashionable seminary. Fortunately, very little geography is worth knowing or remembering, except as generalities, and that little can be taught to those who cannot travel, by maps and blocks and other appeals to the senses. I applaud the English because they boast of their ignorance of American geography; of what worth to them, of what worth to most of us whether Montana be in California, or Alaska be or be not the capital of Arizona?

The system of instruction by lectures and recitations is unpsychological as well as costly and wearisome to teacher and learner. Of the two, recitations are the least extravagant and unsatisfactory. But both methods of education are out of harmony with the laws of the mind, and, in the universities of Great Britain both these methods are in a degree displaced by a system which may be conducted in harmony with psychology; that is, private tutelage. The Harvard professor who says, or used to say, that when students entered his room his desire was, not to find out what they knew but what they did not know, ought to have been born in the twentieth century, and possibly in the thirtieth, for his philosophy is so sound and so well grounded psychology that he cannot hope to have it either received or comprehended in his lifetime; and the innovation that Harvard has just promised, of having the teacher recite and the pupils ask the questions, is one of the few gleams of light in the great darkness by which this whole subject of education has been enveloped.

The universal habit of lecturing, which is so common in Germany, is one which the world ought to slowly outgrow.

Lectures, except they be of a clinical sort, in which appeals are made to the senses, cost so much in nerve-force, in those that listen to them, that the world cannot much longer afford to indulge in them; and the information they give is of a most unsatisfactory sort, since questioning, and interruption, and repetition, and reviewing are scarcely possible; whence it is, that what one derives from listening to lectures is not so much knowledge as a suspicion of knowledge. The human brain is too feeble and limited an organ to catch a new idea when first stated, and if the idea be not new it is useless to state it.

One of the pleasantest memories in my life, is that, during my medical education, I did not attend one lecture out of twelve — save those of a clinical sort — that were delivered (brilliant and able as some of them were) in the college where I studied, and my regret is, that the poverty of medical literature at that time compelled me to attend even those. All the long lectures in my academical course at the college were useful to me — and I think were useful to all my classmates — only by enforcing the necessity, and inspiring the habit of enduring passively and patiently what we know to be in all respects painful and pernicious, providing we have no remedy. It is by reading and constant reviewing, by having our teachers recite to us ; by conversing informally with those who know more than we, by writing—above all, by seeing, and hearing, and tasting, and smelling, and touching, and by reflecting on what we see and hear, and taste, and smell, and touch, that we become truly wise. Work of this kind is healthful, as well as inspiring, and favors longevity ; it is economical, and makes it possible for us to become learned without becoming nervous bankrupts.

The hardest worker, in the best modes of work, and one of the healthiest men I ever knew, is Edison, whose perfect method of intellectual activity makes it safe for him to break almost every known law of health.   Original thinkers and discoverers, and writers are objects of increasing worry on the part of their relatives and friends, lest they break down from overwork ; whereas, it is not so much these great thinkers as the young school-girl or bank clerk that needs our sympathy.

In my own experience I have had a remarkable opportunity to test the value of the sense of sight as a means of scientific and popular instruction. For years I have been writing and lecturing on the subject of trance — which, next to evolution, is the great scientific problem of the century, as is now beginning to be understood by scientific men all over the world—without obtaining any evidence of intelligent interest except with a limited body of experts in psychology ; and I had questioned whether it would ever be possible, in my life time, to obtain any scientific or popular recognition of the importance of this subject ; but, during the past year, I tried the experiment of giving, before the New York Academy of Sciences, a lecture on trance, illustrated by large numbers of experiments of various kinds on living human beings.   The theory and philosophy advanced in that lecture, and very many of the facts also, had been presented by me years before, in that same hall, and before some of the same audience, without exciting even a flash of interest ; but these experiments, made before the eyes, on living human beings, aroused an enthusiasm which has not yet died away, but has developed what would appear to be a permanent and enduring interest in this fascinating and important realm of scientific study· It was, so to speak, an experiment in psychological object teaching, quite uncongenial to my own taste, as I would have much preferred to give the facts, theories, and philosophies without any experiments.

The experience was to me, most instructive and important in its relation to the subject here under review; it was a potent demonstration of the fact that the eye is the widest and most accessible of all the avenues that open to the brain.

More worthy of note is this experience from this; that the lectures were given before scientific audiences whose intellects were supposed to be trained to thinking and to following logical procosses. In England during the last summer, I attempted, without any human beings on whom to experiment, to explain some of the theories and philosophies of trance before an audience composed of the very best physiologists and psychologists of Europe, and with no better success than at home. If I had had but one out of the twenty or thirty cases on whom I have lately experimented, to illustrate and enforce my views, there would have been, I am sure, no difficulty in making clear not only the facts, but what is of chief importance, the interpretation of the facts.

Competitive Examinations.

Modern competitive examinations are but slightly in advance of the system of recitations and lectures. They seem to have been invented by some one who wished to torture rather than benefit mankind, and whose philosophy was, that whatever is disagreeable is useful, and that the temporary accumulation of facts is true wisdom, and an accurate measure of cerebral force. Crammed-knowledge is ignorance; in Montaigne's words, " Knowing by heart is not knowing;" the greatest fool may often pass the best examination; no wise man can always tell what he knows; ideas come by suggestion rather than by order; you must wait for their appearing at their own time and not at ours; we may be ready to shoot them when they fly, like birds on the wing, but we cannot tell when they will rise; he who can always tell what he knows, knows little worth knowing.

Recent Improvement in the American Physique.

Herein is the partial, though not the entire elucidation of the observed fact that, during the last two decades, the well-to-do classes of America have been visibly growing stronger, fuller, healthier. We weigh more than our fathers; the women in all our great centres of population are yearly becoming more plump and more beautiful; and in the leading brain-working occupations our men also are acquiring robustness, amplitude, quantity of being. On all sides there is a visible reversion to the better physical appearance of our English and German ancestors. A thousand girls and boys, a thousand men in the prime of years, taken by accident in any of our large cities, are heavier and more substantial than were the same number of the same age and walk of life twenty-five years ago.

Many years of careful study of the physical appearance of our higher classes, in those places where representative types from all parts of the country are constantly seen — in our leading churches and concert halls, on Fifth Avenue and Broadway — have convinced me long ago that the combined influences of wealth and culture. of better manners and better diet, are already bringing fulness and freshness to the angular cheek of the traditional Yankee; the American race is filling out; the next generation, as the experience of the late war gives us reason to hope, may equal our European ancestors in strength, in solidity, and endurance, as our women have long surpassed them in personal attractiveness and beauty.

This improvement in the *physique* of the Americans of the most favored classes during the last quarter of a century is a fact more and more compelling the inspection both of the physician and the sociologist. Of old it was said that the choicest samples of manly form were to be found in the busy hours of the Exchange at Liverpool; their equals, at least, now walk Broadway and Fifth Avenue. The one need for the perfection of the beauty of the American women — increase of fat — is now supplied.

It could not, in fact, be different, for we have better homes, more suitable clothing, less anxiety, greater ease, and more variety of healthful activity than even the best situated of our immediate ancestors. So inevitable was this result, that had it been otherwise, one might well suspect that the law of causation had been suspended.

The first signs of ascension, as of declension, in nations are seen in women. As the foliage of delicate plants first show the early warmth of spring and the earliest frosts of autumn, so the impressible, susceptive organization of woman appreciates and exhibits far sooner than that of man the manifestations of national progress or decay.

Not long since I had occasion to take a train at Providence on my way to Boston. It was a very stormy morning, and I was surprised to see a large number of ladies in the cars. I observed that the majority of them were, if not handsome, at least strong and vigorous, as though they lived well, and were equal to a long walk or, if necessary, a hard day's work. Still further, I noticed that many of them were of an intellectual cast of feature; various ages were represented, but nearly all were mature. On inquiring what had called out such a host of brave females on so disagreeable a day, I learned that a Woman's Congress had just closed its sessions in Providence, and that the members were returning to their homes. On subsequently reading the reports of the congress, as published in the Providence papers, I was both interested and mildly surprised to find that the essays were of a far higher order in topics and in treatment than I had been accustomed to expect in organizations sustained wholly by women; the subjects selected being more closely related to science, in its various branches, and the discussions were carried on in the scientific spirit; far less was said of politics, and far more of what requires higher and broader intellect than politics — the difficult and complex problems of psychology, physiology, sociology, and educational reform.

A well-trained intellect is itself medicine and hygiene, enabling its possessor to guard successfully against the appeals of passion and the storms of emotion, keeping the mind constantly supplied with the fresh and varied material for thought and action, and rendering the avoidance of exhausting pleasures at once spontaneous and intelligent. The nervous female patients of our time do not come from the most intellectual of the sex. The pioneers in feminine development are often sturdy and patient of physical and mental toil — capable of enduring the fatigue of travel, of public speaking, of literary and philanthropic activity; and if, like George Eliot, of a sensitive frame, yet able to keep themselves out of helpless invalidism and in fair working order.

This improvement in the physical appearance of our women is not equally distributed through all classes, nor has it reached all sections. The late Centennial gave an unusual opportunity to study American physique such as we have not had for a century, since there it was possible to see, on any day, every phase of American society, and from every State. It was observed that the women from many distant country places represented, in size, color, and features, the type that twenty-five years ago was national, almost universal; the wave of physical improvement had not yet reached their class of neighborhood; they were thin, angular, stooping, anxious, pale, and, in not a few cases, emaciated. The wives and daughters of farmers are often in some respects less favored hygienically than the fashionable classes of our great cities; they give far too little thought and care to the preparation and mastication of food; they labor oftentimes out of proportion to their strength, and, in want of temptation to walk out or even to ride during inclement seasons, really suffer more from confinement in excessively heated rooms than their sisters in city or town or village.

American inventions are now assisting both American men and American women to diminish their nervousness; palace cars and elevators and sewing machines are types of recent improvements that help to diminish the friction of modern life. Formerly inventors increased the friction of our lives and made us nervous.

Germanization of America.

The Germanization of America — by which I mean the introduction through very extensive immigration, of German habits and character — is a phenomenon which can now be observed, even by the dullest and nearest-sighted, in the large cities of the Northern portion of our country. As the Germans in their temperament are the opposite of the native Americans, this process promises to be in all respects beneficial, encouraging in every way out-door life and amusements, tending to displace pernicious whiskey by less pernicious beer and wine, setting the example of coolness and calmness, which the nervously exhausted American very much needs. Quite true it is that the second and third generations of Germans do themselves become Americanized, through the effects of climate and the contagion of our institutions; but the pressure of immigration provides, every year, a supply of phleg-matic temperament.

America of the past 'has been but England in a minor key. All that is good, all that is evil in the United States has come directly and mainly from Great Britain — the daughter is but a mild type of the mother. In the angry and inexpert discussions of national characteristics, it is forgotten that the difference between one country and the other is far less than is suggested or commonly alleged. We have been all English in our conservatism, a quality which has increased in proportion as we have gained anything of wealth or character or any mani-festation of force whatsoever, that is worth pre-serving. To supplement the Anglican by German characteristics is a process to be developed during the coming half century.

Americanization of Europe.

Observations in both continents bring into view another process, that is of supreme import in its relation to the future of mankind, the American-ization of Europe. That Americans were more rapid in their movements, more intense in their whole life, and concentrated more activity in a certain period of time than any other people, has been the faith of all travellers, and this belief has a foundation of reality; but in Europe at least, and to a less degree in Continental Europe, we now observe the same eagerness, intensity, concentration, feverishness, and nervousness that have hitherto been supposed to be peculiarly American.

Particularly was I amazed by this when I was in Cork and Cambridge, attending meetings of the British Medical Association. The labor of a month was compressed into a week. Every one was in haste — officers and members having only bits of time to breathe or speak; a procession of suppers, breakfasts, balls, banquets, scientific orations, garden-parties, and excursions at every point of the compass, crowded so closely as to tread upon each other's heels; after such a vacation one needed a vacation. At no gathering outside of political assemblages in America have I seen such excitement, such hurryings, such impatience, such evidences of imminent responsibility as among the leaders and officers of these meetings.

This Americanization of Europe would seem to be the complex resultant of a variety of influences — the increase of travel and trade, and concentration, and intensifying of activity required by the telegraph, railway, and printing-press — the endosmosis and exosmosis of international life — a reciprocity of character. It is clear that even in Europe each generation becomes on the whole rather more sensitive than its predecessor, and in this pathological process even Germany shares; Switzerland, perhaps, being less affected up to the present time than almost any other part of Central Europe.

The nervousness of the third generation of Germans is a fact that comes to my professional notice more and more. Men whose parents on both sides were born in Germany, here develop the American type in all its details — chiselled features, great fineness and silkiness of the hair, delicacy of skin and tapering extremities. Such persons have consulted me for all phases and stages of functional nervous trouble. Indeed, I have seen no more severe examples of nervous suffering than in this class. Englishmen, even those who were born in England, develop either in their own country, or in this, the land of their adoption, many of the prominent symptoms of functional nervous diseases that are supposed to be especially and pre-eminently American. Quite a percentage of my patients are of German and English birth. I am told by one of the leaders of German science, Professor Erb, of Leipsic, whose opportunities for getting facts on this theme are exceptionally good, and whose capacity for observing and for reasoning justly from his observations is very great, that in nearly all parts of Germany there can be found at the present day, and that too without very much seeking, cases of functional nervous disease in all respects the types of what we see in America; and that there has been an increase in these disorders. Within less than nine months after the publication of my work on Nervous Exhaustion, two independent requests for authority to translate it into German were made of me and my publishers by German physicians; this could not probably have happened if the disease were not increasing in Germany. Even Irishmen born in this land or brought here early are not entirely safe from the chances of nervous contagion.

The increasing fluency of speech among English orators is, perhaps, one of the best of all the proofs of the Americanization of Europe. Not only are the " ha, ha's," of which so much sport was once made, heard much less frequently than formerly in public meetings, but there is a positive ease and attractiveness to very many of the English speakers in and out of Parliament, in the pulpit and on the platform, that is thoroughly American; and this is noticeable, not only among orators of renown, like Gladstone or Bright, but in many who are in no wise famous.

While I was in London, during the last year, the House of Commons spent a good portion of a session in recapitulating, to the excessive amusement of readers and listeners, the amount of talking that had been done by both sides. By this inquiry — which was inaugurated by the Marquis of Hartington — it was proved that if all the speakers continued to speak as often and as elaborately as they had been speaking, a number of years would be required before they could adjourn.

This difficulty, American legislative bodies have long recognized; but only lately has it become a matter of formal investigation in Parliament; but outside of Parliament—at public banquets, and on all occasions where oratory is required, there is no more fluent or attractive speaking than in Great Britain to-day. Great Britain has long had great orators — excelled by none of any modern nation, but this universal and widely diffused alertness and facility of speech, the contemplation of which kept Carlyle in a dolorous growl and ferment, is a late development.

The Omnistic Philosophy applied to this subject.

It is a part of the omnistic philosophy — and by omnistic philosophy I mean that which includes optimism on the one hand, and pessimism on the other, and makes the best of both — to see simultaneously the redeeming and the destroying forces of society; to study them with a single eye in their relation to each other.

Applying the omnistic philosophy to our subject, we find that the American people are not coming to complete and immediate overthrow; the forces that renovate and save are mightier far than the forces that emasculate and destroy.

Although mental friction is the most fruitful of all causes of nervousness, yet intellectual activity in the serene realms, is an antidote and a modifier of nervousness and other diseases.

It is not a dream to predict that, under the inspiration of the scientific sense, the last and best expression of the evolution of mind, there shall be developed on this continent a higher order of humanity from which shall be developed what the world, thus far, has never seen, a limited number of philosophers who, in all the eternal problems, shall think for themselves, as though the gods were blind, and they were alone upon their footstool.

The American race, it is said, is dying out; but there is no American race. Americans are the union of European races and peoples, as lakes are fed by many streams, and can only disappear with the exhaustion of its sources. Europe must die before America. In sections of America, as in New England, and in large cities, the number of children to a family in certain classes is too small for increase of population; but these classes are a minority in society, and immigration is as certain as the future. Malthus forgot that the tendency of all evil is, in a certain degree, to cure itself; the poison and the antidote being rooted in the same soil.

The typical American of the highest type will, in the near future, be a union of the coarse and the fine organizations; the solidity of the German, the fire of the Saxon, the delicacy of the American, flowing together as one—sensitive, impressible, readily affected through all the avenues of influence, but trained and held by a will of steel; original, idiosyncratic; learned in this — that he knows what not to know, laborious in knowing what not to do · with more of wiriness than of excess of strength and achieving his purposes not so much through the amount of his force as in wisdom and economy of its use.

INDEX.

Works by George M. Beard, M.D.

AMERICAN NERVOUSNESS; Its Causes and Consequences. 12mo. Cloth. . . . . . .

NERVOUS EXHAUSTION (Neurasthenia); Its Nature, Symptoms, and Treatment. Second Revised Edition. . 1 75

SEA SICKNESS; Its Nature and Treatment. New and Enlarged Edition. 12mo. Cloth. 1 00

STIMULANTS AND NARCOTICS. 4th Edition. 12mo. Cloth. 75

EATING AND DRINKING. 4th Edition. 12mo. Cloth. 75

THE SCIENTIFIC BASIS OF DELUSIONS. 8vo. Paper. (A new theory of trance). 50

IN PRESS.

INDUCED OR MESMERIC TRANCE (so called **HYPNOTISM OR SOMNAMBULISM.** Its nature and phenomena.

G. P. PUTNAM'S SONS,   NEW YORK